EVERYDAY
Slow Cooker
& ONE-DISH RECIPES

TASTE OF HOME BOOKS • RDA ENTHUSIAST BRANDS, LLC • MILWAUKEE, WI

© 2021 RDA Enthusiast Brands, LLC.
1610 N. 2nd St., Suite 102, Milwaukee WI 53212-3906
All rights reserved.
Taste of Home is a registered trademark
of RDA Enthusiast Brands, LLC.

Visit us at **tasteofhome.com** for other Taste of Home
books and products.

ISBN:
D 978-1-61765-989-8
U 978-1-61765-990-4

Component Number:
D 119400100H
U 119400102H

ISSN: 1944-6382

Executive Editor: Mark Hagen
Senior Art Director: Raeann Thompson
Editor: Christine Rukavena
Designer: Jazmin Delgado
Copy Editor: Ann Walter
Food Editor: Rashanda Cobbins

Cover
Photographer: Dan Roberts
Set Stylist: Melissa Franco
Food Stylist: Shannon Norris

Pictured on front cover:
Sausage & Squash Penne, p. 139
Pictured on title page:
Saucy Thai Chicken Pizzas, p. 30
Pictured on back cover:
Marinara-Mozzarella Dip, p. 79
Asparagus Beef Cashew Stir-Fry, p. 93
Turkey & Black Bean Enchilada Casserole, p. 193

Printed in USA
1 3 5 7 9 10 8 6 4 2

**SLOW-COOKER
BREAKFAST BURRITOS
PAGE 43**

Contents

Slow Cooker

BEEF & GROUND BEEF » 10

POULTRY » 24

OTHER ENTREES » 38

SOUPS, SIDES &
  SANDWICHES » 56

SNACKS & SWEETS » 74

Stovetop Suppers

BEEF & GROUND BEEF » 92

POULTRY » 110

PORK » 132

FISH & SEAFOOD » 146

Oven Entrees

BEEF & GROUND BEEF » 162

POULTRY » 178

PORK » 200

FISH & SEAFOOD » 214

Bonus Chapter

CAST-IRON DESSERTS » 230

More ways to connect with us:

SHOPTASTEOFHOME.COM

Stovetop Suppers Are Super Convenient

Stovetop cooking is quick and easy. In fact, many of the stovetop meals in this book need just one pot, making cleanup a breeze. Haul out your favorite skillet and let's get cooking!

CHOOSE THE RIGHT PAN FOR THE JOB.

The right cookware can simplify meal preparation when cooking on the stovetop. The basic skillets every kitchen needs include a 10- or 12-in. skillet with lid and an 8- or 9-in. saute/omelet pan.

Good quality cookware conducts heat quickly and cooks food evenly. The type of metal and thickness of the pan affect performance. Consider these pros and cons for each of the most common cookware metals:

Copper does conduct heat the best, but it is expensive, tarnishes (and usually requires periodic polishing) and reacts with acidic ingredients, which is why the interior of a copper pan is usually lined with tin or stainless steel.

138
148

Aluminum is a good conductor of heat and is less expensive than copper. However, aluminum reacts with acidic ingredients.

Anodized aluminum has the same positive qualities as aluminum, but the surface is electrochemically treated so it will not react to acidic ingredients. The surface is resistant to scratches and is nonstick.

Cast iron conducts heat very well. It is usually heavy. Cast iron also needs regular seasoning to prevent sticking and rusting.

Nonstick is especially preferred for cooking delicate foods, such as eggs, pancakes or thin fish fillets. It won't scorch foods if you're cooking batches. It can be scratched easily and has maximum temperature limitations.

Stainless steel is durable and retains its new look for years. It isn't a good conductor of heat, which is why it often has an aluminum or copper core or bottom.

100

MASTER THESE COMMON STOVETOP COOKING TECHNIQUES.

Sauteeing Add a small amount of oil to a hot skillet and heat over medium-high heat. For best results, cut food into uniform pieces before adding. Don't overcrowd in pan. Stir frequently while cooking.

Frying Pour ¼-½ in. oil into a skillet. Heat over medium-high heat until hot. The oil is ready when it shimmers (gives off visible waves of heat). Never leave the pan unattended, and don't overheat the oil or it will smoke. Pat food dry before frying and, if desired, dip in batter or coat it with crumbs. Fry, uncovered, until food is golden brown and cooked through.

Braising Season meat; coat with flour if recipe directs. In Dutch oven, brown meat in oil in batches. To ensure nice browning, do not crowd. Set meat aside; cook vegetables, adding flour if recipe directs. Add broth gradually, stirring to deglaze pan and to keep lumps from forming. Return meat to pan and stir until mixture comes to a boil.

Steaming Place a steamer basket or bamboo steamer in a pan with water. Bring water to a boil (boiling water shouldn't touch the steamer) and place food in the basket; cover and steam. Add more boiling water to pan as necessary, making sure pan does not run dry.

Slow-Cook with Confidence

Follow these tips for slow-cooking success every time.

PLAN AHEAD TO PREP AND GO.
In most cases, you can prepare and load ingredients into the slow-cooker insert beforehand and store it in the refrigerator overnight. But an insert can crack if exposed to rapid temperature changes. Let the insert sit out just long enough to reach room temperature before placing in the slow cooker.

USE THAWED INGREDIENTS.
Although throwing frozen chicken breasts into the slow cooker may seem easy, it's not a smart shortcut. Thawing foods in a slow cooker can create the ideal environment for bacteria to grow, so thaw frozen meat and veggies ahead of time. The exception: If using a prepackaged slow-cooker meal kit, follow instructions as written.

LINE THE CROCK FOR EASE OF USE.
Some recipes in this book call for a **foil collar** or **sling**. Here's why:

▶ A **foil collar** prevents scorching of rich, saucy dishes near the slow cooker's heating element. To make a collar, fold two 18-in.-long pieces of foil into strips 4 in. wide. Line the crock's perimeter with the strips; spray with cooking spray.

▶ A **sling** helps you lift layered foods out of the crock without much fuss. To make, fold one or more pieces of heavy-duty foil into strips. Place on bottom and up sides of the slow cooker; coat with cooking spray.

TAKE THE TIME TO BROWN.
Give yourself a few extra minutes to brown your meat in a skillet before placing in the slow cooker. Doing so will add rich color and more flavor to the finished dish.

KEEP THE LID CLOSED.
Don't peek! While it's tempting to lift the lid and check on your meal's progress, resist the urge. Every time you open the lid, you'll have to add about 30 minutes to the total cooking time.

ADJUST COOK TIME AS NEEDED.
Live at a high altitude? Slow-cooking will take longer. Add about 30 minutes for each hour of cooking the recipe calls for; legumes will take about twice as long.

Want your food done sooner? Cooking one hour on high is roughly equal to two hours on low, so adjust the recipe to suit your schedule.

Stovetop Suppers Are Super Convenient

Stovetop cooking is quick and easy. In fact, many of the stovetop meals in this book need just one pot, making cleanup a breeze. Haul out your favorite skillet and let's get cooking!

CHOOSE THE RIGHT PAN FOR THE JOB.

The right cookware can simplify meal preparation when cooking on the stovetop. The basic skillets every kitchen needs include a 10- or 12-in. skillet with lid and an 8- or 9-in. saute/omelet pan.

138

148

100

Good quality cookware conducts heat quickly and cooks food evenly. The type of metal and thickness of the pan affect performance. Consider these pros and cons for each of the most common cookware metals:

Copper does conduct heat the best, but it is expensive, tarnishes (and usually requires periodic polishing) and reacts with acidic ingredients, which is why the interior of a copper pan is usually lined with tin or stainless steel.

Aluminum is a good conductor of heat and is less expensive than copper. However, aluminum reacts with acidic ingredients.

Anodized aluminum has the same positive qualities as aluminum, but the surface is electrochemically treated so it will not react to acidic ingredients. The surface is resistant to scratches and is nonstick.

Cast iron conducts heat very well. It is usually heavy. Cast iron also needs regular seasoning to prevent sticking and rusting.

Nonstick is especially preferred for cooking delicate foods, such as eggs, pancakes or thin fish fillets. It won't scorch foods if you're cooking batches. It can be scratched easily and has maximum temperature limitations.

Stainless steel is durable and retains its new look for years. It isn't a good conductor of heat, which is why it often has an aluminum or copper core or bottom.

MASTER THESE COMMON STOVETOP COOKING TECHNIQUES.

Sauteeing Add a small amount of oil to a hot skillet and heat over medium-high heat. For best results, cut food into uniform pieces before adding. Don't overcrowd in pan. Stir frequently while cooking.

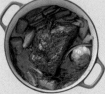

Frying Pour ¼-½ in. oil into a skillet. Heat over medium-high heat until hot. The oil is ready when it shimmers (gives off visible waves of heat). Never leave the pan unattended, and don't overheat the oil or it will smoke. Pat food dry before frying and, if desired, dip in batter or coat it with crumbs. Fry, uncovered, until food is golden brown and cooked through.

Braising Season meat; coat with flour if recipe directs. In Dutch oven, brown meat in oil in batches. To ensure nice browning, do not crowd. Set meat aside; cook vegetables, adding flour if recipe directs. Add broth gradually, stirring to deglaze pan and to keep lumps from forming. Return meat to pan and stir until mixture comes to a boil.

Steaming Place a steamer basket or bamboo steamer in a pan with water. Bring water to a boil (boiling water shouldn't touch the steamer) and place food in the basket; cover and steam. Add more boiling water to pan as necessary, making sure pan does not run dry.

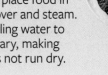

204

202

Oven Entrees Bake Hands-Free

You can't beat a meal-in-one specialty for convenience and comfort. Review these hints while the oven preheats.

CHOOSE THE RIGHT BAKEWARE.

Metal baking pans Excellent conductors of heat, these create nice browning on rolls, coffee cakes and other baked goods. Metal is a safe, smart choice for under the broiler. It may react with acidic foods such as tomato sauce or cranberries and create a metallic taste or discoloration.

Glass baking dishes Glass provides slower, more even baking for egg dishes, custards and casseroles. It takes longer to heat than metal, but once heated, the dish holds the heat longer. This is undesirable for many desserts, as sugary batters may overbrown in glass. If you wish to bake in a glass dish even though the recipe calls for a metal pan, decrease the oven temperature by 25°.

Other baking dishes Ceramic or stoneware baking dishes generally perform much like glass but are more attractive. They may be safe for higher temperatures than glass; refer to the manufacturer's instructions.

CONFIRM THE OVEN'S TEMPERATURE.

Use an oven thermometer to check. Preheat oven to the desired temperature; place an oven thermometer on the center rack. Close the oven door and leave the oven on at the set temperature. Keep thermometer in the oven for 15 minutes before reading. Adjust the oven temperature accordingly to ensure best baking results.

NEGATE HOT OR COOL SPOTS.

To test your oven for uneven temperatures, try the bread test. Heat the oven to 350° while arranging six to nine slices of white bread on a large cookie sheet. Place in oven for 5-10 minutes; check if the slices are starting to brown or burn. If some slices are noticeably darker or lighter than others, the oven may have hot or cool spots. To negate this, rotate pans while baking.

ELIMINATE SPILLS—THE SMART WAY.

Line a rimmed baking sheet with foil and place it on the bottom oven rack directly below the baking dish. Any drips or spills from the recipe will fall onto the foil-lined pan instead of the oven bottom.

We don't recommend lining the bottom of your oven with aluminum foil or other liners, as there's a chance that they could melt and stick to the oven, causing damage.

Want to clean up a drip while it's still hot? Grab your oven mitt, a pair of tongs and a damp dishcloth. Use the tongs to move the cloth and help prevent burns.

224

MARINARA-MOZZARELLA
DIP, PAGE 79

Slow Cooker

For the ultimate in cozy and convenient foods, good cooks love to reach for their slow cookers. Nothing beats coming home to the aroma of dinner waiting for you after a long day. Except, perhaps, waking up to a hot, ready-to-eat breakfast! Irresistible party dips, healthy heartwarming soups, and even homemade bread await your consideration in this section.

BEEF & GROUND BEEF » 10

POULTRY » 24

OTHER ENTREES » 38

SOUPS, SIDES & SANDWICHES » 56

SNACKS & SWEETS » 74

Beef & Ground Beef

SLOW-COOKER BEEF WITH RED SAUCE

A homemade rub spices up this tender beef; vinegar and gingersnaps add depth to the sauce. You can substitute graham crackers for the cookies.
—*Laurie Tietze, Longview, TX*

PREP: 25 min. • **COOK:** 8 hours
MAKES: 8 servings

- 2 Tbsp. canola oil
- 2 Tbsp. baking cocoa
- 1 Tbsp. chili powder
- 2 tsp. dried oregano
- 1 tsp. salt
- 1 tsp. pepper
- 1 tsp. ground cumin
- ½ tsp. ground cloves
- ½ tsp. ground cinnamon
- 1 beef rump roast or bottom round roast (3 lbs.), cut into 1½-in. cubes
- 1 large onion, chopped
- 1 can (28 oz.) whole tomatoes, undrained
- 3 Tbsp. cider vinegar
- 1½ cups crushed gingersnap cookies (about 30 cookies)
- 9 garlic cloves, peeled
- 1 Tbsp. sugar
  Hot cooked noodles, rice or mashed potatoes

1. In a small bowl, combine first 9 ingredients; set aside.
2. Place the beef and onion in a 4-qt. slow cooker; rub beef with spice mixture. Pour tomatoes over the top; sprinkle with vinegar, gingersnaps and garlic.
3. Cover and cook on low for 8-10 hours or until meat is tender. Stir in sugar. Serve with hot cooked noodles.

1 cup: 388 cal., 14g fat (4g sat. fat), 102mg chol., 685mg sod., 27g carb. (9g sugars, 3g fiber), 36g pro.

"We greatly enjoyed eating this recipe. Reminded us of sauerbraten. I did not use the sugar, cut the amount of crushed gingersnaps to ¾ cup, and used crushed tomatoes. We enjoyed it with noodles and steamed Brussels sprouts. I will definitely make this again."
—ANNRMS, TASTEOFHOME.COM

SLOW-COOKER
BEEF WITH RED SAUCE

HOMEMADE CINCINNATI CHILI

The chocolate in this recipe threw me a little at first, but now it's the only way I make chili. You'll find layers of delicious flavor in this heartwarming dish. It's well worth the time it takes!

—*Joyce Alm, Thorp, WA*

PREP: 25 min. • **COOK:** 5 hours
MAKES: 10 servings (2½ qt.)

- 3 lbs. ground beef
- 1½ cups chopped onions
- 1½ tsp. minced garlic
- 2 cans (16 oz. each) kidney beans, rinsed and drained
- 2 cans (15 oz. each) tomato sauce
- 2 cups beef broth
- ¼ cup chili powder
- ¼ cup red wine vinegar
- ¼ cup Worcestershire sauce
- 1 oz. unsweetened chocolate, coarsely chopped
- 1½ tsp. ground cinnamon
- 1½ tsp. ground cumin
- 1 tsp. salt
- 1 tsp. dried oregano
- ½ tsp. pepper
- ⅛ tsp. ground cloves
  Hot cooked spaghetti
  Optional: Shredded cheddar cheese and sliced green onions

1. In a Dutch oven, cook beef and onions over medium heat until the meat is no longer pink. Add garlic; cook 1 minute longer. Drain.
2. In a 5-qt. slow cooker, combine the beans, tomato sauce, broth, chili powder, vinegar, Worcestershire sauce, chocolate, cinnamon, cumin, salt, oregano, pepper and cloves. Stir in beef mixture. Cover and cook on low for 5-6 hours or until heated through.
3. Serve with spaghetti. If desired, serve with cheese and green onions.
Freeze option: Freeze cooled chili in freezer containers. To use, partially thaw in the refrigerator overnight. Heat through in a saucepan, stirring occasionally; add broth or water if necessary. Serve with spaghetti. If desired, serve with cheese and green onions.
1 cup: 358 cal., 14g fat (6g sat. fat), 67mg chol., 1141mg sod., 26g carb. (5g sugars, 7g fiber), 33g pro.

SLOW-COOKER
BEEF TOSTADAS

SLOW-COOKER BEEF TOSTADAS

I dedicate these slow-simmered tostadas to my husband, the only Italian man I know who can't get enough of zesty Mexican flavors. Pile on your best toppings.
—*Teresa DeVono, Red Lion, PA*

PREP: 20 min. • **COOK:** 6 hours
MAKES: 6 servings

- 1 large onion, chopped
- ¼ cup lime juice
- 1 jalapeno pepper, seeded and minced
- 1 serrano pepper, seeded and minced
- 1 Tbsp. chili powder
- 3 garlic cloves, minced
- ½ tsp. ground cumin
- 1 beef top round steak (about 1½ lbs.)
- 1 tsp. salt
- ½ tsp. pepper
- ¼ cup chopped fresh cilantro
- 12 corn tortillas (6 in.)
  Cooking spray

TOPPINGS
- 1½ cups shredded lettuce
- 1 medium tomato, finely chopped
- ¾ cup shredded sharp cheddar cheese
- ¾ cup reduced-fat sour cream, optional

1. Place the first 7 ingredients in a 3- or 4-qt. slow cooker. Cut steak in half and sprinkle with salt and pepper; add to slow cooker. Cook, covered, on low until meat is tender, 6-8 hours.
2. Remove meat; cool slightly. Shred meat with 2 forks. Return beef to slow cooker and stir in cilantro; heat through. Spritz both sides of tortillas with cooking spray. Place tortillas in a single layer on baking sheets; broil for 1-2 minutes on each side or until crisp. Spoon beef mixture over tortillas; top with lettuce, tomato, cheese and, if desired, sour cream.
Note: Wear disposable gloves when cutting hot peppers; the oils can burn skin. Avoid touching your face.
2 tostadas: 372 cal., 13g fat (6g sat. fat), 88mg chol., 602mg sod., 30g carb. (5g sugars, 5g fiber), 35g pro. **Diabetic exchanges:** 4 lean meat, 2 starch, ½ fat.

SAVORY BEEF FAJITAS

My family loves beef and I love to use the slow cooker, so this dish pleases everyone. The meat comes out nice and tender to create these tempting fajitas.
—*Twila Burkholder, Middleburg, PA*

PREP: 15 min. • **COOK:** 7 hours
MAKES: 12 servings

- 1 beef flank steak (2 lbs.), thinly sliced
- 1 cup tomato juice
- 2 garlic cloves, minced
- 1 Tbsp. minced fresh cilantro
- 1 tsp. chili powder
- 1 tsp. ground cumin
- ½ tsp. salt
- ½ tsp. ground coriander
- 1 medium onion, sliced
- 1 medium green pepper, julienned
- 1 medium sweet red pepper, julienned
- 1 medium jalapeno, cut into thin strips
- 12 flour tortillas (6 in.)
  Optional: Sour cream, guacamole, salsa or shredded cheddar cheese

1. Place beef in a 3-qt. slow cooker. Combine the next 7 ingredients; pour over beef. Cover and cook on low for 6-7 hours.
2. Add onion, peppers and jalapeno. Cover and cook 1 hour longer or until meat and vegetables are tender.
3. Using a slotted spoon, place about ½ cup of meat-vegetable mixture on each tortilla. Add desired toppings. Roll up.
Note: Wear disposable gloves when cutting hot peppers; the oils can burn skin. Avoid touching your face.
1 fajita: 225 cal., 7g fat (3g sat. fat), 39mg chol., 264mg sod., 19g carb. (0 sugars, 2g fiber), 20g pro. **Diabetic exchanges:** 2 lean meat, 1 starch, 1 vegetable.

SMOTHERED ROUND STEAK

Try less expensive round steak and gravy served over egg noodles for a hearty meal. Meaty and packed with veggies, this creation takes the worry out of wondering what's for dinner.
—*Kathy Garrett, Camden, WV*

PREP: 15 min. • **COOK:** 6 hours
MAKES: 4 servings

- 1½ lbs. beef top round steak, cut into strips
- ⅓ cup all-purpose flour
- ½ tsp. salt
- ¼ tsp. pepper
- 1 large onion, sliced
- 1 large green pepper, sliced
- 1 can (14½ oz.) diced tomatoes, undrained
- 1 jar (4 oz.) sliced mushrooms, drained
- 3 Tbsp. reduced-sodium soy sauce
- 2 Tbsp. molasses
  Hot cooked egg noodles, optional

1. In a 3-qt. slow cooker, toss beef with flour, salt and pepper. Stir in all remaining ingredients except noodles.
2. Cook, covered, on low until meat is tender, 6-8 hours. If desired, serve with noodles.
1¼ cups beef mixture: 335 cal., 6g fat (2g sat. fat), 95mg chol., 1064mg sod., 28g carb. (14g sugars, 4g fiber), 42g pro.

SMOTHERED ROUND STEAK

INDIAN CURRIED BEEF WITH RICE

BEER-BRAISED BEEF

I modified the ingredients in this main dish to suit my family's tastes. It's quick to put together in the morning, and at the end of the day, all that's left to do is cook the noodles and eat! This recipe can easily be doubled or tripled to serve a large crowd.
—*Geri Faustich, Appleton, WI*

- -

PREP: 20 min. • **COOK:** 6 hours
MAKES: 8 servings

- 3 bacon strips, diced
- 2 lbs. beef stew meat, cut into 1-in. cubes
- ½ tsp. pepper
- ¼ tsp. salt
- 2 Tbsp. canola oil
- 1 medium onion, cut into wedges
- 1 tsp. minced garlic
- 1 bay leaf
- 1 can (12 oz.) beer or nonalcoholic beer
- 1 Tbsp. soy sauce
- 1 Tbsp. Worcestershire sauce
- 1 tsp. dried thyme
- 2 Tbsp. all-purpose flour
- ¼ cup water
  Hot cooked noodles

1. In a large skillet, cook bacon over medium heat until crisp. Remove to paper towels; drain, discarding drippings. Sprinkle beef with pepper and salt. In the same skillet, brown beef in oil in batches; drain.
2. Transfer to a 5-qt. slow cooker. Add the bacon, onion, garlic and bay leaf. Combine the beer, soy sauce, Worcestershire sauce and thyme. Pour over beef mixture.
3. Cover and cook on low for 5½-6 hours or until meat is tender.
4. Combine flour and water until smooth; gradually stir into the slow cooker. Cover and cook on high for 30 minutes or until thickened. Discard bay leaf. Serve beef with noodles.
Freeze option: After discarding bay leaf, freeze cooled stew in freezer containers. To use, partially thaw the stew in refrigerator overnight. Heat through in a saucepan, stirring occasionally; add broth or water if necessary. Serve with noodles.
½ cup: 246 cal., 13g fat (4g sat. fat), 74mg chol., 313mg sod., 5g carb. (3g sugars, 1g fiber), 24g pro. **Diabetic exchanges:** 3 lean meat, 1 fat.

INDIAN CURRIED BEEF WITH RICE

My family loves Indian food. Instead of always going to an Indian restaurant, I created this recipe using chuck roast, spinach and curry.
—*Nancy Heishman, Las Vegas, NV*

- -

PREP: 30 min. • **COOK:** 4½ hours
MAKES: 6 servings

- 1½ tsp. salt, divided
- 1 tsp. ground cardamom
- ½ tsp. ground allspice
- 1 boneless beef chuck roast (2 lbs.), cut into 1 in. cubes
- 1 Tbsp. olive oil
- 2 medium onions, chopped
- 1 Tbsp. minced fresh gingerroot
- 2 garlic cloves, minced
- 2 tsp. curry powder
- 1 tsp. ground cumin
- 1 pkg. (10 oz.) frozen chopped spinach, thawed and squeezed dry
- ¾ cup plain Greek yogurt
  Hot cooked rice
  Optional: Additional plain Greek yogurt and chopped red onion

1. In a large bowl, combine ½ tsp. salt, cardamom and allspice. Add beef; turn to coat. In a large skillet, heat oil over medium heat; brown meat in batches. Transfer meat to a 3- or 4-qt. slow cooker. In the same skillet, cook onions until tender, 4-5 minutes. Add ginger, garlic, curry powder, cumin and remaining 1 tsp. salt; cook 1 minute longer. Transfer to slow cooker.
2. Cook, covered, on low until meat is tender, 4-5 hours. Stir in spinach; cook until heated through, about 30 minutes. Just before serving, stir in yogurt. Serve with rice and, if desired, additional yogurt and red onion.
1 serving: 343 cal., 20g fat (8g sat. fat), 106mg chol., 707mg sod., 8g carb. (3g sugars, 3g fiber), 33g pro.

SLOW-COOKER
ASIAN SHORT RIBS

SLOW-COOKER ASIAN SHORT RIBS

My slow cooker is my best friend—I use it at least three times a week! This rib recipe is one of my favorites. The sauce can be used for other proteins, too.

—*Carole Resnick, Cleveland, OH*

PREP: 15 min. • **COOK:** 6 hours
MAKES: 6 servings

- ¾ cup sugar
- ¾ cup ketchup
- ¾ cup reduced-sodium soy sauce
- ⅓ cup honey
- ¼ cup lemon juice
- 3 Tbsp. hoisin sauce
- 1 Tbsp. ground ginger
- 2 garlic cloves, minced
- 4 lbs. bone-in beef short ribs
  Optional: Sesame seeds and chopped green onions

In a greased 4- or 5-qt. slow cooker, whisk together the first 8 ingredients. Add short ribs and turn to coat; cook, covered, on low until meat is tender, 6-7 hours. If desired, serve with sesame seeds and green onions.

1 serving: 460 cal., 15g fat (6g sat. fat), 73mg chol., 1706mg sod., 56g carb. (51g sugars, 0 fiber), 27g pro.

SHREDDED
GREEN CHILE BEEF

SHREDDED GREEN CHILE BEEF

This Tex-Mex pulled beef roast is tender, slightly spicy, juicy, and so delicious served over mashed potatoes or rice. The beef also makes the best soft tacos you've ever had. Save any leftover pulled beef in the liquid to prevent it from drying out.

—*Colleen Delawder, Herndon, VA*

PREP: 25 min. • **COOK:** 7 hours
MAKES: 12 servings

- 2 large sweet onions, halved and thinly sliced
- 4 Tbsp. packed brown sugar, divided
- 1 Tbsp. paprika
- 1½ tsp. salt
- 1 tsp. cayenne pepper
- 1 tsp. chili powder
- 1 tsp. garlic powder
- ½ tsp. pepper
- 1 boneless beef chuck roast (about 3 lbs.)
- 2 Tbsp. canola oil
- 1 can (28 oz.) green enchilada sauce
  Mashed potatoes, optional

1. Place onions and 3 Tbsp. brown sugar in a 5- or 6-qt. slow cooker. Combine remaining brown sugar and the next 6 ingredients; coat beef with mixture.

2. In a large skillet, heat oil over medium-high heat; brown beef, 1-2 minutes on each side. Transfer to slow cooker; pour enchilada sauce over beef. Cook, covered, on low until beef is tender, 7-9 hours. Remove beef; shred meat with 2 forks. Return to slow cooker; heat through. If desired, serve over potatoes.

1 cup beef mixture: 278 cal., 15g fat (4g sat. fat), 74mg chol., 658mg sod., 14g carb. (8g sugars, 1g fiber), 23g pro. **Diabetic exchanges:** 3 lean meat, 1 starch, ½ fat.

TEST KITCHEN TIP
Try this shredded beef over pepper jack or cheddar mashed potatoes.

PEPPER BEEF GOULASH

I only need a couple of common ingredients to turn beef stew meat into a hearty entree. No one will ever guess the secret behind this flavorful goulash—an envelope of sloppy joe seasoning.
—*Peggy Key, Grant, AL*

PREP: 10 min. • **COOK:** 4 hours
MAKES: 6 servings

- ½ cup water
- 1 can (6 oz.) tomato paste
- 2 Tbsp. cider vinegar
- 1 envelope sloppy joe seasoning
- 2 lbs. beef stew meat (¾-in. cubes)
- 1 celery rib, cut into ½-in. slices
- 1 medium green pepper, cut into ½-in. chunks
  Hot cooked rice or noodles

In a 3-qt. slow cooker, combine the water, tomato paste, vinegar and sloppy joe seasoning. Stir in the beef, celery and green pepper. Cook, covered, on high for 4-5 hours or until meat is tender. Serve with rice.
1 serving: 268 cal., 10g fat (4g sat. fat), 94mg chol., 565mg sod., 11g carb. (3g sugars, 1g fiber), 31g pro. **Diabetic exchanges:** 4 lean meat, 1 starch.

"I was looking for something different to do with stew meat and found this recipe. Simple yet so delicious, this is now part of my recipe file. It's a nice easy dish for a busy weeknight or Sunday dinner."
—BERTBELL, TASTEOFHOME.COM

SLOW-COOKED CORNED BEEF

It's not luck; it's just an amazing Irish recipe. With this dish in the slow cooker by sunrise, you can be sure to fill seats at the dinner table by sundown.
—*Heather Parraz, Rochester, WA*

PREP: 20 min. • **COOK:** 9 hours
MAKES: 6 servings (plus about 14 oz. leftover corned beef)

- 6 medium red potatoes, quartered
- 2 medium carrots, cut into chunks
- 1 large onion, sliced
- 2 corned beef briskets with spice packets (3 lbs. each)
- ¼ cup packed brown sugar
- 2 Tbsp. sugar
- 2 Tbsp. coriander seeds
- 2 Tbsp. whole peppercorns
- 4 cups water

1. In a 6-qt. slow cooker, combine the potatoes, carrots and onion. Add briskets (discard spice packets from corned beef or save for another use). Sprinkle the brown sugar, sugar, coriander and peppercorns over meat. Pour water over top.
2. Cover and cook on low for 9-11 hours or until meat and vegetables are tender.
3. Remove meat and vegetables to a serving platter. Thinly slice 1 brisket across the grain and serve with vegetables.
4 oz. cooked corned beef with ¾ cup vegetables: 557 cal., 31g fat (10g sat. fat), 156mg chol., 1825mg sod., 38g carb. (16g sugars, 4g fiber), 32g pro.

SLOW-COOKED CORNED BEEF

GARLIC BEEF STROGANOFF

FLANK STEAK ROLL-UP

As a working mother of five hungry boys, I rely on my slow cooker to give me a head start on meals. With this dish, I roll stuffing mix and mushrooms into flank steak before simmering it in gravy.
—*Sheryl Johnson, Las Vegas, NV*

PREP: 15 min. • **COOK:** 8 hours
MAKES: 6 servings

- 1 can (4 oz.) mushroom stems and pieces, undrained
- 2 Tbsp. butter, melted
- 1 pkg. (6 oz.) seasoned stuffing mix
- 1 beef flank steak (1¾ lbs.)
- 1 envelope brown gravy mix
- ¼ cup chopped green onions
- ¼ cup dry red wine or beef broth

1. In bowl, toss the mushrooms, butter and dry stuffing mix. Spread over steak to within 1 in. of edges. Roll up jelly-roll style, starting with a long side; tie with kitchen string. Place in a 3-qt. slow cooker.
2. Prepare gravy mix according to package directions; add onions and wine. Pour over meat. Cover and cook on low for 8-10 hours. Remove meat to a serving platter and keep warm. Strain cooking juices and thicken if desired. Remove string from roll-up; slice beef and serve with gravy.
1 slice: 329 cal., 11g fat (4g sat. fat), 63mg chol., 768mg sod., 25g carb. (3g sugars, 2g fiber), 29g pro.

GARLIC BEEF STROGANOFF

I'm a mom and work full time, so I use my slow cooker whenever possible. This Stroganoff is perfect because I can get it ready in the morning before the kids get up.
—*Erika Anderson, Wausau, WI*

PREP: 20 min. • **COOK:** 7 hours
MAKES: 8 servings

- 2 tsp. beef bouillon granules
- 1 cup boiling water
- 1 can (10¾ oz.) condensed cream of mushroom soup, undiluted
- 2 jars (4½ oz. each) sliced mushrooms, drained
- 1 large onion, chopped
- 3 garlic cloves, minced
- 1 Tbsp. Worcestershire sauce
- 1½ to 2 lbs. beef top round steak, cut into thin strips
- 2 Tbsp. canola oil
- 1 pkg. (8 oz.) cream cheese, cubed
  Hot cooked noodles
  Minced fresh parsley, optional

1. In a 3-qt. slow cooker, dissolve bouillon in water. Add the soup, mushrooms, onion, garlic and Worcestershire sauce. In a skillet, brown beef in oil.
2. Transfer beef to the slow cooker. Cover and cook on low until the meat is tender, 7-8 hours. Stir in cream cheese until smooth. Serve with noodles and, if desired, minced fresh parsley.
1 serving: 281 cal., 18g fat (8g sat. fat), 81mg chol., 661mg sod., 7g carb. (2g sugars, 1g fiber), 23g pro.

SLOW-COOKER
MONGOLIAN BEEF

SLOW-COOKED ROPA VIEJA

I traveled to Cuba a few years ago and had some of the best food imaginable. This dish stuck out, and when I returned home I began to experiment. I hope you enjoy the flavors of Cuba as much as I do.
—*Joshua Boyer, Traverse City, MI*

PREP: 35 min. • **COOK:** 8 hours
MAKES: 6 servings

    1   beef flank steak (2 lbs.)
    ½   tsp. salt
    ½   tsp. pepper
    2   cups beef broth
    ½   cup dry vermouth
    ½   cup dry red wine or
        additional beef broth
    1   can (6 oz.) tomato paste
    1   large onion, thinly sliced
    1   large carrot, sliced
    1   small sweet red pepper, thinly sliced
    1   Cubanelle or mild banana pepper, thinly sliced
    3   springs fresh oregano
        Hot cooked rice
        Optional: Additional fresh oregano, lime wedges and sliced green olives with pimientos

1. Cut the steak into 6 pieces; sprinkle with salt and pepper. Heat a large skillet over medium-high heat; brown meat in batches. Transfer meat to a 5- or 6-qt. slow cooker. Add broth, vermouth, wine and tomato paste to pan. Cook 2-3 minutes, stirring to loosen browned bits from pan. Pour over meat.
2. Top with onion, carrot, red pepper, Cubanelle pepper and oregano. Cook, covered, on low 8-10 hours or until meat is tender. Remove oregano sprigs; discard. Remove meat; shred with 2 forks. Return to slow cooker; heat through. Serve with rice and, if desired, additional oregano, lime wedges and green olives.
1 serving: 278 cal., 11g fat (5g sat. fat), 72mg chol., 611mg sod., 10g carb. (5g sugars, 2g fiber), 32g pro. **Diabetic exchanges:** 4 lean meat, 1 vegetable.

SLOW-COOKER MONGOLIAN BEEF

This dish uses inexpensive ingredients to offer big flavor in a small amount of time. The slow cooker makes easy work of it as well—easier than getting takeout!
—*Taste of Home Test Kitchen*

PREP: 10 min. • **COOK:** 4¼ hours
MAKES: 4 servings

    ¾   cup reduced-sodium chicken broth
    2   Tbsp. reduced-sodium soy sauce
    1   Tbsp. hoisin sauce
    2   tsp. minced fresh gingerroot
    2   tsp. sesame oil
    1   tsp. minced garlic
    ½   tsp. salt
    ¼   tsp. crushed red pepper flakes
    1   lb. beef flank steak, cut into thin strips
    2   Tbsp. cornstarch
    2   Tbsp. water
    2   cups hot cooked rice
    5   green onions, cut into 1-in. pieces
        Sesame seeds, optional

1. In a 4- or 5-qt. slow cooker, combine first 8 ingredients. Add the beef and toss to coat. Cook, covered, on low until meat is tender, 4-5 hours.
2. In a small bowl, mix cornstarch and water until smooth; gradually stir into beef. Cook, covered, on high until sauce is thickened, 15-30 minutes. Serve over hot cooked rice. Sprinkle with green onions and, if desired, sesame seeds.
1 serving: 329 cal., 11g fat (4g sat. fat), 54mg chol., 530mg sod., 30g carb. (2g sugars, 1g fiber), 26g pro.

SLOW-COOKED
ROPA VIEJA

MUSHROOM BEEF & NOODLES

I've prepared this flavorful beef dish many times for family and friends. I've also shared the easy six-ingredient recipe with lots of other cooks, and they all think it's great.
—*Virgil Killman, Mascoutah, IL*

PREP: 10 min. • **COOK:** 8 hours
MAKES: 8 servings

- 1 can (10¾ oz.) condensed golden mushroom soup, undiluted
- 1 can (10¾ oz.) condensed beefy mushroom soup, undiluted
- 1 can (10¾ oz.) condensed French onion soup, undiluted
- ¼ cup seasoned bread crumbs
- 2 lbs. beef stew meat, cut into ½-in. cubes
- 1 pkg. (12 oz.) wide egg noodles

In a 3-qt. slow cooker, combine soups and bread crumbs. Stir in beef. Cover and cook on low for 8 hours or until meat is tender. Cook noodles according to package directions; drain. Serve with beef mixture.
1 cup: 408 cal., 12g fat (4g sat. fat), 116mg chol., 985mg sod., 41g carb. (3g sugars, 2g fiber), 31g pro.

"Substituted cream of mushroom soup for the French onion soup, and my family liked it even better that way."
—WOODDUCK62, TASTEOFHOME.COM

TEXAS STEW

I love to experiment with many different types of recipes. But as a mother of young children, I rely on family-friendly ones more and more. Everyone enjoys this stew.
—*Kim Balstad, Lewisville, TX*

PREP: 15 min. • **COOK:** 6 hours
MAKES: 12 servings (3 qt.)

- 1½ lbs. ground beef
- 1 medium onion, chopped
- 1 can (15½ oz.) hominy, drained
- 1 can (15¼ oz.) whole kernel corn, drained
- 1 can (15 oz.) sliced carrots, drained
- 1 can (15 oz.) sliced potatoes, drained
- 1 can (16 oz.) Ranch Style beans (pinto beans in seasoned tomato sauce)
- 1 can (14½ oz.) diced tomatoes, undrained
- 1 cup water
- 1 tsp. beef bouillon granules
- ½ tsp. garlic powder
- Chili powder to taste
- Dash Worcestershire sauce
- Dash hot pepper sauce

1. In a large skillet, cook beef and onion over medium heat until meat is no longer pink; drain. Transfer to a 5-qt. slow cooker. Stir in the remaining ingredients.
2. Cover and cook on low until heated through, 6-8 hours.
1 cup: 223 cal., 8g fat (3g sat. fat), 38mg chol., 710mg sod., 21g carb. (5g sugars, 5g fiber), 15g pro.

TEST KITCHEN TIP
If your family doesn't care for hominy, you can use a 15-oz. can of green beans (drained) instead.

TEXAS STEW

SLOW-COOKER MEAT LOAF

HEARTY GROUND BEEF STEW

I created this chunky soup when looking for something inexpensive and easy to make. The thick and hearty mixture is chock-full of ground beef, potatoes and baby carrots.
—*Sandra Castillo, Janesville, WI*

PREP: 20 min. • **COOK:** 5 hours
MAKES: 8 servings (3 qt.)

- 1 lb. ground beef
- 6 medium potatoes, peeled and cubed
- 1 pkg. (16 oz.) baby carrots
- 3 cups water
- 2 Tbsp. Lipton beefy onion soup mix
- 1 garlic clove, minced
- 1 tsp. Italian seasoning
- 1 to 1½ tsp. salt
- ¼ tsp. garlic powder
- ¼ tsp. pepper
- 1 can (10¾ oz.) condensed tomato soup, undiluted
- 1 can (6 oz.) Italian tomato paste

In a large skillet, cook beef over medium heat until no longer pink; drain. In a 5-qt. slow cooker, combine the next nine ingredients. Stir in the beef. Cover and cook on high for 4-5 hours. Stir in soup and tomato paste; cover and cook for 1 hour longer or until heated through.

1½ cups: 270 cal., 7g fat (3g sat. fat), 35mg chol., 678mg sod., 38g carb. (10g sugars, 4g fiber), 15g pro. **Diabetic exchanges:** 1½ starch, 1 vegetable, 1 lean meat.

SLOW-COOKER MEAT LOAF

An old standby, meat loaf, gets fun Mexican flair and a convenient preparation method with this slow-cooked recipe. Boost the flavor by serving it with your favorite taco sauce or salsa.
—*Julie Sterchi, Campbellsville, KY*

PREP: 10 min. • **COOK:** 6 hours
MAKES: 8 servings

- 1 large egg, beaten
- ⅓ cup taco sauce
- 1 cup coarsely crushed corn chips
- ⅓ cup shredded Mexican cheese blend or cheddar cheese
- 2 Tbsp. taco seasoning
- ½ tsp. salt, optional
- 2 lbs. lean ground beef (90% lean)
  Additional taco sauce or salsa

In a large bowl, combine first 6 ingredients. Crumble beef over mixture and mix lightly but thoroughly. Shape into a round loaf; place in a 3-qt. slow cooker. Cover and cook on low until a thermometer reads 160°, 6-8 hours. Serve with taco sauce or salsa.

1 slice: 258 cal., 11g fat (5g sat. fat), 86mg chol., 471mg sod., 14g carb. (1g sugars, 1g fiber), 24g pro.

MOROCCAN
POT ROAST

❄ MOROCCAN POT ROAST

My husband loves meat and I love veggies, so we're both happy with this spiced twist on pot roast. It's like something you'd eat at a Marrakech bazaar.
—*Catherine Dempsey, Clifton Park, NY*

PREP: 25 min. • **COOK:** 7 hours
MAKES: 8 servings

- 2 **Tbsp. olive oil**
- 3 **small onions, chopped**
- 3 **Tbsp. paprika**
- 1 **Tbsp. plus ½ tsp. garam masala, divided**
- 1¼ **tsp. salt, divided**
- ¼ **tsp. cayenne pepper**
- 2 **Tbsp. tomato paste**
- 1 **can (15 oz.) garbanzo beans or chickpeas, rinsed and drained**
- 1 **can (14½ oz.) beef broth**
- ¼ **tsp. pepper**
- 1 **boneless beef chuck roast (3 lbs.)**
- 4 **medium carrots, cut diagonally into ¾-in. pieces**
- 1 **small eggplant, cubed**
- 2 **Tbsp. honey**
- 2 **Tbsp. minced fresh mint**
  Hot cooked couscous or flatbreads, optional

1. In a large skillet, heat oil over medium heat; saute onions with paprika, 1 Tbsp. garam masala, ½ tsp. salt and cayenne until tender, 4-5 minutes. Stir in tomato paste; cook and stir 1 minute. Stir in chickpeas and broth; transfer to a 5- or 6-qt. slow cooker.
2. Mix pepper and the remaining ½ tsp. garam masala and ¾ tsp. salt; rub over roast. Place in slow cooker. Add carrots and eggplant. Cook, covered, until meat and vegetables are tender, 7-9 hours.
3. Remove roast from slow cooker; break into pieces. Remove vegetables with a slotted spoon; skim fat from cooking juices. Stir in honey. Return beef and vegetables to slow cooker and heat through. Sprinkle with mint. If desired, serve with couscous.
Freeze option: Freeze cooled beef and vegetable mixture in freezer containers. To use, partially thaw in refrigerator overnight. Microwave, covered, on high in a microwave-safe dish until heated through, stirring gently.
1 serving: 435 cal., 21g fat (7g sat. fat), 111mg chol., 766mg sod., 23g carb. (10g sugars, 6g fiber), 38g pro.

SLOW-COOKER BEEF & BROCCOLI

SLOW-COOKER BEEF & BROCCOLI

I love introducing my kids to all kinds of flavors. This Asian-inspired slow-cooker meal is one of their favorites, so I serve it often.
—*Brandy Stansbury, Edna, TX*

PREP: 20 min. • **COOK:** 6½ hours
MAKES: 4 servings

- 2 **cups beef broth**
- ½ **cup reduced-sodium soy sauce**
- ⅓ **cup packed brown sugar**
- 1½ **tsp. sesame oil**
- 1 **garlic cloves, minced**
- 1 **beef top sirloin steak (1½ lbs.), cut into ½-in.-thick strips**
- 2 **Tbsp. cornstarch**
- ¼ **cup cold water**
- 4 **cups fresh broccoli florets**
  Hot cooked rice
  Optional: Sesame seeds and thinly sliced green onions

1. In a 5-qt. slow cooker, combine the first 5 ingredients. Add beef; stir to coat. Cover and cook on low until tender, about 6 hours.
2. In a small bowl, whisk cornstarch and cold water until smooth; stir into slow cooker. Cover and cook on high until thickened, about 30 minutes. Meanwhile, in a large saucepan, place a steamer basket over 1 in. of water. Place broccoli in basket. Bring water to a boil. Reduce heat to maintain a simmer; steam broccoli, covered, until crisp-tender, 3-4 minutes. Stir broccoli into slow cooker. Serve over rice. If desired, garnish with optional ingredients.
1 cup: 366 cal., 9g fat (3g sat. fat), 69mg chol., 1696mg sod., 28g carb. (19g sugars, 2g fiber), 42g pro.

Poultry

BEERGARITA CHICKEN TACOS

The first time I had a "beergarita" I loved it so much that it became the inspiration for these tacos. They have traditional flavors with a fun twist of a margarita!
—*Ashley Lecker, Green Bay, WI*

PREP: 20 min. • **COOK:** 2½ hours
MAKES: 6 servings

- 1 bottle (12 oz.) Mexican beer or chicken broth
- 1 cup thawed nonalcoholic margarita mix
- 1 can (4 oz.) chopped green chiles, undrained
- 2 Tbsp. lime juice
- 1 tsp. grated lime zest
- 1 tsp. salt
- 1 tsp. garlic powder
- 1 tsp. onion powder
- 1 tsp. chili powder
- ½ tsp. ground cumin
- ½ tsp. pepper
- 1½ lbs. boneless skinless chicken breast halves
- 12 taco shells
  Optional toppings: Shredded pepper jack cheese, minced fresh cilantro, thinly sliced radishes and sour cream

1. Combine the first 11 ingredients in a 3- or 4-qt. slow cooker; top with chicken. Cook, covered, on low until a thermometer inserted in chicken reads 165°, 2½-3 hours.
2. Remove the chicken; shred with 2 forks. Return to slow cooker; heat through. Using a slotted spoon, serve in taco shells with toppings as desired.

Freeze option: Freeze cooled meat mixture and juices in freezer containers. To use, partially thaw in refrigerator overnight. Heat through in a saucepan, stirring occasionally; add broth if necessary.

2 tacos: 294 cal., 7g fat (3g sat. fat), 63mg chol., 627mg sod., 32g carb. (16g sugars, 1g fiber), 25g pro.

BEERGARITA CHICKEN TACOS

TURKEY SAUSAGE
CABBAGE ROLLS

SLOW-COOKER SOUTHWESTERN CHICKEN

Prepared salsa and convenient canned corn and beans add color, texture and flavor to this chicken dish. I usually serve it with salad and white rice. Our children love it!
—*Karen Waters, Laurel, MD*

- -

PREP: 10 min. • **COOK:** 6 hours
MAKES: 6 servings

- 2 cans (15¼ oz. each) whole kernel corn, drained
- 1 can (15 oz.) black beans, rinsed and drained
- 1 jar (16 oz.) chunky salsa
- 6 boneless skinless chicken breast halves (4 oz. each)
- 1 cup shredded cheddar cheese

1. In a 5-qt. slow cooker, combine the corn, black beans and ½ cup salsa. Top with the chicken and remaining salsa.
2. Cover and cook on low for 6-8 hours or until chicken is tender. Sprinkle with cheese. Cover and cook 5 minutes longer or until cheese is melted.
1 serving: 348 cal., 10g fat (4g sat. fat), 82mg chol., 1027mg sod., 28g carb. (11g sugars, 6g fiber), 33g pro.

"We love this dish. I make it almost every week. We serve it with Spanish rice or in tortillas. Very flavorful, quick, and easy."
—FINALBOSS, TASTEOFHOME.COM

TURKEY SAUSAGE CABBAGE ROLLS

I practically grew up in my Polish grandmother's kitchen, watching Babci cook and listening to her stories. I made her cabbage roll recipe healthier with whole grains and turkey, but kept the same rich flavors I remember.
—*Fay A. Moreland, Wichita Falls, TX*

- -

PREP: 50 min. • **COOK:** 7 hours
MAKES: 12 servings

- 12 large plus 6 medium cabbage leaves
- 2 packets (3 oz. each) instant multigrain rice mix
- 1 medium onion, finely chopped
- ½ cup finely chopped sweet red pepper
- ¼ cup minced fresh parsley
- 3 tsp. Italian seasoning
- 1¼ tsp. salt
- 1 tsp. garlic powder
- 1 tsp. pepper
- 1½ lbs. lean ground turkey
- 3 Italian turkey sausage links (about 4 oz. each), casings removed
- 1 bottle (46 oz.) V8 juice

1. In batches, cook cabbage leaves in boiling water until crisp-tender, about 5 minutes. Drain; cool slightly.
2. In a large bowl, combine the rice mix, onion, red pepper, parsley and seasonings. Add the turkey and sausage; mix lightly but thoroughly.
3. Line bottom of a 6-qt. slow cooker with medium cabbage leaves, overlapping as needed. Trim thick veins from bottom of large cabbage leaves, making V-shaped cuts. Top each with about ½ cup filling. Pull cut edges together to overlap, then fold over filling; fold in sides and roll up. Layer in slow cooker, seam side down. Pour the vegetable juice over top.
4. Cook, covered, on low until cabbage is tender, 7-9 hours (a thermometer inserted in filling should read at least 165°).
Note: This recipe was tested with Minute Brand Multi-Grain Medley.
1 cabbage roll with 3 Tbsp. sauce: 202 cal., 7g fat (2g sat. fat), 49mg chol., 681mg sod., 19g carb. (5g sugars, 3g fiber), 17g pro.
Diabetic exchanges: 2 lean meat, 1 starch.

SLOW-COOKED GOOSE

My husband and I own a hunting lodge and host about 16 hunters a week at our camp. The slow cooker makes easy work of fixing this flavorful goose dish, which is a favorite of our guests. The recipe makes lots of savory gravy to serve over mashed potatoes.
—*Edna Ylioja, Lucky Lake, SK*

PREP: 20 min. + marinating • **COOK:** 4 hours
MAKES: 6 servings

- ½ cup soy sauce
- 4 tsp. canola oil
- 4 tsp. lemon juice
- 2 tsp. Worcestershire sauce
- 1 tsp. garlic powder
- 2 lbs. cubed goose breast
- ¾ to 1 cup all-purpose flour
- ¼ cup butter, cubed
- 1 can (10¾ oz.) condensed golden mushroom soup, undiluted
- 1⅓ cups water
- 1 envelope onion soup mix
  Hot cooked mashed potatoes, noodles or rice

1. In a large shallow dish, combine soy sauce, oil, lemon juice, Worcestershire sauce and garlic powder. Add goose; turn to coat. Refrigerate for 4 hours or overnight.
2. Drain goose, discarding marinade. Place flour in another large shallow dish; add goose in batches and turn to coat. In a large skillet over medium heat, brown goose in butter on all sides.
3. Transfer to a 3-qt. slow cooker. Add the soup, water and soup mix. Cover and cook on high for 4-5 hours or until meat is tender. Serve with potatoes, noodles or rice.
Note: If goose breast is unavailable, chicken thighs or duck legs will work great in this recipe, too.
1 serving: 378 cal., 15g fat (5g sat. fat), 127mg chol., 1706mg sod., 20g carb. (1g sugars, 1g fiber), 39g pro.

SLOW-COOKER MALAYSIAN CHICKEN

Malaysian food has influences from the Malays, Chinese, Indians, Thai, Portuguese and British. In this dish, Asian ingredients combine for maximum flavor, and the sweet potatoes help to thicken the sauce as the dish slowly cooks.
—*Suzanne Banfield, Basking Ridge, NJ*

PREP: 20 min. • **COOK:** 5 hours
MAKES: 6 servings

- 1 cup coconut milk
- 2 Tbsp. brown sugar
- 2 Tbsp. soy sauce
- 2 Tbsp. creamy peanut butter
- 1 Tbsp. fish sauce
- 2 tsp. curry powder
- 2 garlic cloves, minced
- ½ tsp. salt
- ½ tsp. pepper
- 1 can (14½ oz.) diced tomatoes, undrained
- 2 medium sweet potatoes, peeled and cut into ½-in. thick slices
- 2 lbs. boneless skinless chicken thighs
- 2 Tbsp. cornstarch
- 2 Tbsp. water

1. In a bowl, whisk together the first 9 ingredients; stir in tomatoes. Place sweet potatoes in a 5- or 6-qt. slow cooker; top with the chicken. Pour tomato mixture over top. Cook, covered, on low until chicken is tender and a thermometer reads 170°, 5-6 hours.
2. Remove chicken and sweet potatoes; keep warm. Transfer cooking juices to a saucepan. In a small bowl, mix cornstarch and water until smooth; stir into cooking juices. Bring to a boil; cook and stir 1-2 minutes or until thickened. Serve sauce with chicken and potatoes.
1 serving: 425 cal., 20g fat (10g sat. fat), 101mg chol., 964mg sod., 28g carb. (14g sugars, 4g fiber), 33g pro.

SLOW-COOKER MALAYSIAN CHICKEN

CURRIED CHICKEN
CACCIATORE

CHICKEN WITH STUFFING

With just a few ingredients, you can create a comforting home-style meal of chicken and cornbread stuffing. I sometimes make the recipe with two cans of soup so there's lots of sauce.
—*Susan Kutz, Stillman Valley, IL*

- -

PREP: 5 min. • **COOK:** 4 hours
MAKES: 4 servings

  4   boneless skinless chicken breast
       halves (4 oz. each)
  1   can (10¾ oz.) condensed cream of
       chicken soup, undiluted
1¼   cups water
 ¼   cup butter, melted
  1   pkg. (6 oz.) cornbread stuffing mix

Place chicken in a greased 3-qt. slow cooker. Top with soup. In a bowl, combine the water, butter and stuffing mix; spoon over the chicken. Cover and cook on low for 4 hours or until chicken is tender.
1 serving: 365 cal., 18g fat (8g sat. fat), 52mg chol., 1481mg sod., 37g carb. (5g sugars, 2g fiber), 12g pro.

TEST KITCHEN TIP
Get creative with this recipe to make it your own. Prepare it with pork chops and pork-flavored stuffing, or turkey breast tenderloins and turkey stuffing.

CURRIED CHICKEN
CACCIATORE

With a family, full-time load at college and a part-time job, I've found that the slow cooker is my best friend when it comes to getting hot and homemade meals like this one on the table.
—*Laura Gier, Rensselaer, NY*

- -

PREP: 30 min. • **COOK:** 6¼ hours
MAKES: 4 servings

  1   broiler/fryer chicken (3 to 4 lbs.), cut up and skin removed
  2   small zucchini, halved and sliced
 ½   lb. sliced fresh mushrooms
  1   small green pepper, chopped
  1   small onion, chopped
  1   jar (24 oz.) spaghetti sauce
  1   can (14½ oz.) diced tomatoes, undrained
 ⅔   cup dry red wine
 ⅓   cup chicken broth
  1   Tbsp. minced fresh parsley
  2   garlic cloves, minced
1½   tsp. dried thyme
1½   tsp. curry powder
 ½   tsp. pepper
  2   Tbsp. cornstarch
  2   Tbsp. cold water
       Hot cooked rice

1. Place chicken and vegetables in a 5-qt. slow cooker. In a large bowl, mix spaghetti sauce, tomatoes, wine, broth, parsley, garlic and seasonings; pour over the chicken. Cook, covered, on low 6-8 hours or until chicken is tender.
2. In a small bowl, mix cornstarch and water until smooth; gradually stir into stew. Cook, covered, on high 15 minutes or until sauce is thickened. Serve with rice.
1 serving: 452 cal., 16g fat (4g sat. fat), 115mg chol., 1167mg sod., 33g carb. (17g sugars, 7g fiber), 44g pro.

SLOW-COOKED
PIZZAIOLA MEAT LOAF

SLOW-COOKED PIZZAIOLA MEAT LOAF

I like to add Italian Castelvetrano olives to the meat loaf mixture in this recipe. They're bright green, very mild and fruity, and are available in the deli section of the grocery store.
—*Ann R. Sheehy, Lawrence, MA*

- -

PREP: 35 min. • **COOK:** 4 hours
MAKES: 8 servings

- 2 Tbsp. canola oil
- 1 large onion, chopped
- 1 cup chopped sweet red, yellow or green peppers
- 1½ cups sliced fresh mushrooms
- 2 garlic cloves, minced
- 2 large eggs, lightly beaten
- 1 cup seasoned bread crumbs
- 1 cup shredded Italian cheese blend
- 1 tsp. Italian seasoning
- ½ tsp. salt
- 1¼ lbs. ground turkey
- 1 lb. meat loaf mix (equal parts ground beef, pork and veal)
  Optional: Pizza sauce and shredded Parmesan cheese

1. Cut three 25x3-in. strips of heavy-duty foil; crisscross so they resemble the spokes of a wheel. Place strips on bottom and up sides of a 5- or 6-qt. slow cooker. Coat strips with cooking spray.
2. In a large skillet, heat oil over medium-high heat. Add onion, peppers and mushrooms; cook and stir until tender, 4-6 minutes. Add garlic; cook 1 minute longer. Remove from the heat and cool slightly.
3. In a large bowl, combine eggs, bread crumbs, cheese, Italian seasoning, salt and reserved cooked vegetables. Add turkey and meat loaf mix; mix lightly but thoroughly. Shape into a loaf; transfer to slow cooker.
4. Cook, covered, on low until a thermometer reads at least 160°, 4-5 hours. Using foil strips as handles, remove meat loaf to a platter. If desired, serve with pizza sauce and shredded Parmesan cheese.
Note: If you don't have meat loaf mix on hand, you may substitute 1 lb. ground beef.
1 slice: 356 cal., 19g fat (6g sat. fat), 139mg chol., 551mg sod., 14g carb. (3g sugars, 1g fiber), 31g pro.

ZA'ATAR CHICKEN

ZA'ATAR CHICKEN

It's hard to find a dinner that both my husband and kids will enjoy—and even harder to find one that's fast and easy. This is it! No matter how much I make of this dish, it's gone to the last bite.
—*Esther Erani, Brooklyn, NY*

- -

PREP: 20 min. • **COOK:** 5 hours
MAKES: 6 servings

- ¼ cup za'atar seasoning
- ¼ cup olive oil
- 3 tsp. dried oregano
- 1 tsp. salt
- ½ tsp. ground cumin
- ½ tsp. ground turmeric
- 3 lbs. bone-in chicken thighs
- 1 cup pimiento-stuffed olives
- ½ cup dried apricots
- ½ cup pitted dried plums
- ¼ cup water
  Hot cooked basmati rice, optional

1. In a large bowl, combine first 6 ingredients. Add chicken; toss to coat.
2. Arrange olives, apricots and plums on the bottom of a 4- or 5-qt. slow cooker. Add ¼ cup water; top with the chicken. Cook, covered, on low until chicken is tender, 5-6 hours. If desired, serve with rice.
1 serving: 484 cal., 32g fat (7g sat. fat), 107mg chol., 1367mg sod., 18g carb. (10g sugars, 2g fiber), 30g pro.

TEST KITCHEN TIP
Za'atar seasoning may become your new favorite spice. Add it to melted butter and toss with popcorn, mix it with olive oil for a dipping sauce, or toss it with potatoes before roasting.

SWEET & TANGY CHICKEN

My slow cooker comes in handy during the haying and harvest seasons. We're so busy that if supper isn't prepared before I serve lunch, it never seems to get done on time. This fuss-free recipe is ready when we are.
—*Joan Airey, Rivers, MB*

- -

PREP: 15 min. • **COOK:** 4 hours
MAKES: 4 servings

1	medium onion, chopped
1½	tsp. minced garlic
1	broiler/fryer chicken (3 lbs.), cut up, skin removed
⅔	cup ketchup
⅓	cup packed brown sugar
1	Tbsp. chili powder
1	Tbsp. lemon juice
1	tsp. dried basil
½	tsp. salt
¼	tsp. pepper
⅛	tsp. hot pepper sauce
2	Tbsp. cornstarch
3	Tbsp. cold water

1. In a 3-qt. slow cooker, combine onion and garlic; top with the chicken. In a small bowl, combine the ketchup, brown sugar, chili powder, lemon juice, basil, salt, pepper and pepper sauce; pour over chicken. Cover and cook on low until juices run clear, 4-5 hours. Remove chicken to a serving platter; keep warm.
2. Skim fat from cooking juices; transfer to a small saucepan. Bring liquid to a boil. Combine cornstarch and water until smooth. Gradually stir into the pan. Bring to a boil; cook and stir 2 minutes or until thickened. Serve with chicken.
1 serving: 385 cal., 9g fat (3g sat. fat), 110mg chol., 892mg sod., 38g carb. (25g sugars, 2g fiber), 38g pro.

SAUCY THAI
CHICKEN PIZZAS

SAUCY THAI CHICKEN PIZZAS

I serve this sweet and salty chicken with rice. You can give it a fresh spin and turn the slow-cooked favorite into a Thai-style pizza.
—Taste of Home *Test Kitchen*

- -

PREP: 4¼ hours • **BAKE:** 10 min.
MAKES: 2 pizzas (6 slices each)

3	lbs. boneless skinless chicken thighs
¾	cup sugar
¾	cup reduced-sodium soy sauce
⅓	cup cider vinegar
1	garlic clove, minced
¾	tsp. ground ginger
¼	tsp. pepper
1	cup Thai peanut sauce
2	prebaked 12-in. pizza crusts
2	cups coleslaw mix
2	cups shredded part-skim mozzarella cheese
4	green onions, thinly sliced
½	cup chopped salted peanuts
¼	cup minced fresh cilantro

1. Place chicken in a 4- or 5-qt. slow cooker. In a small bowl, mix sugar, soy sauce, vinegar, garlic, ginger and pepper; pour over chicken. Cook, covered, on low 4-5 hours or until the chicken is tender.
2. Preheat oven to 450°. Remove chicken from slow cooker; discard cooking juices. Shred chicken with 2 forks; transfer to large bowl. Add peanut sauce; toss to coat.
3. Place crusts on 2 ungreased 12-in. pizza pans or baking sheets. Spoon the chicken mixture over crusts; top with coleslaw mix and cheese. Bake 10-12 minutes or until cheese is melted. Sprinkle with green onions, peanuts and cilantro.
1 slice: 522 cal., 23g fat (6g sat. fat), 88mg chol., 803mg sod., 40g carb. (9g sugars, 2g fiber), 37g pro.

HERBED SLOW-COOKER TURKEY BREAST

A holiday meal warrants an elegant and satisfying entree. This one promises to deliver. The turkey comes out of the slow cooker moist and tender, and the herbs make a flavorful gravy.
—Lorie Miner, Kamas, UT

PREP: 15 min. • **COOK:** 5 hours + standing
MAKES: 12 servings

1 bone-in turkey breast (6 to 7 lbs.), thawed and skin removed
½ cup water
⅔ cup spreadable garden vegetable cream cheese
¼ cup butter, softened
¼ cup soy sauce
2 Tbsp. minced fresh parsley
1 tsp. dried basil
1 tsp. rubbed sage
1 tsp. dried thyme
½ tsp. pepper

1. Place turkey breast and water in a 6-qt. slow cooker. In a small bowl, mix remaining ingredients; rub over turkey. Cook, covered, on low 5-6 hours or until turkey is tender.
2. Remove turkey from slow cooker; tent with foil. Let stand 15 minutes before slicing.
5 oz. cooked turkey: 264 cal., 8g fat (5g sat. fat), 130mg chol., 486mg sod., 1g carb. (0 sugars, 0 fiber), 44g pro. **Diabetic exchanges:** 6 lean meat.

HERBED SLOW-COOKER TURKEY BREAST

PROSCIUTTO CHICKEN CACCIATORE

I tailored my mother's recipe so I can slow-cook this hearty entree and enjoy it on busy weeknights.
—Sandra Putnam, Corvallis, MT

PREP: 30 min. • **COOK:** 4 hours
MAKES: 8 servings

2 lbs. boneless skinless chicken thighs
1½ lbs. boneless skinless chicken breast halves
½ cup all-purpose flour
1 tsp. salt
¼ tsp. pepper
3 Tbsp. olive oil
1 can (14½ oz.) chicken broth
1 can (14½ oz.) diced tomatoes, undrained
1 cup sliced fresh mushrooms
1 medium onion, chopped
1 pkg. (3 oz.) thinly sliced prosciutto or deli ham, coarsely chopped
1 Tbsp. diced pimientos
2 garlic cloves, minced
½ tsp. Italian seasoning
   Hot cooked linguine
   Grated Parmesan cheese

1. Cut chicken into serving-size pieces. In a large shallow dish, combine the flour, salt and pepper. Add chicken, a few pieces at a time, and turn to coat.
2. In a large skillet, brown chicken in oil in batches. Transfer to a 5-qt. slow cooker.
3. Stir in the broth, tomatoes, mushrooms, onion, prosciutto, pimientos, garlic and Italian seasoning. Cover and cook on low for 4-4½ hours or until chicken juices run clear. Serve with a slotted spoon over linguine; sprinkle with cheese.
1 serving: 373 cal., 17g fat (4g sat. fat), 133mg chol., 909mg sod., 11g carb. (3g sugars, 1g fiber), 43g pro.

TEMPTING TERIYAKI
CHICKEN STEW

SLOW-COOKER BUFFALO CHICKEN SALAD

My husband and boys love chicken with blue cheese, so I created this salad. You can even make the chicken the day before and reheat when ready to serve.
—*Shauna Havey, Roy, UT*

PREP: 20 min. • **COOK:** 2½ hours
MAKES: 6 servings

1½ lbs. boneless skinless
    chicken breast halves
¾ cup Buffalo wing sauce
3 Tbsp. butter
1 envelope ranch salad dressing mix
1 pkg. (10 oz.) hearts of romaine salad mix
1 cup julienned carrot
1 medium ripe avocado, peeled and cubed
½ cup crumbled blue cheese
½ cup blue cheese salad dressing

1. Place chicken in a 1½- or 3-qt. slow cooker. Top with wing sauce, butter and ranch dressing mix. Cook, covered, on low until thermometer inserted in chicken reads 165°, 2½-3 hours.
2. Remove chicken; shred with 2 forks. Reserve ⅓ cup cooking juices; discard remaining juices. Return chicken and reserved juices to slow cooker; heat through.
3. Add romaine salad mix to a serving dish. Top with shredded chicken, carrots, avocado and blue cheese; drizzle with blue cheese dressing. Serve immediately.
1 salad: 385 cal., 26g fat (9g sat. fat), 93mg chol., 1693mg sod., 12g carb. (2g sugars, 4g fiber), 28g pro.

TEMPTING TERIYAKI CHICKEN STEW

I created this dish that combines two of my favorite tastes, salty and sweet. I'm always looking for new ideas for my slow cooker, and this one's a keeper!
—*Amy Siegel, Clifton, NJ*

PREP: 20 min. • **COOK:** 7 hours
MAKES: 6 servings

1 Tbsp. olive oil
6 bone-in chicken thighs (about 2 lbs.)
2 medium sweet potatoes, cut into 1-in. pieces
3 medium carrots, cut into 1-in. pieces
1 medium parsnip, peeled and cut into 1-in. pieces
1 medium onion, sliced
1 cup apricot preserves
½ cup maple syrup
½ cup teriyaki sauce
½ tsp. ground ginger
⅛ tsp. cayenne pepper
2 Tbsp. cornstarch
2 Tbsp. cold water

1. In a large skillet, heat oil over medium-high heat; brown chicken on both sides. Place vegetables in a 4-qt. slow cooker; add chicken. In a small bowl, mix the preserves, maple syrup, teriyaki sauce, ginger and cayenne; pour over chicken.
2. Cover and cook on low for 6-8 hours or until chicken is tender. Remove chicken and vegetables to a platter; keep warm.
3. Transfer the cooking liquid to a small saucepan. Skim fat. Bring cooking liquid to a boil. In a small bowl, combine cornstarch and water until smooth; gradually stir into pan. Return to a boil, stirring constantly; cook and stir for 2 minutes or until thickened. Serve with chicken and vegetables.
1 chicken thigh with ½ cup vegetables and ½ cup sauce: 576 cal., 17g fat (4g sat. fat), 81mg chol., 937mg sod., 82g carb. (52g sugars, 4g fiber), 26g pro.

DID YOU KNOW?
Ranch dressing was created by Nebraska cowboy-turned-cook Steve Henson more than 60 years ago. While cooking for a work crew in Alaska in the 1940s, Steve perfected his recipe for buttermilk salad dressing. It later became the house dressing at Hidden Valley Ranch, a dude ranch he bought with his wife, Gayle, outside Santa Barbara, California.

SLOW-COOKER BUFFALO
CHICKEN SALAD

CHICKEN VEGGIE ALFREDO

My family loves this dinner—it's easy to make and a great way to save time after a busy day. If you'd like, add other veggies to suit your family's tastes.
—*Jennifer Jordan, Hubbard, OH*

- -

PREP: 10 min. • **COOK:** 6 hours
MAKES: 4 servings

- 4 boneless skinless chicken breast halves (4 oz. each)
- 1 Tbsp. canola oil
- 1 jar (16 oz.) Alfredo sauce
- 1 can (15¼ oz.) whole kernel corn, drained
- 1 cup frozen peas, thawed
- 1 jar (4½ oz.) sliced mushrooms, drained
- ½ cup chopped onion
- ½ cup water
- ½ tsp. garlic salt
- ¼ tsp. pepper
  Hot cooked linguine

1. In a large skillet, brown chicken in oil. Transfer to a 3-qt. slow cooker. In a large bowl, combine the Alfredo sauce, corn, peas, mushrooms, onion, water, garlic salt and pepper.

2. Pour over chicken. Cover and cook on low for 6-8 hours or until a thermometer reads 165°. Serve with linguine.

1 serving: 435 cal., 19g fat (9g sat. fat), 94mg chol., 1202mg sod., 30g carb. (11g sugars, 5g fiber), 33g pro.

"I liked this recipe. I cut the chicken into smaller portions—and I used more peas for more color."
—BONITO15, TASTEOFHOME.COM

SLOW-COOKER CHICKEN TIKKA MASALA

Just a small dash of garam marsala adds lots of flavor. The bright red sauce coats the caramelized chicken beautifully.
—*Anwar Khan, Iriving, TX*

- -

PREP: 25 min. • **COOK:** 3 hours 10 min.
MAKES: 4 Servings

- 1 can (15 oz.) tomato puree
- 1 small onion, grated
- 3 garlic cloves, minced
- 2 Tbsp. tomato paste
- 1 tsp. grated lemon zest
- 1 Tbsp. lemon juice
- 1 tsp. hot pepper sauce
- 1 Tbsp. canola oil
- 1 tsp. curry powder
- 1 tsp. salt
- ¼ tsp. pepper
- ¼ tsp. garam masala
- 4 bone-in chicken thighs
- 3 Tbsp. plain Greek yogurt, plus more for topping
- 1 Tbsp. unsalted butter, melted
  Optional: Chopped cilantro and grated lemon zest
  Hot cooked rice

1. Combine first 12 ingredients in a 3- or 4-qt. slow cooker. Add chicken thighs and stir gently to coat. Cook, covered, on low 3-4 hours or until chicken is tender.

2. Preheat broiler. Using a slotted spoon, transfer chicken to a broiler-safe baking pan lined with foil. Broil 4-6 in. from heat until lightly charred, 3-4 minutes on each side.

3. Meanwhile, transfer cooking juices from slow cooker to saucepan. Cook, uncovered, over medium-high heat until the mixture is slightly thickened, 6-8 minutes. Remove from heat and gently stir in yogurt and butter. Serve chicken with sauce. If desired, garnish with chopped cilantro, lemon zest and additional yogurt. Serve with hot cooked rice.

1 chicken thigh: 364 cal., 22g fat (7g sat. fat), 91mg chol., 705mg sod., 12g carb. (4g sugars, 3g fiber), 25g pro.

SLOW-COOKER CHICKEN TIKKA MASALA

GREEK-STYLE CHICKEN WITH GREEN BEANS

My Greek grandmother made the most delicious Greek-style green beans with a lemon-tomato flavor; whenever I make this recipe I think of her. The juices from the chicken flavor the green beans, but the beans can be prepared alone as a side dish without the chicken.
—*Elizabeth Lindemann, Driftwood, TX*

- -

PREP: 20 min. • **COOK:** 4 hours
MAKES: 4 servings

- 1   lb. fresh green beans, trimmed
- 2   large tomatoes, chopped
- 1   medium onion, chopped
- 1   cup chicken broth
- ¼   cup snipped fresh dill
- 2 to 3 Tbsp. lemon juice
- 2   garlic cloves, minced
- 4   bone-in chicken thighs (about 1½ lbs.)
- 1   Tbsp. olive oil
- ¾   tsp. salt
- ¼   tsp. pepper
  Optional: Lemon wedges and additional snipped fresh dill

1. Combine the first seven ingredients in a 5- or 6-qt. slow cooker. Top with chicken. Drizzle with oil; sprinkle with salt and pepper. Cook, covered, on low 4-6 hours or until a thermometer inserted in chicken reads 170°-175°.
2. Preheat broiler. Place chicken on a greased rack of a broiler pan. Broil 4-6 in. from heat until golden brown, 3-4 minutes. Serve with bean mixture and, if desired, lemon wedges and additional fresh dill.
1 serving: 324 cal., 18g fat (5g sat. fat), 82mg chol., 769mg sod., 16g carb. (7g sugars, 6g fiber), 26g pro.

CURRIED SWEET POTATO
PINEAPPLE CHICKEN

CURRIED SWEET POTATO PINEAPPLE CHICKEN

This dish is a delicious combination of sweet and savory flavors. I like to add a bit more spice. Make sure to keep the sweet potato chunks large so they keep their integrity over the long cooking time.
—*Trisha Kruse, Eagle, ID*

- -

PREP: 25 min. • **COOK:** 5 hours 20 min.
MAKES: 8 servings

- 8   boneless skinless chicken thighs (about 2 lbs.)
- 2 to 3 tsp. curry powder
- 1   tsp. granulated garlic
- ½   tsp. salt
- 2   Tbsp. canola oil
- 2   large sweet potatoes, peeled and cut into 1 in. pieces
- 1   medium onion, chopped
- 1   can (8 oz.) unsweetened crushed pineapple
- 1   cup apricot-pineapple preserves or ½ cup each apricot and pineapple preserves
- 1   Tbsp. soy sauce
- 2   Tbsp. cornstarch
  Minced fresh parsley, optional

1. Sprinkle chicken with curry powder, garlic and salt. In a large nonstick skillet, heat oil over medium heat. Add chicken and cook until golden brown, 3-4 minutes on each side. Place sweet potatoes and onion in a 5- or 6-qt. slow cooker, top with chicken. Drain pineapple, reserving juice. Add drained pineapple, preserves and soy sauce to slow cooker. Cook, covered, on low until chicken and potatoes are tender, 5-6 hours.
2. In a small bowl, mix cornstarch and reserved pineapple juice until smooth; gradually stir into slow cooker. Cook, covered, on high until sauce is thickened, 20-25 minutes. If desired, sprinkle with minced fresh parsley.
1 serving: 383 cal., 8g fat (2g sat. fat), 76mg chol., 352mg sod., 55g carb. (31g sugars, 3g fiber), 23g pro.

Other Entrees

CANTONESE PORK

CANTONESE PORK

This is our favorite way to prepare pork loin. We love it with fried rice and veggies, but it's also delicious sliced and served cold as an appetizer. Try dipping it in soy sauce, hot mustard and sesame seeds.
—*Carla Mendres, Winnipeg, MB*

PREP: 10 min. + marinating • **COOK:** 3 hours
MAKES: 10 servings

3	Tbsp. honey
2	Tbsp. soy sauce
1	Tbsp. sesame oil
1	Tbsp. Chinese cooking wine or mirin (sweet rice wine)
4	garlic cloves, crushed
1	tsp. minced fresh gingerroot
1	tsp. hoisin sauce
1	tsp. oyster sauce
1	tsp. Chinese five-spice powder
1	tsp. salt
1	tsp. red food coloring, optional
1	boneless pork loin roast (about 4 lbs.)

1. In a bowl, combine first 10 ingredients and, if desired, red food coloring. Cut pork roast lengthwise in half. Add pork; turn to coat. Cover and refrigerate at least 24 hours.
2. Transfer pork and marinade to a 5-qt. slow cooker. Cook, covered, on low 3-4 hours or until a thermometer inserted in roast reads 145° and meat is tender. Let roast stand for 10-15 minutes before slicing.

5 oz. cooked pork: 262 cal., 10g fat (3g sat. fat), 91mg chol., 498mg sod., 6g carb. (5g sugars, 0 fiber), 36g pro. **Diabetic exchanges:** 5 lean meat.

DID YOU KNOW?

Cantonese cuisine is from the Guangdong province of southeast China, near Hong Kong. Hallmarks of the cuisine are light, simple flavors that let the star ingredient (usually meat or seafood) shine. Sweet and sour pork and char siu (Chinese barbecue) pork are popular Cantonese dishes.

**NEW ZEALAND
ROSEMARY LAMB SHANKS**

SOUTHWEST SHREDDED PORK SALAD

This knockout shredded pork makes a healthy, delicious and hearty salad with black beans, corn, Cotija cheese and plenty of fresh salad greens.
—*Mary Shivers, Ada, OK*

- -

PREP: 20 min. • **COOK:** 6 hours
MAKES: 12 servings

- 1   boneless pork loin roast (3 to 4 lbs.)
- 1½   cups apple cider or juice
- 1   can (4 oz.) chopped green chiles, drained
- 3   garlic cloves, minced
- 1½   tsp. salt
- 1½   tsp. hot pepper sauce
- 1   tsp. chili powder
- 1   tsp. pepper
- ½   tsp. ground cumin
- ½   tsp. dried oregano
- 12   cups torn mixed salad greens
- 1   can (15 oz.) black beans, rinsed and drained
- 2   medium tomatoes, chopped
- 1   small red onion, chopped
- 1   cup fresh or frozen corn
- 1   cup crumbled Cotija or shredded part-skim mozzarella cheese
      Salad dressing of your choice

1. Place pork in a 5- or 6-qt. slow cooker. In a small bowl, mix cider, green chiles, garlic, salt, pepper sauce, chili powder, pepper, cumin and oregano; pour over pork. Cook, covered, on low 6-8 hours or until meat is tender.
2. Remove roast from slow cooker; discard cooking juices. Shred pork with 2 forks. Arrange salad greens on a large serving platter. Top with pork, black beans, tomatoes, onion, corn and cheese. Serve with salad dressing.
Freeze option: Place shredded pork in a freezer container; top with cooking juices. Cool and freeze. To use, partially thaw in refrigerator overnight. Heat through in a saucepan, stirring occasionally.
1 serving: 233 cal., 8g fat (4g sat. fat), 67mg chol., 321mg sod., 12g carb. (2g sugars, 3g fiber), 28g pro. **Diabetic exchanges:** 4 lean meat, 1 vegetable, ½ starch.

NEW ZEALAND ROSEMARY LAMB SHANKS

When I was young, my family lived in New Zealand for two years. One item that was always available was lamb shanks. Mother cooked them all the time with root vegetables, and to this day I love lamb!
—*Nancy Heishman, Las Vegas, NV*

- -

PREP: 25 min. • **COOK:** 6 hours
MAKES: 8 servings

- 1   tsp. salt
- ¾   tsp. pepper
- 4   lamb shanks (about 20 oz. each)
- 1   Tbsp. butter
- ½   cup white wine
- 3   medium parsnips, peeled and cut into 1-in. chunks
- 2   large carrots, peeled and cut into 1-in. chunks
- 2   medium turnips, peeled and cut into 1-in. chunks
- 2   large tomatoes, chopped
- 1   large onion, chopped
- 4   garlic cloves, minced
- 2   cups beef broth
- 1   pkg. (10 oz.) frozen peas, thawed
- ⅓   cup chopped fresh parsley
- 2   Tbsp. minced fresh rosemary

1. Rub salt and pepper over lamb. In a large skillet, heat butter over medium-high heat; brown meat. Transfer meat to a 6- or 7-qt. slow cooker. Add wine to skillet; cook and stir 1 minute to loosen brown bits. Pour over lamb. Add the parsnips, carrots, turnips, tomatoes, onion, garlic and broth. Cook, covered, on low for 6-8 hours or until meat is tender.
2. Remove lamb; keep warm. Stir in peas, parsley and rosemary; heat through. Serve lamb with vegetables.
½ lamb shank with 1 cup vegetables: 350 cal., 15g fat (6g sat. fat), 103mg chol., 668mg sod., 22g carb. (8g sugars, 6g fiber), 31g pro. **Diabetic exchanges:** 4 lean meat, 1 starch, 1 vegetable, ½ fat.

CARNITAS TACOS

The house smells fantastic all day when I'm making this slow-cooked recipe. The tacos have so much flavor, you'd never guess they use just five ingredients. I love that they're ready when you need them at the end of the day.
—*Mary Wood, Maize, KS*

PREP: 15 min. • **COOK:** 6 hours
MAKES: 12 servings

- 1 boneless pork shoulder butt roast (3 to 4 lbs.)
- 1 envelope taco seasoning
- 1 can (10 oz.) diced tomatoes and green chiles, undrained
- 12 flour tortillas (8 in.), warmed
- 2 cups shredded Colby-Monterey Jack cheese
  Sour cream, optional

1. Cut roast in half; place in a 4- or 5-qt. slow cooker. Sprinkle with taco seasoning. Pour tomatoes over top. Cover and cook on low for 6-8 hours or until meat is tender.
2. Remove meat from slow cooker; shred with 2 forks. Skim fat from cooking juices. Return meat to slow cooker; heat through. Using a slotted spoon, place ½ cup on each tortilla; top with cheese. Serve with sour cream if desired.

1 taco: 414 cal., 20g fat (8g sat. fat), 84mg chol., 789mg sod., 30g carb. (1g sugars, 0 fiber), 28g pro.

PORK CHOP DINNER

Family and friends call me the slow-cooker queen. Of my many specialties, this one is my husband's favorite.
—*Janet Phillips, Meadville, PA*

PREP: 15 min. • **COOK:** 4 hours
MAKES: 6 servings

- 6 bone-in pork loin chops (7 oz. each)
- 1 Tbsp. canola oil
- 1 large onion, sliced
- 1 medium green pepper, chopped
- 1 can (4 oz.) mushroom stems and pieces, drained
- 1 can (8 oz.) tomato sauce
- 1 Tbsp. brown sugar
- 2 tsp. Worcestershire sauce
- 1½ tsp. cider vinegar
- ½ tsp. salt
  Baked potatoes or hot cooked rice, optional

In a skillet, brown pork chops on both sides in oil; drain. Place chops in a 3-qt. slow cooker. Add onion, green pepper and mushrooms. In a bowl, combine the tomato sauce, brown sugar, Worcestershire sauce, vinegar and salt. Pour over meat and vegetables. Cover and cook on low for 4-5 hours or until meat is tender. If desired, serve with baked potatoes or hot cooked rice.

1 serving: 338 cal., 19g fat (6g sat. fat), 97mg chol., 527mg sod., 8g carb. (5g sugars, 2g fiber), 33g pro. **Diabetic exchanges:** 4 lean meat, ½ fat.

PORK CHOP
DINNER

SLOW-COOKED
VEGETABLE CURRY

PIZZA RIGATONI

Everyone will want seconds of this casserole loaded with cheese, sausage, pepperoni and olives. It's all the things you love about pizza, in an easy slow-cooked meal.
—*Marilyn Cowan, North Manchester, IN*

PREP: 15 min. • **COOK:** 4 hours
MAKES: 8 servings

- 1½ lbs. bulk Italian sausage
- 3 cups uncooked rigatoni or large tube pasta
- 4 cups shredded part-skim mozzarella cheese
- 1 can (10¾ oz.) condensed cream of mushroom soup, undiluted
- 1 small onion, chopped
- 2 cans (one 15 oz., one 8 oz.) pizza sauce
- 1 pkg. (3½ oz.) sliced pepperoni
- 1 can (6 oz.) pitted ripe olives, drained and halved

1. In a skillet, cook sausage until no longer pink; drain. Cook pasta according to package directions; drain.
2. In a 5-qt. slow cooker, layer half of the sausage, pasta, cheese, soup, onion, pizza sauce, pepperoni and olives. Repeat layers. Cover and cook on low for 4 hours.
1 cup: 525 cal., 30g fat (13g sat. fat), 78mg chol., 1573mg sod., 32g carb. (7g sugars, 3g fiber), 30g pro.

"I made this for company last week and it was a huge hit! So easy to put together. I used two jars of pizza sauce. Yum!"
—FACSGIRL, TASTEOFHOME.COM

SLOW-COOKED VEGETABLE CURRY

I love the fuss-free nature of the slow cooker, but I don't want to sacrifice flavor for convenience. This cozy, spiced-up dish has both.
—*Susan Smith, Mead, WA*

PREP: 35 min. • **COOK:** 5 hours
MAKES: 6 servings

- 1 Tbsp. canola oil
- 1 medium onion, finely chopped
- 4 garlic cloves, minced
- 3 tsp. ground coriander
- 1½ tsp. ground cinnamon
- 1 tsp. ground ginger
- 1 tsp. ground turmeric
- ½ tsp. cayenne pepper
- 2 Tbsp. tomato paste
- 2 cans (15 oz. each) garbanzo beans or chickpeas, rinsed and drained
- 3 cups cubed peeled sweet potatoes (about 1 lb.)
- 3 cups fresh cauliflower florets (about 8 oz.)
- 4 medium carrots, cut into ¾-in. pieces (about 2 cups)
- 2 medium tomatoes, seeded and chopped
- 2 cups chicken broth
- 1 cup light coconut milk
- ½ tsp. pepper
- ¼ tsp. salt
  Minced fresh cilantro
  Hot cooked brown rice
  Lime wedges
  Plain yogurt, optional

1. In a large skillet, heat oil over medium heat; saute onion until soft and lightly browned, 5-7 minutes. Add garlic and spices; cook and stir 1 minute. Add tomato paste; cook 1 minute longer. Transfer to a 5- or 6-qt. slow cooker.
2. Mash 1 can of beans until smooth; add to slow cooker. Stir in remaining beans, vegetables, broth, coconut milk, pepper and salt.
3. Cook, covered, on low 5-6 hours or until vegetables are tender. Sprinkle with cilantro. Serve with rice, lime and, if desired, yogurt.
1⅔ cups curry: 304 cal., 8g fat (2g sat. fat), 2mg chol., 696mg sod., 49g carb. (12g sugars, 12g fiber), 9g pro.

SLOW-COOKED THAI
DRUNKEN NOODLES

SLOW-COOKED THAI DRUNKEN NOODLES

I really love pad kee mao and was inspired to try my recipe in the slow cooker on a really busy day. It came out tasting great! I was so happy to have it ready to go when we got home. You can easily substitute chicken, turkey or beef for the pork.
—*Lori McLain, Denton, TX*

- -

PREP: 25 min. • **COOK:** 5 hours + standing
MAKES: 6 servings

- 1   lb. boneless pork ribeye chops, chopped
- 1   medium onion, halved and sliced
- 1   can (8¾ oz.) whole baby corn, drained, optional
- 1   small sweet red pepper, sliced
- 1   small green pepper, sliced
- 1¾ cups sliced fresh mushrooms
- ½   cup chicken broth
- ½   cup soy sauce
- ¼   cup honey
- 2   garlic cloves, minced
- 2   tsp. Sriracha chili sauce
- ¼   tsp. ground ginger
- 8   oz. thick rice noodles or linguine
- 1   cup fresh snow peas
      Thinly sliced fresh basil

1. Place pork, onion, corn, if desired, peppers and mushrooms in a 6- or 7-qt. slow cooker. Whisk chicken broth, soy sauce, honey, garlic, Sriracha chili sauce and ginger until blended; pour over top. Cook, covered, on low for 5-6 hours or until pork is cooked through and vegetables are tender.
2. Meanwhile, cook pasta according to package directions; do not overcook. Drain noodles; rinse under cold water. Stir noodles and snow peas into slow cooker; let stand 15 minutes. Garnish with basil.
1½ cups: 360 cal., 9g fat (3g sat. fat), 44mg chol., 1467mg sod., 47g carb. (14g sugars, 2g fiber), 21g pro.

SLOW-COOKER BREAKFAST BURRITOS

SLOW-COOKER BREAKFAST BURRITOS

Prep these tasty, hearty burritos the night before for a quick breakfast in the morning, or let them cook while you are away on a weekend afternoon for an easy supper.
—*Anna Miller, Churdan, IA*

- -

PREP: 25 min. • **COOK:** 3¾ hours + standing
MAKES: 12 servings

- 1   pkg. (12 oz.) uncooked breakfast sausage links
- 1   pkg. (28 oz.) frozen O'Brien potatoes, thawed
- 2   cups shredded sharp cheddar cheese
- 12 large eggs
- ½   cup 2% milk
- ¼   tsp. seasoned salt
- ⅛   tsp. pepper
- 12 flour tortillas (8 in.)
      Optional toppings: Salsa, sliced jalapenos, chopped tomatoes, sliced green onions and cubed avocado

1. Remove sausage from casings. In a large skillet, cook sausage over medium heat until no longer pink, 8-10 minutes, breaking into crumbles; drain.
2. In a greased 4- or 5-qt. slow cooker, layer potatoes, sausage and cheese. In a large bowl, whisk eggs, milk, seasoned salt and pepper until blended; pour over top.
3. Cook, covered, on low 3¾-4¼ hours or until eggs are set and a thermometer reads 160°. Uncover and let stand 10 minutes. Serve in tortillas with the toppings of your choice.
1 burrito: 382 cal., 21g fat (9g sat. fat), 221mg chol., 711mg sod., 29g carb. (2g sugars, 3g fiber), 18g pro.

SLOW-COOKER RED BEANS & SAUSAGE

Being from Louisiana, my go-to comfort food is red beans and rice. The slow cooker makes it easy and the recipe reminds me of Sunday family dinners going back generations. Dig in with some hot buttered cornbread.
—Lisa Summers, Las Vegas, NV

- -

PREP: 30 min. • **COOK:** 8 hours
MAKES: 8 servings (2¾ qt.)

- 1 lb. dried red beans
- 1 Tbsp. olive oil
- 1 lb. fully cooked andouille sausage links, cut into ¼-in. slices
- 1 large onion, chopped
- 1 medium green pepper, chopped
- 2 celery ribs, finely chopped
- 3 tsp. garlic powder
- 3 tsp. Creole seasoning
- 2 tsp. smoked paprika
- 2 tsp. dried thyme
- 1½ tsp. pepper
- 6 cups chicken broth
  Hot cooked rice

1. Rinse and sort beans; soak according to package directions.
2. In a large skillet, heat oil over medium-high heat. Brown sausage. Remove with a slotted spoon. Add onion, green pepper and celery to skillet; cook and stir 5-6 minutes or until crisp-tender.
3. In a 5- or 6-qt. slow cooker, combine beans, sausage, vegetables and seasonings. Stir in broth. Cook, covered, on low for 8-10 hours or until beans are tender.
4. Remove 2 cups of the bean mixture to a bowl. Mash gently with a potato masher. Return to slow cooker; heat through. Serve with rice.

1⅓ cups: 283 cal., 14g fat (4g sat. fat), 77mg chol., 1534mg sod., 43g carb. (4g sugars, 27g fiber), 25g pro.

OVERNIGHT BACON & SWISS BREAKFAST

When we have overnight guests, I like to prepare things ahead of time so we can enjoy our company. It often gets crazy when everyone first wakes up, and I like to have food available whenever people are ready to eat. I devised this slow-cooker breakfast recipe when I was feeding 22 people for breakfast at a destination wedding!
—Donna Gribbins, Shelbyville, KY

- -

PREP: 15 min. • **COOK:** 4 hours + standing
MAKES: 12 servings

- 1 pkg. (28 oz.) frozen O'Brien potatoes, thawed
- 1 lb. bacon strips, cooked and crumbled
- 2 cups shredded Swiss cheese
- 12 large eggs
- 2 cups 2% milk
- 1 tsp. seasoned salt
- 1 tsp. pepper
  Minced chives, optional

In a greased 4- or 5-qt. slow cooker, layer potatoes, bacon and cheese. In a large bowl, whisk eggs, milk, seasoned salt and pepper; pour over top. Cook, covered, on low until eggs are set, 4-5 hours. Turn off slow cooker. Remove crock insert to a wire rack; let stand, uncovered, for 30 minutes before serving. Garnish with minced chives, if desired.

1 serving: 277 cal., 16g fat (7g sat. fat), 220mg chol., 507mg sod., 13g carb. (3g sugars, 2g fiber), 18g pro.

OVERNIGHT BACON & SWISS BREAKFAST

GERMAN SCHNITZEL
& POTATOES WITH
GORGONZOLA CREAM

PORK ROAST WITH PEACH SAUCE

My husband loves this roast with spiced peaches and sauce. Easy to make, it's ideal for special occasions or weeknight meals when it's chilly here in the Northwoods.
—*Janice Christofferson, Eagle River, WI*

PREP: 20 min. • **COOK:** 6 hours
MAKES: 8 servings (2½ cups sauce)

- 1   boneless pork loin roast (3 to 4 lbs.)
- 2   tsp. canola oil
- ¼   tsp. onion salt
- ¼   tsp. pepper
- 1   can (15¼ oz.) sliced peaches
- ½   cup chili sauce
- ⅓   cup packed brown sugar
- 3   Tbsp. cider vinegar
- 1   tsp. pumpkin pie spice
- 2   Tbsp. cornstarch
- 2   Tbsp. cold water

1. Cut roast in half. In a large skillet, brown pork in oil on all sides. Transfer to a 4- or 5-qt. slow cooker. Sprinkle with onion salt and pepper.
2. Drain peaches, reserving juice in a small bowl; stir the chili sauce, brown sugar, vinegar and pie spice into the juice. Spoon peaches over roast; top with juice mixture. Cover and cook on low for 6-8 hours or until meat is tender.
3. Remove meat and peaches to a serving platter; keep warm. Skim fat from cooking juices; transfer to a small saucepan. Bring liquid to a boil. Combine cornstarch and water until smooth; gradually stir into the pan. Bring to a boil; cook and stir for 2 minutes or until thickened. Serve with pork and peaches.

1 serving: 318 cal., 8g fat (3g sat. fat), 85mg chol., 344mg sod., 25g carb. (22g sugars, 0 fiber), 33g pro. **Diabetic exchanges:** 4 lean meat, 1 starch, ½ fruit.

GERMAN SCHNITZEL & POTATOES WITH GORGONZOLA CREAM

I lived in Germany for five years and ate a lot of schnitzel. I developed this recipe so it wasn't so time-consuming to make. I get asked for the recipe every time I make it.
—*Beth Taylor, Pleasant Grove, UT*

PREP: 20 min. • **COOK:** 4 hours
MAKES: 4 servings

- 1   pork tenderloin (1 lb.)
- 1   cup dry bread crumbs
- 2   lbs. medium Yukon Gold potatoes, peeled and cut into ¼-in. slices
- 2   cups heavy whipping cream
- ⅔   cup crumbled Gorgonzola cheese
- 1   tsp. salt
- ¼   cup minced fresh Italian parsley
     Lemon wedges

1. Cut tenderloin into 12 slices. Pound with a meat mallet to ¼-in. thickness. Place 4 slices in a 3- or 4-qt. slow cooker. Layer with ¼ cup bread crumbs and a third of the potatoes. Repeat layers twice; top with the remaining bread crumbs.
2. In a small bowl, combine whipping cream, Gorgonzola and salt. Pour over pork mixture; cook on low, covered, 4-6 hours or until the meat and potatoes are tender. Sprinkle with parsley; serve with lemon wedges.
3 slices pork with 1 cup potato mixture:
926 cal., 54g fat (33g sat. fat), 216mg chol., 1132mg sod., 73g carb. (9g sugars, 5g fiber), 38g pro.

TEST KITCHEN TIP

Often fried, schnitzel made in the slow cooker is satisfying without all the mess of frying. Add some dried herbs to make this dish your own. Just add a teaspoon or two to the bread crumbs.

PUMPKIN SPICE
OATMEAL

GREEN CHILE ADOBADO POUTINE

Canadian comfort food is even better when served southwestern style. You can also bake the ribs at 325°, covered with foil, for about 45 minutes. Then uncover and bake another 20 minutes.
—*Johnna Johnson, Scottsdale, AZ*

- -

PREP: 50 min. • **COOK:** 3 hours
MAKES: 8 servings

- 3 garlic cloves, unpeeled
- 4 dried guajillo or ancho chiles, stemmed and seeded
- 1 can (10 oz.) enchilada sauce, divided
- 3 cans (4 oz. each) chopped green chiles, divided
- 1 Tbsp. cider vinegar
- 2 tsp. dried oregano
- ½ tsp. ground cumin
- ½ tsp. salt
- ½ tsp. pepper
- ⅛ tsp. ground cinnamon
- 2 lbs. boneless country-style pork ribs, cut into 2-in. pieces
- 1 pkg. (32 oz.) frozen french-fried potatoes
- 1 cup queso fresco
     Pico de gallo, optional

1. Lightly smash garlic cloves with the bottom of a heavy skillet to flatten. Cook in a large skillet over medium-low heat until softened and browned, 10 minutes. Cool and peel. In same pan at the same time, cook dried chiles, pressing them against the bottom with a spatula or tongs until lightly toasted and fragrant, 1-2 minutes. Place in a bowl. Add boiling water to cover; let stand 15 minutes. Drain.
2. Place chiles and garlic in a food processor. Add ½ cup enchilada sauce, 2 cans green chiles, vinegar, oregano, cumin, salt, pepper and cinnamon; process until blended. Stir in remaining enchilada sauce and green chiles. Transfer to a 5- or 6-qt. slow cooker. Add ribs; turn to coat. Cover and cook on high 3-4 hours or until meat is tender. During the final 30 minutes, cook fries according to package directions.
3. Remove pork from slow cooker; shred with 2 forks. Top fries with meat, cheese, enchilada gravy and, if desired, pico de gallo.
1 serving: 434 cal., 19g fat (7g sat. fat), 75mg chol., 1065mg sod., 31g carb. (2g sugars, 5g fiber), 28g pro.

PUMPKIN SPICE OATMEAL

There's nothing like a warm cup of oatmeal in the morning, and my spiced version works in a slow cooker.
—*Jordan Mason, Brookville, PA*

- -

PREP: 10 min. • **COOK:** 5 hours
MAKES: 6 servings

- 1 can (15 oz.) solid-pack pumpkin
- 1 cup steel-cut oats
- 3 Tbsp. brown sugar
- 1½ tsp. pumpkin pie spice
- 1 tsp. ground cinnamon
- ¾ tsp. salt
- 3 cups water
- 1½ cups 2% milk
     Optional toppings: Toasted chopped pecans, ground cinnamon, and additional brown sugar and milk

In a large bowl, combine first 6 ingredients; stir in water and milk. Transfer to a greased 3-qt. slow cooker. Cook, covered, on low for 5-6 hours or until oats are tender, stirring once. Serve with toppings as desired.
1 cup: 183 cal., 3g fat (1g sat. fat), 5mg chol., 329mg sod., 34g carb. (13g sugars, 5g fiber), 6g pro. **Diabetic exchanges:** 2 starch, ½ fat.

TEST KITCHEN TIP
To make gingerbread oatmeal, replace half the brown sugar with molasses and sprinkle chopped candied ginger over the top.

SLOW-COOKER SAUSAGE LASAGNA

On especially cold winter days, my family loves this stick-to-your-ribs lasagna. If you prefer to heat things up a bit, use a spicy Italian sausage to give it more zing.
—*Cindi DeClue, Anchorage, AK*

- -

PREP: 40 min. • **COOK:** 3½ hours + standing
MAKES: 8 servings

- 1 lb. ground beef
- 1 lb. ground mild Italian sausage
- 1 medium onion, finely chopped
- 1 garlic clove, minced
- 1 jar (24 oz.) spaghetti sauce
- 1 can (14½ oz.) diced tomatoes in sauce, undrained
- ½ cup water
- 1 tsp. dried basil
- 1 tsp. dried oregano
- 1 carton (15 oz.) whole-milk ricotta cheese
- 2 large eggs, lightly beaten
- ½ cup grated Parmesan cheese
- 9 uncooked lasagna noodles
- 4 cups shredded part-skim mozzarella cheese
  Minced fresh basil, optional

1. Line sides of an oval 6-qt. slow cooker with heavy-duty foil; coat foil with cooking spray. In a Dutch oven, cook beef, sausage, onion and garlic over medium heat 8-10 minutes or until meat is no longer pink, breaking up beef and sausage into crumbles; drain. Stir in spaghetti sauce, tomatoes, water and herbs; heat through.

2. In a small bowl, mix ricotta cheese, eggs and Parmesan cheese. Spread 1½ cups meat sauce onto bottom of prepared slow cooker. Layer with 3 noodles (breaking to fit), ¾ cup ricotta mixture, 1 cup mozzarella cheese and 2 cups meat sauce. Repeat layers twice. Sprinkle with remaining mozzarella.

3. Cook, covered, on low 3½-4 hours or until noodles are tender. Turn off slow cooker; remove insert. Let stand 15 minutes. If desired, sprinkle with fresh basil.

1 serving: 667 cal., 37g fat (17g sat. fat), 164mg chol., 1310mg sod., 41g carb. (14g sugars, 4g fiber), 42g pro.

SLOW-COOKER
SAUSAGE LASAGNA

LIGHT HAM TETRAZZINI

This creamy pasta is an easy way to serve a hungry crowd. If you're bringing this tetrazzini to a potluck, cook and add the spaghetti to the slow cooker just before heading our to the gathering.
—*Susan Blair, Sterling, MI*

- -

PREP: 15 min. • **COOK:** 4 hours
MAKES: 10 servings

- 2 cans (10¾ oz. each) reduced-fat reduced-sodium condensed cream of mushroom soup, undiluted
- 2 cups cubed fully cooked ham
- 2 cups sliced fresh mushrooms
- 1 cup fat-free evaporated milk
- ¼ cup white wine or water
- 2 tsp. prepared horseradish
- 1 pkg. (14½ oz.) multigrain spaghetti
- 1 cup shredded Parmesan cheese

1. In a 5-qt. slow cooker, mix the first 6 ingredients. Cook, covered, on low for 4-5 hours or until heated through.

2. To serve, cook spaghetti according to package directions; drain. Add spaghetti and cheese to slow cooker; toss to combine.

1 cup: 279 cal., 5g fat (2g sat. fat), 26mg chol., 734mg sod., 37g carb. (5g sugars, 4g fiber), 20g pro. **Diabetic exchanges:** 2½ starch, 1 lean meat, ½ fat.

SPICY KALE
& HERB PORCHETTA

BBQ CHICKEN
& SMOKED SAUSAGE

My party-ready barbecue recipe works for weeknights, too. With just a few minutes of prep time, you get that low-and-slow flavor everybody craves.
—*Kimberly Young, Mesquite, TX*

- -

PREP: 30 min. • **COOK:** 4 hours
MAKES: 8 servings

- 1 **medium onion, chopped**
- 1 **large sweet red pepper, cut into 1-in. pieces**
- 4 **bone-in chicken thighs, skin removed**
- 4 **chicken drumsticks, skin removed**
- 1 **pkg. (12 oz.) smoked sausage links, cut into 1-in. pieces**
- 1 **cup barbecue sauce**
  Sliced seeded jalapeno pepper, optional

1. Place first 5 ingredients in a 4- or 5-qt. slow cooker; top with barbecue sauce. Cook, covered, on low 4-5 hours or until chicken is tender and a thermometer inserted in chicken reads at least 170°-175°.
2. Remove chicken, sausage and vegetables from slow cooker; keep warm. Transfer cooking juices to a saucepan; bring to a boil. Reduce heat; simmer, uncovered, until mixture is thickened, 15-20 minutes, stirring occasionally.
3. Serve chicken, sausage and vegetables with sauce. If desired, top with jalapeno.
1 serving: 331 cal., 18g fat (6g sat. fat), 91mg chol., 840mg sod., 17g carb. (13g sugars, 1g fiber), 24g pro.

SPICY KALE
& HERB PORCHETTA

Serve this classic Italian specialty as a main entree or with a loaf of crusty artisan bread for sandwiches. Use the liquid from the slow cooker with your favorite seasonings to make a sauce or gravy.
—*Sandi Sheppard, Norman, OK*

- -

PREP: 30 min. + chilling • **COOK:** 5 hours
MAKES: 12 servings

- 1½ **cups packed torn fresh kale leaves (no stems)**
- ¼ **cup each chopped fresh sage, rosemary and parsley**
- 2 **Tbsp. kosher salt**
- 1 **Tbsp. crushed fennel seed**
- 1 **tsp. crushed red pepper flakes**
- 4 **garlic cloves, halved**
- 1 **boneless pork shoulder roast (about 6 lbs.), butterflied**
- 2 **tsp. grated lemon zest**
- 1 **large sweet onion, thickly sliced**
- ¼ **cup white wine or chicken broth**
- 1 **Tbsp. olive oil**
- 3 **Tbsp. cornstarch**
- 3 **Tbsp. water**

1. In a blender or food processor, pulse the first 8 ingredients until finely chopped. In a 15x10x1-in. baking pan, open roast flat. Spread herb mixture evenly over meat to within ½ in. of edges; sprinkle lemon zest over herb mixture.
2. Starting at a long side, roll up jelly-roll style. Using a sharp knife, score fat on outside of roast. Tie at 2-in. intervals with kitchen string. Secure ends with toothpicks. Refrigerate, covered, at least 4 hours or overnight.
3. In a 6-qt. slow cooker, combine onion and wine. Place porchetta seam side down on top of onion. Cook, covered, on low 5-6 hours or until tender. Remove toothpicks. Reserve cooking juices.
4. In a large skillet, heat oil over medium heat. Brown porchetta on all sides; remove from heat. Tent with foil. Let stand 15 minutes.
5. Meanwhile, strain and skim fat from cooking juices. Transfer to a large saucepan; bring to a boil. In a small bowl, mix cornstarch and water until smooth; stir into juices. Return to a boil, stirring constantly; cook and stir until thickened, 1-2 minutes. Serve with roast.
1 serving: 402 cal., 24g fat (8g sat. fat), 135mg chol., 1104mg sod., 5g carb. (1g sugars, 1g fiber), 39g pro.

CARNITAS HUEVOS RANCHEROS

When I was in college, I was a church counselor in Colorado and had my first taste of Mexican food. Recently I've learned to make more authentic dishes, like these pork huevos rancheros. It's one of my favorite recipes to serve for dinner.
—*Lonnie Hartstack, Clarinda, IA*

PREP: 35 min. • **COOK:** 7 hours
MAKES: 12 servings

- 1 boneless pork shoulder butt roast (3 lbs.), halved
- 2 tsp. olive oil
- 3 garlic cloves, thinly sliced
- ½ tsp. salt
- ½ tsp. pepper
- 1 medium onion, chopped
- 2 cans (4 oz. each) chopped green chiles
- 1 cup salsa
- ½ cup minced fresh cilantro
- ½ cup chicken broth
- ½ cup tequila or additional chicken broth
- 1 can (15 oz.) black beans, rinsed and drained

ASSEMBLY

- 12 large eggs
- 1 jar (16 oz.) salsa
- 12 flour tortillas (6 in.), warmed and quartered
- 4 medium ripe avocados, peeled and sliced

1. Rub roast with oil, garlic, salt and pepper. Place in a 4- or 5-qt. slow cooker. Top with onion, green chiles, salsa, cilantro, broth and tequila. Cook, covered, on low 7-8 hours or until meat is tender.
2. Remove roast; shred with 2 forks. Discard cooking juices, reserving 1 cup. Return the cooking juices and meat to slow cooker. Stir in beans; heat through.
3. Meanwhile, coat a large skillet with cooking spray; place over medium-high heat. Working in batches, break eggs, 1 at a time, into pan; reduce heat to low. Cook until whites are set and yolks begin to thicken, turning once if desired. Divide the pork mixture among 12 bowls. Top with salsa, eggs, avocados and additional cilantro. Serve with tortillas.
1 serving: 509 cal., 27g fat (8g sat. fat), 254mg chol., 858mg sod., 32g carb. (3g sugars, 7g fiber), 31g pro.

MUSHROOM PORK RAGOUT

🍎 MUSHROOM PORK RAGOUT

Savory, slow-cooked pork is luscious served in a delightful tomato gravy over noodles. It's a nice change from regular pork roast. I serve it with broccoli or green beans on the side.
—*Connie McDowell, Greenwood, DE*

PREP: 20 min. • **COOK:** 3 hours
MAKES: 2 servings

- 1 pork tenderloin (¾ lb.)
- ⅛ tsp. salt
- ⅛ tsp. pepper
- 1 Tbsp. cornstarch
- ¾ cup canned crushed tomatoes, divided
- 1 Tbsp. chopped sun-dried tomatoes (not packed in oil)
- 1¼ tsp. dried savory
- 1½ cups sliced fresh mushrooms
- ⅓ cup sliced onion
- 1½ cups hot cooked egg noodles

1. Rub pork with salt and pepper; cut in half. In a 1½-qt. slow cooker, combine the cornstarch, ½ cup crushed tomatoes, sun-dried tomatoes and savory. Top with mushrooms, onion and pork. Pour remaining tomatoes over pork. Cover and cook on low until meat is tender, 3-4 hours.
2. Remove meat and cut into slices. Stir cooking juices until smooth; serve with pork and noodles.
1 serving: 360 cal., 7g fat (2g sat. fat), 122mg chol., 309mg sod., 32g carb. (3g sugars, 3g fiber), 40g pro. **Diabetic exchanges:** 5 lean meat, 2 vegetable, 1 starch.

RASPBERRY COCONUT FRENCH TOAST SLOW-COOKER STYLE

I put the ingredients in the crock the night before, refrigerate it, then pop the crock into the slow cooker in the morning. You can use regular milk or half-and-half, your favorite jam, and almond extract instead of vanilla.
—*Teri Rasey, Cadillac, MI*

- -

PREP: 20 min. + chilling • **COOK:** 2¾ hours.
MAKES: 12 servings

- 6 large eggs
- 1½ cups refrigerated sweetened coconut milk
- 1 tsp. vanilla extract
- 1 loaf (1 lb.) French bread, cubed
- 1 pkg. (8 oz.) cream cheese, cubed
- ⅔ cup seedless raspberry jam
- ½ cup sweetened shredded coconut
  Whipped cream, fresh raspberries and toasted sweetened shredded coconut

1. In a large bowl, whisk eggs, coconut milk and vanilla until blended. Place half of the bread in a greased 5- or 6-qt. slow cooker; layer with half of the cream cheese, jam, coconut and egg mixture. Repeat layers. Refrigerate, covered, overnight.
2. Cook, covered, on low 2¾-3¼ hours or until a knife inserted in the center comes out clean. Serve warm with whipped cream, raspberries and toasted coconut.
1 cup: 280 cal., 12g fat (7g sat. fat), 112mg chol., 338mg sod., 35g carb. (16g sugars, 1g fiber), 9g pro.

MOROCCAN LAMB LETTUCE WRAPS

MOROCCAN LAMB LETTUCE WRAPS

I am a huge fan of both lamb and lettuce wraps. This combination—with the creamy dressing and crunchy cucumber—makes a tasty slow-cooked dish. The wine and chili powder add extra flavor elements, too.
—*Arlene Erlbach, Morton Grove, IL*

- -

PREP: 25 min. • **COOK:** 5 hours
MAKES: 8 servings

- 2 lbs. lamb stew meat
- 1 cup chunky salsa
- ⅓ cup apricot preserves
- 6 Tbsp. dry red wine, divided
- 1 to 2 Tbsp. Moroccan seasoning (ras el hanout)
- 2 tsp. chili powder
- ½ tsp. garlic powder
- 1 English cucumber, very thinly sliced
- 2 Tbsp. prepared ranch salad dressing
- 16 Bibb or Boston lettuce leaves

1. Combine lamb, salsa, preserves, 4 Tbsp. wine, Moroccan seasoning, chili powder and garlic powder. Transfer to a 3-qt. slow cooker. Cook, covered, on low 5-6 hours or until lamb is tender. Remove lamb; shred with 2 forks. Strain cooking juices and skim fat. Return lamb and cooking juices to slow cooker; heat through. Stir in remaining 2 Tbsp. wine; heat through.
2. Combine cucumber and ranch dressing; toss to coat. Serve lamb mixture in lettuce leaves; top with cucumber mixture.
2 filled lettuce wraps: 221 cal., 8g fat (2g sat. fat), 74mg chol., 257mg sod., 13g carb. (8g sugars, 1g fiber), 24g pro. **Diabetic exchanges:** 3 lean meat, 1 starch.

SPICY SAUSAGE MEATBALL SAUCE

I threw together three favorite veggies and spicy sausage for this incredible sauce that makes our mouths water the whole time it's cooking. Besides serving this with pasta (refrigerated tortellini is best), we've had it with brown basmati rice, as sloppy subs on toasted Italian rolls, and as a stew with hot garlic bread.

—*Ann R. Sheehy, Lawrence, MA*

PREP: 40 min. • **COOK:** 5 hours
MAKES: 12 servings (3¾ qt.)

- 2 cans (28 oz. each) crushed tomatoes
- 2 cans (14½ oz. each) diced tomatoes, undrained
- ¾ lb. sliced fresh mushrooms
- 5 garlic cloves, minced
- 4 tsp. Italian seasoning
- 1 tsp. pepper
- ¼ tsp. salt
- ¼ tsp. crushed red pepper flakes
- 1 large sweet onion
- 1 large green pepper
- 1 medium sweet red pepper
- 1 medium sweet orange pepper
- 1 medium sweet yellow pepper
- 10 hot Italian sausage links (4 oz. each), casings removed
- ¼ cup all-purpose flour
- 2 Tbsp. canola oil
  Hot cooked pasta

1. Place first 8 ingredients in a 6-qt. slow cooker. Chop onion and peppers; stir into tomato mixture.

2. Shape sausage into 1¾-in. balls; roll in flour to coat lightly. In a large skillet, heat oil over medium-high heat; cook meatballs in batches until lightly browned, 5-8 minutes, turning occasionally. Drain on paper towels. Add to slow cooker, stirring gently into sauce.

3. Cook, covered, on low 5-6 hours or until meatballs are cooked through and vegetables are tender. Serve with pasta.

Freeze option: Freeze cooled meatball mixture in freezer containers. To use, partially thaw in refrigerator overnight. Place meatball mixture in a large skillet; heat through, stirring occasionally and adding a little water to skillet if necessary.

1¼ cups: 343 cal., 23g fat (7g sat. fat), 51mg chol., 984mg sod., 22g carb. (11g sugars, 5g fiber), 15g pro.

TEST KITCHEN TIP
This is a hearty take on meatballs with sauce. If you aren't a fan of heat, use sweet sausage links.

SPICY SAUSAGE
MEATBALL SAUCE

SLOW-COOKER
GOETTA

GERMAN BRATWURST WITH SAUERKRAUT & APPLES

I created this Old World favorite from a dish I had in my travels. This flavorful dish is perfect for weeknights or special occasions. I like to serve it with pasta.
—*Gerald Hetrick, Erie, PA*

- -

PREP: 15 min. • **COOK:** 6 hours
MAKES: 15 servings

- 4 lbs. uncooked bratwurst links
- 3 bottles (12 oz. each) German-style beer or 4½ cups reduced-sodium chicken broth
- 1 jar (32 oz.) sauerkraut, rinsed and well drained
- 4 medium Granny Smith apples (about 1¼ lbs.), cut into wedges
- 1 medium onion, halved and thinly sliced
- 1½ tsp. caraway seeds
- ¼ tsp. pepper

1. In batches, in a large nonstick skillet, brown sausages over medium-high heat. Transfer to a 7-qt. slow cooker. Add the remaining ingredients.
2. Cook, covered, on low 6-8 hours or until a thermometer inserted in sausage reads at least 160°.
1 serving: 445 cal., 35g fat (12g sat. fat), 90mg chol., 1424mg sod., 13g carb. (6g sugars, 3g fiber), 17g pro.

TEST KITCHEN TIP
This recipe pairs well with spaetzle. Also try serving the bratwurst on pretzel buns.

❄

SLOW-COOKER GOETTA

My husband's grandfather, a German, introduced goetta to me when we first got married. I found a slow-cooker recipe and changed some of the ingredients to make the best goetta around. Now, many people request my recipe. It makes a lot of sausage, but it freezes well.
—*Sharon Geers, Wilmington, OH*

- -

PREP: 45 min. + chilling
COOK: 4 hours 10 min.
MAKES: 2 loaves (16 slices each)

- 6 cups water
- 2½ cups steel-cut oats
- 6 bay leaves
- 3 Tbsp. beef bouillon granules
- ¾ tsp. salt
- 1 tsp. each garlic powder, rubbed sage and pepper
- ½ tsp. ground allspice
- ½ tsp. crushed red pepper flakes
- 2 lbs. bulk pork sausage
- 2 medium onions, chopped

1. In a 5-qt. slow cooker, combine water, oats and seasonings. Cook, covered, on high 2 hours. Remove bay leaves.
2. In a large skillet, cook sausage and onions over medium heat 8-10 minutes or until meat is no longer pink, breaking up sausage into crumbles. Drain, reserving 2 Tbsp. drippings. Stir sausage mixture and reserved drippings into oats. Cook, covered, on low 2 hours.
3. Transfer mixture to 2 waxed paper-lined 9x5-in. loaf pans. Refrigerate, covered, overnight.
4. To serve, slice each loaf into 16 slices. In a large skillet, cook goetta, in batches, over medium heat 3-4 minutes on each side or until lightly browned and heated through.
Freeze option: After shaping the goetta in loaf pans, cool and freeze, covered, until firm. Transfer the goetta to freezer containers or wrap securely in foil; return to freezer. Partially thaw in refrigerator overnight; slice and cook as directed.
2 slices: 242 cal., 14g fat (4g sat. fat), 30mg chol., 900mg sod., 20g carb. (2g sugars, 2g fiber), 10g pro.

GERMAN BRATWURST WITH
SAUERKRAUT & APPLES

Soups, Sides & Sandwiches

BUFFALO CHICKEN SLIDERS

My family loves spicy foods, and this is a great combination of sweet and spicy. You won't be able to have just one!

—*Christina Addison, Blanchester, OH*

PREP: 20 min. • **COOK:** 3 hours
MAKES: 6 servings

- 1 lb. boneless skinless chicken breasts
- 2 Tbsp. plus ⅓ cup Louisiana-style hot sauce, divided
- ¼ tsp. pepper
- ¼ cup butter, cubed
- ¼ cup honey
- 12 Hawaiian sweet rolls, warmed
  Optional ingredients: Lettuce leaves, sliced tomato, thinly sliced red onion and crumbled blue cheese

1. Place chicken in a 3-qt. slow cooker. Toss with 2 Tbsp. hot sauce and pepper; cook, covered, on low 3-4 hours or until tender.
2. Remove chicken; discard cooking juices. In a small saucepan, combine butter, honey and remaining hot sauce; cook and stir over medium heat until blended. Shred chicken with 2 forks; stir into sauce and heat through. Serve chicken on Hawaiian sweet rolls with desired optional ingredients.
Freeze option: Freeze cooled chicken mixture in freezer containers. To use, partially thaw in refrigerator overnight. Microwave, covered, on high in a microwave-safe dish until heated through, stirring occasionally; add water or broth if necessary.
2 sliders: 396 cal., 15g fat (8g sat. fat), 92mg chol., 873mg sod., 44g carb. (24g sugars, 2g fiber), 24g pro.

BUFFALO CHICKEN SLIDERS

SLOW-COOKER
BAKED POTATOES

SWEET & SAVORY SLOW-COOKED BEEF

There's plenty of sweet and a little heat from the chipotle pepper in this family-friendly shredded beef recipe. Add your favorite barbecue sauce or stir things up each time you make it by varying the flavor to see which way you like it best.
—*David Kleiman, New Bedford, MA*

- -

PREP: 20 min. • **COOK:** 8 hours
MAKES: 16 servings

1	beef top round roast (4 lbs.)
1	bottle (18 oz.) barbecue sauce
½	cup water
¼	cup packed brown sugar
1	chipotle pepper in adobo sauce, chopped
2	Tbsp. Worcestershire sauce
2	Tbsp. steak sauce
1½	tsp. reduced-sodium soy sauce
1	tsp. celery salt
1	tsp. garlic salt
1	tsp. seasoned salt
1	tsp. pepper
16	onion rolls, split

1. Cut roast in half; place in a 6-qt. slow cooker. Combine the barbecue sauce, water, brown sugar, chipotle pepper, Worcestershire sauce, steak sauce, soy sauce and seasonings. Pour over meat.
2. Cover and cook on low for 8-10 hours or until meat is tender. Remove roast and cool slightly. Skim fat from cooking juices. Shred meat with 2 forks and return to slow cooker; heat through. Serve on rolls.
1 sandwich: 374 cal., 6g fat (2g sat. fat), 63mg chol., 974mg sod., 45g carb. (20g sugars, 1g fiber), 32g pro.

SLOW-COOKER BAKED POTATOES

This baked potato recipe is so easy—just add your favorite toppings. Save any extra potatoes to make baked potato soup the next day.
—*Teresa Emrick, Tipp City, OH*

- -

PREP: 10 min. • **COOK:** 8 hours
MAKES: 6 potatoes

6	medium russet potatoes
3	Tbsp. butter, softened
3	garlic cloves, minced
1	cup water
	Salt and pepper to taste
	Optional: Sour cream, butter, crumbled bacon, minced chives, guacamole, shredded cheddar cheese and minced fresh cilantro

1. Scrub potatoes; pierce several times with a fork. In a small bowl, mix butter and garlic. Rub potatoes with butter mixture. Wrap each tightly with a piece of foil.
2. Pour water into a 6-qt. slow cooker; add potatoes. Cook, covered, on low 8-10 hours or until tender. Season and top as desired.
1 potato: 217 cal., 6g fat (4g sat. fat), 15mg chol., 59mg sod., 38g carb. (2g sugars, 5g fiber), 5g pro.

TEST KITCHEN TIP

Serve the potatoes right in their foil packets to get the most out of the garlic butter. This is an easy way to make potatoes for a baked potato bar at the office.

SIMPLY
INCREDIBLE GRITS

SIMPLY INCREDIBLE GRITS

Since moving to the South, I have come to love grits! I also love my slow cooker, and worked to find a way to make perfect grits without having to stir them on the stovetop. I knew this recipe was a winner when my mother-in-law overheard someone say at a church potluck that it just wasn't right that a Midwesterner could make such good grits!
—Tacy Fleury, Clinton, SC

PREP: 10 min. • **COOK:** 2½ hours
MAKES: 6 servings

- 2⅔ cups water
- 1½ cups uncooked old-fashioned grits
- 1½ cups 2% milk
- 3 Tbsp. butter, cubed
- 2 tsp. chicken bouillon granules
- ½ tsp. salt
- 1 cup shredded cheddar cheese
- ⅓ cup grated Parmesan cheese

Combine the first 6 ingredients in a greased 3-qt. slow cooker. Cook, covered, on low until liquid is absorbed and grits are tender, 2½-3 hours, stirring every 45 minutes. Stir in cheeses until melted. Serve immediately.
¾ cup: 334 cal., 15g fat (9g sat. fat), 43mg chol., 755mg sod., 38g carb. (3g sugars, 2g fiber), 11g pro.

TEST KITCHEN TIP
To make a vegetarian version of these grits, substitute vegetable bouillon (enough to flavor 2 cups of liquid) for the chicken bouillon granules.

SLOW-COOKER
CITRUS CARROTS

SLOW-COOKER CITRUS CARROTS

These carrots are yummy and so simple. The recipe is from my mom, who tweaked it a bit to suit her tastes. You can make this dish a day in advance and refrigerate until needed. Then reheat it right before the party.
—Julie Puderbaugh, Berwick, PA

PREP: 10 min. • **COOK:** 4¼ hours
MAKES: 12 servings

- 12 cups frozen sliced carrots (about 48 oz.), thawed
- 1¾ cups orange juice
- ½ cup sugar
- 3 Tbsp. butter, cubed
- ½ tsp. salt
- 3 Tbsp. cornstarch
- ¼ cup cold water
  Minced fresh parsley, optional

1. In a 3- or 4-qt. slow cooker, combine the first 5 ingredients. Cook, covered, on low 4-5 hours or until carrots are tender.
2. In a small bowl, mix cornstarch and water until smooth; gradually stir into slow cooker. Cook, covered, on high until the sauce is thickened, 15-30 minutes. Garnish with fresh parsley, if desired.
¾ cup: 136 cal., 4g fat (2g sat. fat), 8mg chol., 208mg sod., 25g carb. (18g sugars, 5g fiber), 1g pro.
Pressure-Cooker Citrus Carrots: In a 6-qt. electric pressure cooker, combine the first 5 ingredients. Lock lid; close pressure-release valve. Adjust to pressure-cook on high for 2 minutes. Quick-release pressure. Press cancel. In a small bowl, mix cornstarch and water until smooth; stir into pressure cooker. Select saute setting and adjust for low heat. Simmer, stirring constantly, until thickened, 1-2 minutes.

CHEESE-STUFFED SWEET ONIONS

HEARTY MANHATTAN CLAM CHOWDER

This veggie-packed clam chowder is savory and satisfying. Butter up some crusty bread and you have yourself a complete meal.
—*Carol Bullick, Royersford, PA*

PREP: 20 min. • **COOK:** 7 hours
MAKES: 6 servings (about 2¼ qt.)

- 1½ lbs. potatoes (about 3 medium), peeled and cut into ¾-in. cubes
- 1 large onion, chopped
- 2 medium carrots, shredded (about ¾ cup)
- 3 celery ribs, sliced
- 4 cans (6½ oz. each) chopped clams, undrained
- 5 bacon strips, cooked and crumbled
- 1 Tbsp. dried parsley flakes
- 1 bay leaf
- 1½ tsp. dried thyme
- ¼ tsp. coarsely ground pepper
- 1 can (28 oz.) diced tomatoes, undrained

Place all ingredients in a 4- or 5-qt. slow cooker. Cook, covered, on low until vegetables are tender, 7-9 hours. Remove bay leaf before serving.

1½ cups: 203 cal., 4g fat (1g sat. fat), 50mg chol., 995mg sod., 29g carb. (8g sugars, 5g fiber), 15g pro.

CHEESE-STUFFED SWEET ONIONS

These onions are cooked in vegetable broth and stuffed with a delicious blend of cheeses. Experiment to find the blend you like. Instead of goat cheese, try mascarpone or cream cheese. Instead of blue cheese, you can use Gorgonzola, and in place of Romano, you can use Parmesan. It's all delicious!
—*Sonya Labbe, West Hollywood, CA*

PREP: 25 min. • **COOK:** 4 hours
MAKES: 8 servings

- 4 large Vidalia or other sweet onions
- ¾ cup crumbled goat cheese
- ¾ cup crumbled blue cheese
- 1 tsp. minced fresh thyme
- 2 cups vegetable stock
- 1 Tbsp. olive oil
- ¼ tsp. salt
- ⅛ tsp. pepper
- ¼ cup grated Romano or Parmesan cheese
  Fresh thyme leaves

1. Peel onions. Cut a ½-in. slice off top of each onion; remove centers with a melon baller, leaving ½-in. shells. Chop removed onion, reserving 3 cups (save remaining onion for another use). Mix together goat and blue cheeses, minced thyme and reserved onion; spoon into onions.

2. Place onions and stock in a 6-qt. slow cooker; drizzle with oil. Sprinkle with salt, pepper and Romano cheese. Cook, covered, on low 4-5 hours or until tender. Cut in half to serve; sprinkle with thyme leaves.

½ stuffed onion: 137 cal., 9g fat (5g sat. fat), 23mg chol., 471mg sod., 8g carb. (3g sugars, 2g fiber), 7g pro.

DID YOU KNOW?

Sweet onions are easy to recognize by their shape. They are shorter from pole to pole and bigger around than regular cooking onions. Many carry the names from the place they're grown, such as Vidalia (from Vidalia, Georgia), Walla Walla (from Washington) and Hawaii's Maui onion.

HEARTY MANHATTAN
CLAM CHOWDER

SANTA FE CHILI

This has been my husband's favorite chili for years. It makes a lot, so it's perfect for those who like to prepare meals for an entire week. I use three kinds of beans and heirloom shoepeg corn in my meaty chili.
—*Laura Manning, Lilburn, GA*

PREP: 20 min. • **COOK:** 4 hours
MAKES: 16 servings (4 qt.)

- 2 lbs. ground beef
- 1 medium onion, chopped
- 2 cans (16 oz. each) kidney beans, rinsed and drained
- 2 cans (15 oz. each) black beans, rinsed and drained
- 2 cans (15 oz. each) pinto beans, rinsed and drained
- 3 cans (7 oz. each) white or shoepeg corn, drained
- 1 can (14½ oz.) diced tomatoes, undrained
- 1 can (10 oz.) diced tomatoes and green chiles
- 1 can (11½ oz.) V8 juice
- 2 envelopes ranch salad dressing mix
- 2 envelopes taco seasoning
  Optional: Sour cream, shredded cheddar cheese and corn chips

1. In a large skillet, cook beef and onion over medium heat until meat is no longer pink; drain. Transfer to a 5- or 6-qt. slow cooker. Stir in the beans, corn, tomatoes, juice, salad dressing mix and taco seasoning.
2. Cover and cook on high for 4-6 hours or until heated through. Serve with sour cream, cheese and corn chips if desired.
Freeze option: Freeze cooled chili in freezer containers. To use, partially thaw in the refrigerator overnight. Heat through in a saucepan, stirring occasionally and adding a little broth or water if necessary.
1 cup: 224 cal., 5g fat (2g sat. fat), 28mg chol., 1513mg sod., 28g carb. (4g sugars, 4g fiber), 15g pro.

SAUSAGE, KALE & SQUASH BREAD PUDDING

SAUSAGE, KALE & SQUASH BREAD PUDDING

Who said bread pudding has to be for dessert? I love to serve this as a brunch or dinner side when I want something hearty and special.
—*Lauren Knoelke, Des Moines, IA*

PREP: 25 min. • **COOK:** 3 hours
MAKES: 12 servings

- 1 lb. bulk spicy pork sausage
- 1½ cups chopped sweet onion (about 1 medium)
- 3 garlic cloves, minced
- ½ cup white wine
- 1 loaf sourdough bread (about 1 lb.), lightly toasted and cubed
- 4 cups chopped fresh kale
- 3 cups cubed peeled butternut squash
- 1 cup shredded Gruyere or Swiss cheese
- 1 cup chicken broth
- 4 large eggs
- ½ cup heavy whipping cream
- 1 Tbsp. minced fresh thyme
- 1 tsp. salt
- ½ tsp. coarsely ground pepper

1. In a large skillet, cook and crumble sausage over medium heat until no longer pink, 6-8 minutes. Remove with a slotted spoon; drain on paper towels.
2. In same skillet, cook and stir onion over medium-low heat until just softened, 2-3 minutes. Add garlic; cook 1 minute longer. Add wine, stirring to loosen browned bits from pan. Cook until liquid is almost evaporated, 2-4 minutes. Transfer to a large bowl. Add sausage, bread, kale, squash, cheese and broth; toss to combine.
3. In another bowl, whisk eggs, cream, thyme, salt and pepper until blended. Pour over bread mixture; toss to coat. Transfer to a greased 6-qt. slow cooker. Cook, covered, on low 3-4 hours or until squash is tender. Serve warm.
¾ cup: 330 cal., 17g fat (7g sat. fat), 104mg chol., 831mg sod., 28g carb. (4g sugars, 2g fiber), 14g pro.

SLOW-COOKER CORDON BLEU SOUP

I've taken this creamy slow-cooker soup to potlucks and teacher luncheons, and I bring home an empty crock every time. When my son's school recently created a cookbook, this was the first recipe he asked me to submit, and his teachers were glad he did.
—*Erica Winkel, Ada, MI*

PREP: 40 min. • **COOK:** 3 hours
MAKES: 8 servings (2½ qt.)

3 Tbsp. butter, melted
¼ tsp. garlic powder
¼ tsp. pepper
4 cups cubed French bread

SOUP
1 small onion, diced
1 celery rib, diced
1 garlic clove, minced
¼ tsp. salt
¼ tsp. pepper
3 cans (14½ oz. each) reduced-sodium chicken broth
⅓ cup all-purpose flour
⅓ cup water
¼ cup white wine or additional reduced-sodium chicken broth
8 oz. reduced-fat cream cheese, cubed
1½ cups Swiss cheese, shredded
½ cup shredded cheddar cheese
½ lb. diced rotisserie chicken
½ lb. diced deli ham

1. For croutons, preheat oven to 375°. In a large bowl, mix melted butter, garlic powder and pepper. Add bread cubes; toss to coat. Transfer croutons to a 15x10x1-in. baking pan; bake, stirring every 5 minutes, until golden brown, 15-20 minutes. Cool in pan on a wire rack.

2. Meanwhile, in a 4- or 5-qt. slow cooker, combine first 5 soup ingredients; pour in broth. Cook, covered, on low about 2 hours or until vegetables are tender.

3. Increase slow-cooker heat setting to high. Mix flour and water until smooth; whisk mixture into broth. Cook until thickened, 30-40 minutes. Stir in wine. Whisk in cheeses until melted. Add chicken and ham; heat through. Serve with croutons.

Freeze option: Before adding croutons, freeze cooled soup in freezer containers. Freeze croutons separately. To use, partially thaw soup in refrigerator overnight. Heat soup through in a saucepan, stirring occasionally; add broth or water if necessary. While soup is heating, thaw croutons at room temperature; sprinkle over soup.

1¼ cups plus ½ cup croutons: 384 cal., 23g fat (13g sat. fat), 100mg chol., 1112mg sod., 15g carb. (3g sugars, 1g fiber), 29g pro.

> **TEST KITCHEN TIP**
> Add some shredded carrots to soup for a little pop of color and a Vitamin A boost!

SLOW-COOKER
CORDON BLEU SOUP

MOJITO
PULLED PORK

MOJITO PULLED PORK

This fork-tender pulled pork tastes fabulous on a bun or in a tortilla. My kids like to eat it spooned over rice in its citrus-flavored juices.
—*Mindy Oswalt, Winnetka, CA*

PREP: 20 min. • **COOK:** 7 hours
MAKES: 16 servings

- 1 boneless pork shoulder roast (4 to 5 lbs.)
- 2 tsp. salt
- 2 tsp. each oregano, ground cumin, paprika and pepper
- 1 bunch fresh cilantro, divided
- 2 medium onions, halved and sliced
- ¼ cup canned chopped green chiles
- 4 garlic cloves, minced
- 2 cans (14½ oz. each) reduced-sodium chicken broth
- ⅔ cup orange juice
- ½ cup lime juice
- 16 sandwich buns, split
  Barbecue sauce and pickle chips

1. Cut roast in half. Combine the salt, oregano, cumin, paprika and pepper; rub over pork. Place in a 4- or 5-qt. slow cooker.
2. Mince cilantro to measure ¼ cup; set aside. Trim remaining cilantro, discarding stems. Add the whole cilantro leaves, onions, chiles and garlic to the slow cooker. Combine the broth, orange juice and lime juice; pour over roast. Cover and cook on low for 7-9 hours or until meat is tender.
3. Remove roast; cool slightly. Skim fat from cooking juices; set aside 3 cups juices. Discard remaining juices. Shred pork with 2 forks and return to slow cooker. Stir in minced cilantro and reserved cooking juices; heat through. Spoon ½ cup meat onto each bun. Serve with barbecue sauce and pickle chips.
1 serving: 418 cal., 16g fat (5g sat. fat), 67mg chol., 916mg sod., 40g carb. (8g sugars, 2g fiber), 29g pro.

GREEN BEANS WITH SMOKED TURKEY BACON

GREEN BEANS WITH SMOKED TURKEY BACON

I really like cooking with curry, and this is a wonderful favorite of mine. Made with fresh green beans, turkey bacon and garbanzo beans, it has loads of flavor. Keep this recipe on hand for the summer when green beans are abundant. It can be a main dish or a side. For vegetarians, eliminate the bacon.
—*Nancy Heishman, Las Vegas, NV*

PREP: 25 min. • **COOK:** 5 hours
MAKES: 10 servings

- 2 lbs. fresh green beans, trimmed
- 1 can (15 oz.) garbanzo beans or chickpeas, rinsed and drained
- 1 large red onion, chopped
- 1 large sweet red pepper, chopped
- 8 turkey bacon strips, chopped
- 1 can (15 oz.) crushed tomatoes
- ¼ cup lemon juice
- 2 Tbsp. minced fresh parsley
- 3 garlic cloves, minced
- 3 tsp. curry powder
- 1 tsp. freshly ground pepper
- ¾ tsp. salt
- ¼ cup minced fresh basil
- 1½ cups (6 oz.) crumbled feta cheese

1. Place first 4 ingredients in a 6-qt. slow cooker. In a large nonstick skillet, cook turkey bacon over medium heat until crisp, stirring occasionally. Add to slow cooker.
2. In a small bowl, mix tomatoes, lemon juice, parsley, garlic and dry seasonings. Pour over bean mixture.
3. Cook, covered, on low 5-6 hours or until green beans are tender. Stir in basil. Top with cheese before serving.
¾ cup: 168 cal., 6g fat (3g sat. fat), 21mg chol., 633mg sod., 21g carb. (7g sugars, 7g fiber), 9g pro. **Diabetic exchanges:** 1 starch, 1 medium-fat meat, 1 vegetable.

ITALIAN SAUSAGES WITH PROVOLONE

Here's an easy recipe everyone will rave about. These tangy sausages with their pepper and onion topping will disappear quickly. Better make a double batch!
—*Shelly Bevington, Hermiston, OR*

- -

PREP: 15 min. • **COOK:** 4 hours
MAKES: 10 servings

- 10 Italian sausage links (4 oz. each)
- 1 Tbsp. canola oil
- 1 each small sweet red, yellow and orange peppers, cut into strips
- 2 medium onions, halved and sliced
- 2 cups Italian salad dressing
- 10 slices provolone cheese
- 10 brat buns, split

1. In a large skillet, brown sausages in batches in oil. Drain. Transfer to a 5-qt. slow cooker. Add the peppers, onions and salad dressing. Cover and cook on low for 4-5 hours or until a thermometer reads 160° and vegetables are tender.
2. Place sausages and cheese in buns; using a slotted spoon, top with pepper mixture.
1 serving: 543 cal., 31g fat (10g sat. fat), 60mg chol., 1267mg sod., 41g carb. (9g sugars, 2g fiber), 25g pro.

SLOW-COOKER SRIRACHA CORN

A restaurant here advertised Sriracha corn on the cob, but I knew I could make my own. The golden ears cooked up a little sweet, a little smoky and a little hot—perfect, if you ask my three teenage boys!
—*Julie Peterson, Crofton, MD*

- -

PREP: 15 min. • **COOK:** 3 hours
MAKES: 8 servings

- ½ cup butter, softened
- 2 Tbsp. honey
- 1 Tbsp. Sriracha chili sauce
- 1 tsp. smoked paprika
- ½ tsp. kosher salt
- 8 small ears sweet corn, husks removed
- ¼ cup water
  Additional smoked paprika, optional

1. Mix first 5 ingredients. Place each ear of corn on a 12x12-in. piece of heavy-duty foil; spread with 1 Tbsp. butter mixture. Wrap foil around corn, sealing tightly. Place in a 6-qt. slow cooker.
2. Add water; cook, covered, on low for 3-4 hours or until corn is tender. If desired, sprinkle corn with additional smoked paprika before serving.
1 ear of corn: 209 cal., 13g fat (8g sat. fat), 31mg chol., 287mg sod., 24g carb. (11g sugars, 2g fiber), 4g pro.

SLOW-COOKER SRIRACHA CORN

MEXICAN PORK & HOMINY SOUP

SLOW-COOKER BACON MAC & CHEESE

I'm all about easy slow-cooker meals. Using more cheese than ever, I've developed an addictive spin on this casserole favorite.
—*Kristen Heigl, Staten Island, NY*

- -

PREP: 20 min. • **COOK:** 3 hours + standing
MAKES: 18 servings

- 2 large eggs, lightly beaten
- 4 cups whole milk
- 1 can (12 oz.) evaporated milk
- ¼ cup butter, melted
- 1 Tbsp. all-purpose flour
- 1 tsp. salt
- 1 pkg. (16 oz.) small pasta shells
- 1 cup shredded provolone cheese
- 1 cup shredded Manchego or Monterey Jack cheese
- 1 cup shredded white cheddar cheese
- 8 bacon strips, cooked and crumbled

1. In a large bowl, whisk the first 6 ingredients until blended. Stir in pasta and cheeses; transfer to a 4- or 5-qt. slow cooker.
2. Cook, covered, on low until pasta is tender, 3-3½ hours. Turn off slow cooker; remove insert. Let stand, uncovered, 15 minutes before serving. Top with bacon.
½ cup: 272 cal., 14g fat (8g sat. fat), 59mg chol., 400mg sod., 24g carb. (5g sugars, 1g fiber), 13g pro.

❄
MEXICAN PORK & HOMINY SOUP

This pork and hominy soup, also known as pozole, is a delicious southwestern delicacy. I moved it to the slow cooker so it can simmer away on its own. It tastes like a tamale in a bowl! Want to make it healthier? Add some sliced cabbage to the mix.
—*Joan Hallford, N. Richland Hills, TX*

- -

PREP: 30 min. • **COOK:** 6 hours
MAKES: 8 servings (2¾ qt.)

- 2 cups water
- 1 large poblano pepper, seeded and chopped
- 1 jalapeno pepper, seeded and chopped
- 1 can (14½ oz.) fire-roasted diced tomatoes, undrained
- 1 medium onion, chopped
- 4 garlic cloves, minced
- 2 tsp. ground cumin
- ½ tsp. dried oregano
- 2 lbs. boneless country-style pork ribs, cubed
- 1 can (29 oz.) hominy, rinsed and drained
- 2 cups reduced-sodium chicken broth
- 1 Tbsp. lime juice
- 1 tsp. kosher salt
- ¼ tsp. pepper
  Optional ingredients: Fried tortillas, cubed avocado, sliced radishes, lime wedges and minced cilantro

1. In a small saucepan, combine water, poblano and jalapeno. Bring to a boil. Reduce heat; simmer until tender, about 10 minutes. Remove from heat; cool slightly. Place the mixture in a blender. Add tomatoes, onion, garlic, cumin and oregano; cover and process until smooth.
2. Transfer to a 5- or 6-qt. slow cooker. Stir in pork, hominy, broth, lime juice, kosher salt and pepper. Cook, covered, on low 6-8 hours or until pork is tender. If desired, serve with optional ingredients.
Freeze option: Freeze cooled stew in freezer containers. To use, partially thaw in the refrigerator overnight. Heat through in a saucepan, stirring occasionally and adding a little broth if necessary.
Note: Wear disposable gloves when cutting hot peppers; the oils can burn skin. Avoid touching your face.
1⅓ cups: 257 cal., 10g fat (4g sat. fat), 65mg chol., 1005mg sod., 16g carb. (3g sugars, 4g fiber), 22g pro.

SLOW-COOKED
VEGETABLES
WITH CHEESE SAUCE

SLOW-COOKED VEGETABLES WITH CHEESE SAUCE

Who can pass up veggies smothered in cheese? No one I know! This is an inviting recipe to serve kids who normally shy away from vegetables.
—*Teresa Flowers, Sacramento, CA*

PREP: 5 min. • **COOK:** 3 hours
MAKES: 6 servings

- 1 pkg. (16 oz.) frozen Italian vegetables, thawed
- 3 cups frozen broccoli florets, thawed
- 1 pkg. (8 oz.) cubed Velveeta
- 1½ cups frozen cut kale, thawed and squeezed dry
- ⅓ cup chicken broth
- 1 Tbsp. butter
- ¼ tsp. salt
- ¼ tsp. pepper

Place all ingredients in a 3- or 4-qt. slow cooker. Cook, covered, on low 3-4 hours or until cheese is melted, . Stir before serving.
¾ cup: 209 cal., 16g fat (7g sat. fat), 42mg chol., 704mg sod., 14g carb. (6g sugars, 4g fiber), 10g pro.

Pressure-Cooker Vegetables with Cheese Sauce: Increase broth to 1 cup; place in a 6-qt. electric pressure cooker. Add the Italian vegetables, broccoli, kale, butter, salt and pepper. Lock lid; close pressure-release valve. Adjust to pressure-cook on high for 3 minutes. Quick-release pressure. Drain vegetables and return to pressure cooker. Select saute setting; adjust for low heat. Add cheese; cook and stir until melted, 1-2 minutes.

CARROT & LENTIL CHILI

CARROT & LENTIL CHILI

This chili is one of my favorite plant-based meals. I love to make it in the fall and spring for the satisfying combination of fresh carrots and hearty lentils. Serve it with yogurt, sour cream or plant-based cheese.
—*Rebekah Ranes, Sedona, AZ*

PREP: 30 min. • **COOK:** 4 hours
MAKES: 8 servings

- 2 Tbsp. olive oil
- 1 medium onion, chopped
- ¾ cup dried green lentils, rinsed
- ¾ cup dried red lentils, rinsed
- 6 garlic cloves, minced
- 6 cups chopped carrots (about 10 medium carrots)
- 1 carton (32 oz.) reduced-sodium vegetable broth
- 1 Tbsp. ground cumin
- 1 tsp. salt
- 2 tsp. paprika
- 1 tsp. chili powder
- 1 can (15 oz.) crushed tomaatoes, undrained
- 2 medium ripe avocados, peeled and cubed
  Optional: Sour cream, sliced red onion and additional paprika

1. In a large skillet, heat oil over medium-high heat. Add onion; cook and stir until tender, 4-5 minutes. Add lentils and garlic; cook 1 minute longer. Transfer to a 5- or 6-qt. slow cooker. Stir in carrots, broth and seasonings. Cook, covered, on low 4-6 hours or until vegetables and lentils are tender.
2. Stir in diced tomatoes; cook, covered, 30 minutes longer. Serve with avocados and, if desired, sour cream, red onion and additional paprika.

Freeze option: Freeze cooled chili in freezer containers. To use, partially thaw in the refrigerator overnight. Heat through in a saucepan, stirring occasionally and adding a little broth or water if necessary.
1¼ cups: 310 cal., 10g fat (1g sat. fat), 0 chol., 574mg sod., 47g carb. (11g sugars, 12g fiber), 13g pro.

SLOW-COOKED SHREDDED PORK

The tasty pork filling for these sandwiches requires very little work because it's prepared in the slow cooker. The mild, sweet sauce is so appealing.

—*Shirleymae Haefner, O'Fallon, MO*

PREP: 15 min. • **COOK:** 6 hours
MAKES: 8 servings

- 1   boneless pork loin roast (2 to 3 lbs.)
- 1   large onion, thinly sliced
- 1   cup beer or nonalcoholic beer
- 1   cup chili sauce
- 2   Tbsp. brown sugar
- 1   Tbsp. prepared horseradish
- 8   sandwich rolls, split

1. Cut roast in half; place in a 3-qt. slow cooker. Top with onion. Combine the beer, chili sauce, brown sugar and horseradish; pour over pork and onion. Cover and cook on low for 6-6½ hours or until meat is tender.
2. Remove pork; shred with 2 forks. Return meat to cooking juices; heat through. Use a slotted spoon to serve on rolls.
1 serving: 413 cal., 10g fat (4g sat. fat), 56mg chol., 847mg sod., 50g carb. (17g sugars, 2g fiber), 29g pro.

BEEF & VEGGIE SOUP

I adapted this recipe from one that I saw in a cookbook in an effort to add more vegetables to our diet. Our two young sons eat this up without hesitation.

—*Teresa King, Chambersburg, PA*

PREP: 20 min. • **COOK:** 8 hours
MAKES: 10 servings (about 2½ qt.)

- 1   lb. ground beef
- 1   medium onion, chopped
- 1   garlic clove, minced
- 2   cans (8 oz. each) tomato sauce
- 2   cans (16 oz. each) kidney beans, rinsed and drained, optional
- 1   pkg. (10 oz.) frozen corn
- 1   cup shredded carrots
- 1   cup chopped green pepper
- 1   cup chopped sweet red pepper
- 1   cup chopped fresh tomato
- 1   Tbsp. chili powder
- ½   tsp. dried basil
- ½   tsp. salt
- ¼   tsp. pepper
      Optional: Shredded cheddar cheese, sour cream and tortilla chips

1. In a skillet, cook beef and onion over medium heat until the meat is no longer pink. Add garlic; cook 1 minute longer. Drain.
2. Transfer to a 5-qt. slow cooker. Stir in the tomato sauce, beans if desired, vegetables and seasonings. Cover and cook on low for 8 hours or until thick and bubbly, stirring occasionally. Serve with cheese, sour cream and chips if desired.
1 cup: 220 cal., 6g fat (2g sat. fat), 28mg chol., 531mg sod., 27g carb. (5g sugars, 7g fiber), 16g pro. **Diabetic exchanges:** 2 starch, 2 medium-fat meat.

"Delicious. I decided to make this late in the day so made it on the stove. Since my husband likes either pasta or potatoes in his soup, I added extra broth and tomato sauce along with ¾ cup baby pasta shells. A thick soup for a cold day."
—LESLIEH, TASTEOFHOME.COM

BARBECUED BEEF CHILI

Served with a hot loaf of bread and a side salad, this slow-cooker chili makes a hearty meal. The recipe was inspired by two friends when we were talking about foods we love at a potluck barbecue.

—*Phyllis Shyan, Elgin, IL*

PREP: 10 min. • **COOK:** 6 hours
MAKES: 12 servings (3 qt.)

- 7   tsp. chili powder
- 1   Tbsp. garlic powder
- 2   tsp. celery seed
- 1   tsp. coarsely ground pepper
- ¼ to ½ tsp. cayenne pepper
- 1   fresh beef brisket (3 to 4 lbs.)
- 1   medium green pepper, chopped
- 1   small onion, chopped
- 1   bottle (12 oz.) chili sauce
- 1   cup ketchup
- ½   cup barbecue sauce
- ⅓   cup packed brown sugar
- ¼   cup cider vinegar
- ¼   cup Worcestershire sauce
- 1   tsp. ground mustard
- 1   can (16 oz.) hot chili beans, undrained
- 1   can (15½ oz.) great northern beans, rinsed and drained
      Optional toppings: Shredded cheddar cheese, chopped white onion and sliced jalapeno peppers

1. Combine the first 5 ingredients; rub over brisket. Cut into 8 pieces; place in a 5-qt. slow cooker. Combine the green pepper, onion, chili sauce, ketchup, barbecue sauce, brown sugar, vinegar, Worcestershire sauce and mustard; pour over meat. Cover and cook on high for 5-6 hours or until meat is tender.
2. Remove meat; cool slightly. Meanwhile, skim fat from cooking juices. Shred meat with 2 forks; return to slow cooker. Reduce heat to low. Stir in the beans. Cover and cook for 1 hour or until heated through. If desired, top with shredded cheddar cheese, chopped white onion and sliced jalapenos.
Freeze option: Freeze cooled chili in freezer containers. To use, partially thaw in the refrigerator overnight. Heat through in a saucepan, stirring occasionally and adding a little broth or water if necessary.
1 cup: 302 cal., 6g fat (2g sat. fat), 48mg chol., 1037mg sod., 36g carb. (20g sugars, 5g fiber), 28g pro.

BARBECUED
BEEF CHILI

**GENERAL TSO'S
CHICKEN SOUP**

GENERAL TSO'S CHICKEN SOUP

I love Asian food and wanted a chili-like soup with the distinctive flavors of General Tso's chicken. The slow cooker makes this recipe super easy, and you can use any meat you like. Besides chicken, it's great with turkey, ground meat or leftover pork.
—*Lori McLain, Denton, TX*

PREP: 10 min. • **COOK:** 2 hours
MAKES: 6 servings (1½ qt.)

- 1 cup tomato juice
- ½ cup pickled cherry peppers, chopped
- 2 Tbsp. soy sauce
- 2 Tbsp. hoisin sauce
- 1 Tbsp. peanut oil
- 1 to 2 tsp. crushed red pepper flakes
- 1 lb. shredded cooked chicken
- 1½ cups chopped onion
- 1 cup chopped fresh broccoli
- ¼ cup chopped green onions
- 1 tsp. sesame seeds, toasted

In a 4- or 5-qt. slow cooker, combine the first 6 ingredients. Stir in chicken, onion and broccoli. Cook, covered, on low for about 2 hours, until vegetables are tender. Top with green onions and sesame seeds to serve.
1 cup: 222 cal., 9g fat (2g sat. fat), 67mg chol., 791mg sod., 10g carb. (5g sugars, 2g fiber), 25g pro. **Diabetic exchanges:** 3 lean meat, 2 vegetable, ½ fat.

"This was a very easy and delicious recipe! I took a shortcut and made this in the pressure cooker with great results. It is a thicker soup so if you wanted to thin it down, I recommend more tomato juice or chicken broth. Great flavor!"
—LPHJKITCHEN, TASTEOFHOME.COM

SLOW-COOKER POTATO & HAM SOUP

SLOW-COOKER POTATO & HAM SOUP

In our house, this recipe is a win-win. It's easy for me to whip up and easy for my family to devour. Serving it with crusty bread for dipping doesn't hurt, either.
—*Linda Haglund, Buffalo, MN*

PREP: 10 min. • **COOK:** 6¼ hours
MAKES: 8 servings (2½ qt.)

- 1 carton (32 oz.) chicken broth
- 1 pkg. (30 oz.) frozen shredded hash brown potatoes, thawed
- 1 small onion, finely chopped
- ¼ tsp. pepper
- 4 oz. cream cheese, softened and cubed
- 1 cup cubed deli ham
- 1 can (5 oz.) evaporated milk
  Optional: Sour cream and chopped green onions

1. In a 4- or 5-qt. slow cooker, combine broth, potatoes, onion and pepper. Cook, covered, on low for 6-8 hours or until the vegetables are tender.
2. Mash potatoes to desired consistency. Whisk in cream cheese until melted. Stir in ham and milk. Cook, covered, until heated through, 15-20 minutes longer. Serve with sour cream and green onions if desired.
1¼ cups: 257 cal., 10g fat (5g sat. fat), 45mg chol., 1053mg sod., 31g carb. (6g sugars, 2g fiber), 12g pro.

Snacks & Sweets

**PUMPKIN
LATTE CUSTARD**

PUMPKIN LATTE CUSTARD

We love this traditional slow-cooker pumpkin spice custard. The added espresso powder gives it a latte effect!
—*Shelly Bevington, Hermiston, OR*

PREP: 10 min. • **COOK:** 6 hours
MAKES: 8 servings

- 1   can (29 oz.) pumpkin
- 1½ cups sugar
- 1   can (12 oz.) evaporated milk
- 4   large eggs, room temperature, lightly beaten
- 1   Tbsp. pumpkin pie spice
- 1   Tbsp. instant espresso powder
- 1   tsp. salt
     Gingersnap cookies, crushed
     Whipped cream, optional

1. Pour 1 in. water into a 6-qt. slow cooker. Layer two 24-in. pieces of foil; roll up lengthwise to make a 1-in.-thick roll. Shape into a ring; place in slow cooker to make a rack.

2. Whisk together first 7 ingredients. Transfer to a greased 2-qt. baking dish; set aside. Fold an 18x12-in. piece of foil lengthwise into thirds, making a sling. Use the sling to lower the baking dish onto foil rack, not allowing sides to touch slow cooker. Cover the slow cooker with a double layer of white paper towels; place lid securely over towels.

3. Cook, covered, on low 6-7 hours or until a thermometer reads 160°. Remove baking dish from slow cooker using sling. Top with crushed gingersnap cookies and, if desired, whipped cream.

1 serving: 280 cal., 6g fat (3g sat. fat), 108mg chol., 381mg sod., 52g carb. (46g sugars, 3g fiber), 7g pro.

TEST KITCHEN TIP
This recipe can also be prepared directly in a smaller slow cooker. Whisk together first 7 ingredients. Transfer to a greased 3-qt. slow cooker. Cook, covered, on low 6-7 hours or until a thermometer reads 160°. Top with crushed gingersnap cookies and, if desired, whipped cream.

ROOT BEER PULLED PORK NACHOS

CRANBERRY CHILI MEATBALLS

Packaged meatballs help save time in the kitchen, and these are just as tasty as homemade. My friends look forward to enjoying these meatballs at our holiday gatherings and there are never leftovers! The sauce is tangy yet sweet, and the festive color is perfect for any holiday party.
—*Amy Scamerhorn, Indianapolis, IN*

- -

PREP: 10 min. • **COOK:** 2 hours
MAKES: about 5 dozen

- 1   can (14 oz.) jellied cranberry sauce
- 1   bottle (12 oz.) chili sauce
- ¾   cup packed brown sugar
- ½   tsp. chili powder
- ½   tsp. ground cumin
- ¼   tsp. cayenne pepper
- 1   pkg. (32 oz.) frozen fully cooked homestyle meatballs, thawed

1. In a large saucepan over medium heat, combine the first 6 ingredients; stir until sugar is dissolved.
2. Place meatballs in a 4-qt. slow cooker. Add sauce. Cook, covered, on low 2-3 hours or until heated through.
Freeze option: Freeze cooled meatball mixture in freezer containers. To use, partially thaw in refrigerator overnight. Microwave, covered, on high in a microwave-safe dish until heated through, gently stirring and adding a little water if necessary.
1 meatball: 74 cal., 4g fat (2g sat. fat), 6mg chol., 191mg sod., 8g carb. (5g sugars, 0 fiber), 2g pro.

"These are delicious and the easiest thing to make ever! I really like the chili sauce and cranberry flavors better than barbecue sauce. Will be making these again for the holidays."
—SE58, TASTEOFHOME.COM

ROOT BEER PULLED PORK NACHOS

I count on my slow cooker to do the honors when I have a house full of summer guests. Teenagers especially love DIY nachos. Try cola, ginger ale or lemon-lime soda if you're not into root beer.
—*James Schend, Pleasant Prairie, WI*

- -

PREP: 20 min. • **COOK:** 8 hours
MAKES: 12 servings

- 1   boneless pork shoulder butt roast (3 to 4 lbs.)
- 1   can (12 oz.) root beer or cola
- 12   cups tortilla chips
- 2   cups shredded cheddar cheese
- 2   medium tomatoes, chopped
      Optional: Pico de gallo, chopped green onions and sliced jalapeno peppers

1. In a 4- or 5-qt. slow cooker, combine pork roast and root beer. Cook, covered, on low 8-9 hours or until meat is tender.
2. Remove roast; cool slightly. When cool enough to handle, shred meat with 2 forks. Return to slow cooker; keep warm.
3. To serve, drain pork. Layer tortilla chips with pork, cheese, tomatoes and optional toppings as desired. Serve immediately.
1 serving: 391 cal., 23g fat (8g sat. fat), 86mg chol., 287mg sod., 20g carb. (4g sugars, 1g fiber), 25g pro.

PINEAPPLE RUMCHATA SHORTCAKES

OLD-FASHIONED STEAMED MOLASSES BREAD

When I was growing up, the smell of this bread greeted me as I walked in the door from school. I thought everyone baked bread in a slow cooker. My grandmother, my mother and I—and now my daughters—all bake this. It's comfort food at its best!
—*Bonnie Geavaras, Chandler, AZ*

PREP: 20 min. • **COOK:** 3 hours + cooling
MAKES: 16 servings

- 2 cups All-Bran
- 1 cup all-purpose flour
- 1 cup whole wheat flour
- 1 cup dried cranberries
- 1½ tsp. baking powder
- 1 tsp. baking soda
- 1 tsp. salt
- ½ tsp. ground cinnamon
- 1 large egg
- 1¾ cups buttermilk
- ½ cup molasses
- 2 Tbsp. honey

1. Layer two 24-in. pieces of foil. Starting with a long side, roll up foil to make a 1-in.-wide strip; shape into a coil. Place on bottom of a 5-qt. slow cooker to make a rack.
2. Combine bran, flours, cranberries, baking powder, baking soda, salt and cinnamon. In another bowl, beat egg, buttermilk, molasses and honey. Stir into flour mixture just until blended (do not overbeat). Pour into a greased and floured 2-qt. baking dish. Tightly cover with lightly greased foil. Place in prepared slow cooker. Cook, covered, on high about 3 hours, until a thermometer reads 190-200°.
3. Remove dish to a wire rack; cool for 10 minutes before inverting loaf onto the rack. Serve warm or cold.

1 wedge: 157 cal., 1g fat (0 sat. fat), 13mg chol., 351mg sod., 36g carb. (19g sugars, 4g fiber), 4g pro.

PINEAPPLE RUMCHATA SHORTCAKES

This deliciously different dessert is made in the slow cooker in jars instead of the oven. When done, add final touches to the cooled shortcake jars and serve.
—*Joan Hallford, N. Richland Hills, TX*

PREP: 20 min. • **COOK:** 1½ hours + cooling
MAKES: 6 servings

- 1½ cups all-purpose flour
- ¼ cup sugar
- 1 tsp. baking powder
- ½ tsp. salt
- ¼ tsp. baking soda
- ⅓ cup cold butter
- 1 large egg, room temperature
- 3 Tbsp. RumChata liqueur
- ¾ cup sour cream

TOPPING
- 1½ cups fresh pineapple, cut into ½-in. pieces
- 3 Tbsp. sugar, divided
- 1 to 2 Tbsp. RumChata liqueur
- 1 tsp. grated lime zest
- ½ cup heavy whipping cream
- 1 medium lime, thinly sliced, optional

1. In a large bowl, whisk flour, sugar, baking powder, salt and baking soda. Cut in butter until mixture resembles coarse crumbs. In another bowl, whisk egg, sour cream and RumChata. Add to flour mixture; stir just until moistened.
2. Spoon mixture into 6 greased half-pint jars. Center lids on jars and screw on bands until fingertip tight. Place jars in a 6- or 7-qt. oval slow cooker; add enough hot water to reach half way up the jars, about 5 cups. Cook, covered, on high 1½-2 hours or until a toothpick inserted in center of shortcake comes out clean.
3. Meanwhile, combine pineapple, 2 Tbsp. sugar, RumChata and lime zest. Refrigerate, covered, at least 1 hour. Remove jars from slow cooker to wire racks to cool completely. In a large, beat cream until it begins to thicken. Add remaining 1 Tbsp. sugar; beat until soft peaks form.
4. Top shortcakes with pineapple mixture, whipped cream and, if desired, lime slices.
1 serving: 463 cal., 28g fat (17g sat. fat), 101mg chol., 442mg sod., 47g carb. (20g sugars, 1g fiber), 6g pro.

OLD-FASHIONED STEAMED
MOLASSES BREAD

MOM'S HAZELNUT & CHOCOLATE BREAD PUDDING

Mom combined her love of Nutella and bread pudding into one delicious recipe. I adapted it for my slow cooker to save time in the kitchen. It's a great make-ahead dessert for game day.
—*Jo Hahn, Newport News, VA*

PREP: 15 min. • **COOK:** 4 hours
MAKES: 12 servings

- ¼   cup unsalted butter
- 2   Tbsp. semisweet chocolate chips
- 8   cups cubed challah or brioche
- ½   cup chopped hazelnuts
- 4   large eggs
- 1½ cups fat-free milk
- ½   cup fat-free half-and-half
- ½   cup Nutella
- ¼   cup sugar
- ½   tsp. vanilla extract
- ¼   tsp. salt
     Sweetened whipped cream, optional

1. Microwave butter and chocolate chips until melted, 30-45 seconds; stir until smooth. Cool. In a 3- or 4-qt. slow cooker coated with cooking spray, combine bread cubes and hazelnuts. In a large bowl, combine next 7 ingredients, mixing well. Add chocolate mixture to bowl; whisk until smooth.
2. Pour the egg mixture over bread and hazelnuts, gently pressing bread cubes to help them absorb liquid. Cook, covered, on low 4-5 hours or until a knife inserted in center comes out clean. Serve warm, dolloped with whipped cream if desired.
½ cup: 259 cal., 14g fat (4g sat. fat), 85mg chol., 190mg sod., 28g carb. (15g sugars, 1g fiber), 7g pro.

SO-EASY STICKY CHICKEN WINGS

My neighbor once shared these tangy wings with me at a potluck, and they have been a family favorite ever since.
—*Jo Vanderwolf, Lillooet, BC*

PREP: 20 min. • **COOK:** 3 hours
MAKES: about 40 pieces

- 4   lbs. chicken wings
- 1   cup barbecue sauce
- 1   cup soy sauce
- 6   green onions, chopped, divided
- 1   Tbsp. sesame seeds

Using a sharp knife, cut through the 2 wing joints; discard wing tips. Place remaining wing pieces in a 4 or 5-qt. slow cooker. Stir in barbecue sauce, soy sauce and ¼ cup chopped green onions. Cook, covered, on high 3-4 hours or until tender. Sprinkle with sesame seeds and remaining green onions.
1 piece: 68 cal., 4g fat (1g sat. fat), 14mg chol., 452mg sod., 3g carb. (2g sugars, 0 fiber), 6g pro

SO-EASY STICKY CHICKEN WINGS

MARINARA-MOZZARELLA DIP

GOOEY PEANUT BUTTER & CHOCOLATE CAKE

Here in Wisconsin, winter weather is extreme. A hot dessert is just the thing to warm us up. This chocolaty delight gets its crunch from a sprinkling of peanuts.
—*Lisa L. Erickson, Ripon, WI*

PREP: 20 min. • **COOK:** 2 hours
MAKES: 8 servings

- 1¾ **cups sugar, divided**
- 1 **cup 2% milk**
- ¾ **cup creamy peanut butter**
- 3 **Tbsp. canola oil**
- 2 **cups all-purpose flour**
- ¾ **cup baking cocoa, divided**
- 3 **tsp. baking powder**
- 2 **cups boiling water**
  Chopped salted peanuts, optional

1. In a large bowl, beat 1 cup sugar, milk, peanut butter and oil until well blended. In another bowl, whisk flour, ½ cup cocoa and baking powder; gradually beat into peanut butter mixture (batter will be thick). Transfer to a greased 5-qt. slow cooker.
2. In a small bowl, mix the remaining sugar and cocoa. Stir in water. Pour over batter (do not stir).
3. Cook, covered, on high 2-2½ hours or until a toothpick inserted in cake portion comes out with moist crumbs. If desired, sprinkle with peanuts. Serve warm.
1 serving: 512 cal., 19g fat (3g sat. fat), 2mg chol., 298mg sod., 79g carb. (48g sugars, 4g fiber), 11g pro.

MARINARA-MOZZARELLA DIP

Talk about easy! With three ingredients and two loaves of baguette-style French bread, you have an easy appetizer that will please everyone. For a variation, try using goat cheese instead of mozzarella.
—*Janie Colle, Hutchinson, KS*

PREP: 10 min. • **COOK:** 2½ hours
MAKES: 12 servings (3 cups)

- 2 **cups marinara sauce**
- 1 **carton (8 oz.) fresh mozzarella cheese pearls, drained**
- 2 **Tbsp. minced fresh basil**
  French bread baguette, thinly sliced and toasted
  Crushed red pepper flakes and additional fresh minced basil, optional

Pour marinara into a 1½-qt. slow cooker. Cook, covered, on low about 2 hours, until hot. Stir in mozzarella and basil. Cook until cheese is melted, about 30 minutes longer. If desired, top with crushed red pepper flakes and additional basil. Serve with toasted baguette slices.
¼ cup: 76 cal., 5g fat (3g sat. fat), 16mg chol., 219mg sod., 4g carb. (3g sugars, 1g fiber), 4g pro.

TEST KITCHEN TIP
This recipe works well with jarred pasta sauce, so use your favorite brand and flavor.

BACK PORCH
MEATBALLS

❄ BACK PORCH MEATBALLS

This idea came to me while sitting on the back porch. The combination of meats and ingredients in the sauce produces meatballs unlike others I've had.
—*Justin Boudreaux, Walker, LA*

PREP: 30 min. • **COOK:** 3 hours
MAKES: 6 dozen

- 2 **large eggs, lightly beaten**
- 2 **cups seasoned bread crumbs**
- 2 **cups salsa**
- ½ **cup grated onion**
- ⅔ **lb. ground turkey**
- ⅔ **lb. ground pork**
- ⅔ **lb. ground beef**
  SAUCE
- 3 **cups tomato sauce**
- 1 **medium onion, grated**
- 1 **cup beef stock**
- 1 **cup mixed fruit jelly**
- 1 **cup molasses**
- ½ **cup packed brown sugar**
- ½ **cup canola oil**
- ½ **cup red wine vinegar**
- ⅓ **cup prepared mustard**
- ⅓ **cup Worcestershire sauce**
- 1 **tsp. salt**

1. Preheat oven to 400°. In a large bowl, combine egg, bread crumbs, salsa and onion. Add turkey, pork and beef; mix lightly but thoroughly. Shape into 1½-in. balls. Place the meatballs on greased racks in two 15x10x1-in. baking pans. Bake until meat is browned, 18-22 minutes.
2. In a 6-qt. slow cooker, combine sauce ingredients. Add meatballs; gently stir to coat. Cook, covered, on low 3-4 hours or until meatballs are cooked through.
Freeze option: Freeze cooled meatball mixture in freezer containers. To use, partially thaw in refrigerator overnight. Microwave, covered, on high in a microwave-safe dish until heated through, gently stirring and adding a little water if necessary.
1 meatball: 87 cal., 3g fat (1g sat. fat), 13mg chol., 195mg sod., 11g carb. (8g sugars, 0 fiber), 3g pro.

SLOW-COOKED
CHAI TEA

SLOW-COOKED CHAI TEA

A friend of my mother's brought chai tea to her house. She told us in India it is served every day. I had never had it before, but I liked it so much that I came up with a recipe to re-create it.
—*Patty Crouse, Warren, PA*

PREP: 10 min. • **COOK:** 4 hours
MAKES: 8 servings

- 6 **cups water**
- 1 **cup sugar**
- 1 **cup nonfat dry milk powder**
- 6 **black tea bags**
- 1 **tsp. ground ginger**
- 1 **tsp. ground cinnamon**
- ½ **tsp. pepper**
- ½ **tsp. ground cardamom**
- ½ **tsp. ground cloves**
- ½ **tsp. vanilla extract**

Place all ingredients in a 3- or 4-qt. slow cooker. Cook, covered, on high 3-4 hours or until heated through. Discard tea bags. Serve tea warm.
¾ cup: 131 cal., 0 fat (0 sat. fat), 2mg chol., 48mg sod., 30g carb. (30g sugars, 0 fiber), 3g pro.

❄ BBQ TURKEY MEATBALLS

What's a party without meatballs? We have these at all our big gatherings. The recipe can also be made with ground beef or even store-bought meatballs.
—*Lisa Harms, Moline, MI*

PREP: 45 min. • **COOK:** 3 hours
MAKES: about 4 dozen

- 1 large egg, lightly beaten
- ⅔ cup soft bread crumbs
- ¼ cup finely chopped onion
- ½ tsp. pepper
- 2 lbs. ground turkey

SAUCE
- 1 bottle (20 oz.) ketchup
- ¼ cup packed brown sugar
- 2 Tbsp. Worcestershire sauce
- 1 tsp. garlic salt
- ½ to 1 tsp. hot pepper sauce

1. Preheat oven to 375°. Combine egg, bread crumbs, onion and pepper. Add turkey; mix lightly but thoroughly. Shape into 1-in. balls. Place on a greased rack in a 15x10x1-in. pan. Bake until lightly browned, 15-20 minutes.
2. Transfer meatballs to a 3-qt. slow cooker. Mix sauce ingredients; pour over top. Cook, covered, on low 3-4 hours or until meatballs are cooked through.
Freeze option: Freeze cooled meatball mixture in freezer containers. To use, partially thaw in refrigerator overnight. Microwave, covered, on high in a microwave-safe dish until heated through, gently stirring and adding a little water if necessary.
1 meatball: 44 cal., 1g fat (0 sat. fat), 16mg chol., 188mg sod., 4g carb. (4g sugars, 0 fiber), 4g pro.

PEACHY SUMMER CHEESECAKE

🍎 PEACHY SUMMER CHEESECAKE

This cool, always refreshing dessert is fancy enough to take to a gathering.
—*Joan Engelhardt, Latrobe, PA*

PREP: 25 min. • **COOK:** 2½ hours + chilling
MAKES: 6 servings

- 1 pkg. (8 oz.) reduced-fat cream cheese
- 4 oz. fat-free cream cheese
- ½ cup sugar
- ½ cup reduced-fat sour cream
- 2 Tbsp. unsweetened apple juice
- 1 Tbsp. all-purpose flour
- ½ tsp. vanilla
- 3 large eggs, lightly beaten
- 2 medium ripe peaches, peeled and thinly sliced

1. Pour 1 in. water into a 6-qt. slow cooker. Layer two 24-in. pieces of foil; roll up lengthwise to make a 1-in.-thick roll. Shape into a ring; place in slow cooker to make a rack.
2. Grease a 6-in. springform pan; place on a double thickness of heavy-duty foil (about 12 in. square). Wrap securely around pan.
3. In a large bowl, beat cream cheeses and sugar until smooth. Beat in sour cream, apple juice, flour and vanilla. Add eggs; beat on low speed just until blended. Pour into prepared pan. Center pan on foil rack, not allowing sides to touch slow cooker. Cover slow cooker with a double layer of white paper towels; place lid securely over towels. Cook, covered, on low 2½ hours.
4. Turn off slow cooker, but do not remove lid. Let stand 1 hour. Remove springform pan from slow cooker; remove foil from pan. Cool cheesecake on a wire rack 1 hour.
5. Loosen the sides from pan with a knife. Refrigerate overnight, covering when cooled. To serve, remove rim from springform pan. Serve with peaches.
1 serving: 268 cal., 12g fat (7g sat. fat), 129mg chol., 342mg sod., 27g carb. (25g sugars, 1g fiber), 12g pro.

SLOW-COOKER SPUMONI CAKE

I created this cake for a holiday potluck one year. It has become one of my most requested desserts. If you prefer, you can use all semisweet chips instead of a mix.
—*Lisa Renshaw, Kansas City, MO*

- -

PREP: 10 min. • **COOK:** 4 hours + standing
MAKES: 10 servings

- 3 cups cold 2% milk
- 1 pkg. (3.40 oz.) instant pistachio pudding mix
- 1 pkg. white cake mix
- ¾ cup chopped maraschino cherries
- 1 cup white baking chips
- 1 cup semisweet chocolate chips
- 1 cup pistachios, chopped

1. In a large bowl, whisk milk and pudding mix for 2 minutes. Transfer to a greased 5-qt. slow cooker. Prepare cake mix batter according to package directions, folding cherries into batter. Pour into slow cooker.
2. Cook, covered, on low about 4 hours, until edges of cake are golden brown.
3. Remove slow-cooker insert; sprinkle cake with baking chips and chocolate chips. Let cake stand, uncovered, 10 minutes. Sprinkle with pistachios before serving.
1 serving: 588 cal., 27g fat (9g sat. fat), 9mg chol., 594mg sod., 79g carb. (54g sugars, 3g fiber), 10g pro.

TEST KITCHEN TIP
To take this dessert right over the top, serve it with vanilla, cherry, pistachio or chocolate ice cream.

❄ SLOW-COOKER PEAR BUTTER

This is a tasty spread for toast, muffins, biscuits or any of your favorite breads. It is easy to make and has a rich pear flavor with hints of cinnamon, star anise and lemon.
—*Geraldine Saucier, Albuquerque, NM*

- -

PREP: 25 min. • **COOK:** 6 hours
MAKES: 6 cups

- 1 cinnamon stick (3 in.)
- 4-5 star anise points (about ½ whole)
- 5 lbs. pears, peeled and chopped (about 12 cups)
- 1 cup packed light brown sugar
- 1 tsp. grated lemon zest

1. Place spices on a double thickness of cheesecloth. Gather corners of cloth to enclose spices; tie securely with string. In a 5- or 6-qt. slow cooker, toss remaining ingredients. Add the spice bag, covering with pears.
2. Cook, covered, on low 5-6 hours or until pears are tender. Remove spice bag.
3. Puree pear mixture using an immersion blender. Or, cool slightly and puree mixture in a blender in batches; return to slow cooker.
4. Cook, uncovered, on high 1-2 hours or until the mixture is thickened to desired consistency, stirring occasionally. Store cooled pear butter in an airtight container in the refrigerator up to 1 week.
Freeze option: Freeze cooled pear butter in freezer containers up to 3 months. To use, thaw in refrigerator.
2 Tbsp.: 41 cal., 0 fat (0 sat. fat), 0 chol., 2mg sod., 11g carb. (9g sugars, 1g fiber), 0 pro.

SLOW-COOKER SPUMONI CAKE

SLOW-COOKER BERRY COMPOTE

SLOW-COOKER CRAB & GREEN ONION DIP

This creamy dip reminds me of my dad, who took us crabbing as kids. Our fingers were tired after those excursions, but eating the fresh crab was worth it.
—*Nancy Zimmerman, Cape May Court House, NJ*

- -

PREP: 10 min. • **COOK:** 3 hours
MAKES: 16 servings (4 cups)

- 3 pkg. (8 oz. each) cream cheese, cubed
- 2 cans (6 oz. each) lump crabmeat, drained
- 4 green onions, chopped
- ¼ cup 2% milk
- 2 tsp. prepared horseradish
- 2 tsp. Worcestershire sauce
- ¼ tsp. salt
  Baked pita chips and assorted fresh vegetables

In a greased 3-qt. slow cooker, combine the first 7 ingredients. Cook, covered, on low 3-4 hours or until heated through, stirring occasionally. Serve with chips.
¼ cup: 167 cal., 15g fat (8g sat. fat), 68mg chol., 324mg sod., 2g carb. (2g sugars, 0 fiber), 7g pro.

"This recipe was fantastic! I prepped it the night before and stuck in the crock the next day. It was a huge hit. Next time I'm going to have to triple the recipe. It's a keeper!"
— SPOILEDBASHER, TASTEOFHOME.COM

SLOW-COOKER BERRY COMPOTE

This is a decades-old recipe my grandma made when I was younger, and it reminds me of her. She always added extra blueberries to help thicken the sauce.
—*Diane Higgins, Tampa, FL*

- -

PREP: 15 min. • **COOK:** 3 hours
MAKES: 4 cups

- ¼ cup sugar
- 2 Tbsp. cornstarch
- 1 cup water
- 1 can (15 oz.) pitted dark sweet cherries, undrained
- 1 pint fresh or frozen unsweetened blueberries
- 1 cup packed brown sugar
- ½ cup chopped walnuts
- ¼ cup all-purpose flour
- ¼ cup sliced almonds
- ¼ cup old-fashioned oats
- 1 tsp. ground cinnamon
- ¼ tsp. ground nutmeg
  Dash salt
- ½ cup cold butter
  Vanilla ice cream, optional

1. In a small bowl, mix sugar, cornstarch and water until smooth. Transfer to a greased 3-qt. slow cooker. Stir in cherries and blueberries. In a large bowl, combine brown sugar, chopped walnuts, flour, almonds, oats, cinnamon, nutmeg and salt; cut in butter until crumbly. Sprinkle over fruit mixture.
2. Cook, covered, on high about 3 hours, until bubbly and thickened. If desired, serve warm with vanilla ice cream.
¼ cup: 256 cal., 12g fat (5g sat. fat), 20mg chol., 80mg sod., 37g carb. (30g sugars, 2g fiber), 2g pro.

SLOW-COOKER CRAB &
GREEN ONION DIP

SLOW-COOKED STUFFED APPLES

This irresistible dessert is slow-cooker easy. Warm and comforting, the tender apples are filled with chewy pecans and yummy caramel topping.
—*Pam Kaiser, Mansfield, MO*

PREP: 20 min. • **COOK:** 3 hours
MAKES: 6 servings

- 6 large tart apples
- 2 tsp. lemon juice
- ⅓ cup chopped pecans
- ¼ cup chopped dried apricots
- ¼ cup packed brown sugar
- 3 Tbsp. butter, melted
- ¾ tsp. ground cinnamon
- ¼ tsp. ground nutmeg
  Granola and caramel ice cream topping, optional

1. Core apples and peel top third of each; brush peeled portions with lemon juice. Place in a 6-qt. slow cooker.
2. Combine the pecans, apricots, brown sugar, butter, cinnamon and nutmeg. Place a heaping tablespoonful of mixture in each apple. Pour 2 cups water around apples.
3. Cover and cook on low for 3-4 hours or until apples are tender. Serve with granola and caramel topping if desired.
1 serving: 256 cal., 11g fat (4g sat. fat), 15mg chol., 50mg sod., 43g carb. (34g sugars, 6g fiber), 1g pro.

SLOW-COOKER HONEY NUT GRANOLA

I lightened up my friend's recipe and changed the add-ins to our tastes. It's now a family favorite! You can vary this recipe to suit your own family, changing the nuts, seeds or dried fruits as desired.
—*Tari Ambler, Shorewood, IL*

PREP: 20 min. • **COOK:** 1½ hours + cooling
MAKES: 8 cups

- 4½ cups old-fashioned oats
- ½ cup sunflower kernels
- ⅓ cup toasted wheat germ
- ¼ cup unsweetened shredded coconut
- ¼ cup sliced almonds
- ¼ cup chopped pecans
- ¼ cup chopped walnuts
- ¼ cup ground flaxseed
- ½ cup honey
- ⅓ cup water
- 3 Tbsp. canola oil
- 1 tsp. ground cinnamon
- 1 tsp. vanilla extract
- ½ tsp. ground nutmeg
  Dash salt
- ¾ cup dried cranberries
- ¾ cup raisins
  Yogurt, optional

1. In a 3- or 4-qt. slow cooker, combine the first 8 ingredients. In a small bowl, whisk honey, water, oil, cinnamon, vanilla, nutmeg and salt until blended; stir into oat mixture. Cook, covered, on high 1½-2 hours or until crisp, stirring well every 20 minutes.
2. Stir in cranberries and raisins. Spread evenly onto waxed paper or baking sheets; cool completely. Store in airtight containers. If desired, serve with yogurt.
½ cup: 267 cal., 12g fat (2g sat. fat), 0 chol., 43mg sod., 39g carb. (19g sugars, 5g fiber), 6g pro.

SLOW-COOKER HONEY NUT GRANOLA

**BACON-RANCH
SPINACH DIP**

CRANBERRY APPLE CIDER

I love to start this soothing cider in the slow cooker on nights before my husband goes hunting. Then he can fill his thermos and take it with him out into the cold. The cider has a terrific fruit flavor we both enjoy.
—*Jennifer Naboka, North Plainfield, NJ*

PREP: 10 min. • **COOK:** 2 hours
MAKES: 10 servings (about 2½ qt.)

- 4　cups water
- 4　cups apple juice
- 1　can (12 oz.) frozen apple juice concentrate, thawed
- 1　medium apple, peeled and sliced
- 1　cup fresh or frozen cranberries
- 1　medium orange, peeled and sectioned
- 1　cinnamon stick

In a 5-qt. slow cooker, combine all ingredients. Cover and cook on low for 2 hours or until cider reaches desired temperature. Discard cinnamon stick. If desired, remove fruit with a slotted spoon before serving.

1 cup: 118 cal., 0 fat (0 sat. fat), 0 chol., 12mg sod., 29g carb. (27g sugars, 1g fiber), 0 pro.

WINE-POACHED PEARS

These pears look beautiful on a plate. The rosy color and wonderful flavor set the scene for a memorable holiday dinner.
—*Patricia Stiehr, Eureka, MO*

PREP: 10 min. • **COOK:** 3 hours
MAKES: 12 servings

- 2　cups port wine
- 2　cups sugar
- 1　tsp. grated lemon zest
- 6　medium Bosc pears, peeled

1. Place wine, sugar and lemon zest in a 5-qt. slow cooker; stir until sugar dissolves. Add peeled pears.

2. Cook, covered, on low 3-4 hours or until pears are tender, turning pears halfway through cooking. Using a slotted spoon, remove pears; cut into slices (save cooking liquid for another use).

1 serving: 74 cal., 0 fat (0 sat. fat), 0 chol., 1mg sod., 18g carb. (13g sugars, 3g fiber), 0 pro.

BACON-RANCH SPINACH DIP

During the hectic holiday season, my slow cooker works overtime. I fill it with a savory bacon dip and watch everyone line up for a helping. Keep the recipe in mind for tailgating, too.
—*Crystal Schlueter, Northglenn, CO*

PREP: 15 min. • **COOK:** 2 hours
MAKES: 6 cups

- 2　pkg. (8 oz. each) cream cheese, softened
- 1½　cups bacon ranch salad dressing
- ¼　cup 2% milk
- 2　cups shredded sharp cheddar cheese
- 1　can (14 oz.) water-packed artichoke hearts, rinsed, drained and chopped
- 1　pkg. (10 oz.) frozen chopped spinach, thawed and squeezed dry
- 2　plum tomatoes, seeded and finely chopped
- ½　cup crumbled cooked bacon
- 4　green onions, thinly sliced
  Assorted crackers and fresh vegetables

1. In a large bowl, beat cream cheese, salad dressing and milk until blended. Stir in the cheese, artichokes, spinach, tomatoes, bacon and green onions. Transfer to a 4- or 5-qt. slow cooker.

2. Cook, covered, on low 2-3 hours or until heated through. Serve with crackers and vegetables.

¼ cup: 195 cal., 17g fat (7g sat. fat), 34mg chol., 344mg sod., 4g carb. (2g sugars, 0 fiber), 6g pro.

CHICKEN CORDON
BLEU SLIDERS

CHICKEN CORDON BLEU SLIDERS

I'm always searching for sandwich ideas, because they're my favorite food! I like sloppy joes and decided to try different variations. This recipe was an experiment that met with the whole family's approval.
—*Carolyn Eskew, Dayton, OH*

- -

PREP: 20 min. • **COOK:** 2½ hours + standing
MAKES: 2 dozen

- 1½ lbs. boneless skinless chicken breasts
- 1 garlic clove, minced
- ¼ tsp. salt
- ¼ tsp. pepper
- 1 pkg. (8 oz.) cream cheese, cubed
- 2 cups shredded Swiss cheese
- 1¼ cups finely chopped fully cooked ham
- 2 pkg. (12 oz. each) Hawaiian sweet rolls, split
  Chopped green onions

1. Place chicken breasts in a greased 3-qt. slow cooker; sprinkle with garlic, salt and pepper. Top with cream cheese. Cook, covered, on low 2½-3 hours or until a thermometer inserted in chicken reads 165°. Remove chicken; shred with 2 forks. Return to slow cooker.
2. Stir in Swiss cheese and ham. Cover and let stand 15 minutes until cheese is melted. Stir before serving on rolls. Sprinkle with green onion.
1 slider: 209 cal., 10g fat (5g sat. fat), 53mg chol., 254mg sod., 17g carb. (6g sugars, 1g fiber), 14g pro.

**APPLE BETTY
WITH ALMOND CREAM**

APPLE BETTY WITH ALMOND CREAM

I love making this treat for friends during the peak of apple season. I plan a quick soup and bread meal, so we can get right to the dessert!
—*Elizabeth Godecke, Chicago, IL*

- -

PREP: 15 min. • **COOK:** 3 hours
MAKES: 8 servings

- 3 lbs. tart apples, peeled and sliced
- 10 slices cinnamon-raisin bread, cubed
- ¾ cup packed brown sugar
- ½ cup butter, melted
- 1 tsp. almond extract
- ½ tsp. ground cinnamon
- ¼ tsp. ground cardamom
- ⅛ tsp. salt

ALMOND CREAM
- 1 cup heavy whipping cream
- 2 Tbsp. sugar
- 1 tsp. grated lemon zest
- ½ tsp. almond extract

1. Place apples in an ungreased 4- or 5-qt. slow cooker. In a large bowl, combine the bread, brown sugar, butter, extract, cinnamon, cardamom and salt; spoon over apples. Cover and cook on low for 3-4 hours or until apples are tender.
2. In a small bowl, beat cream until it begins to thicken. Add the sugar, lemon zest and extract; beat until soft peaks form. Serve with apple mixture.
1 cup with ¼ cup almond cream: 468 cal., 23g fat (14g sat. fat), 71mg chol., 224mg sod., 65g carb. (45g sugars, 5g fiber), 5g pro.

"We added a touch of tangerine zest to the recipe. Great addition! Second time making in two days. Yum!"
— GREATMOM4GIRLS, TASTEOFHOME.COM

SODA POP CHOPS WITH
SMASHED POTATOES
PAGE 140

155

114

99

Stovetop Suppers

What's not to love about dinners prepared on the cooktop? Quick, convenient and healthy, they include best-loved meals like tacos, pasta, fish cakes and chops. Stovetop dishes keep the kitchen cool on a hot day. And on a cold one, nothing warms the heart like a cozy pot of stew bubbling away on the stove.

154

BEEF & GROUND BEEF » 92

POULTRY » 110

PORK » 132

FISH & SEAFOOD » 146

Beef & Ground Beef

TACOS IN
A BOWL

TACOS IN A BOWL

This easy skillet dish tastes like tacos for a fun dinner for two. Garnish each serving with sour cream and salsa and top with crushed tortilla chips for added crunch!
—*Sue Schoening, Sheboygan, WI*

- -

TAKES: 25 min. • **MAKES:** 2 servings

½   lb. lean ground beef (90% lean)
2   Tbsp. finely chopped onion
¾   cup canned diced tomatoes, drained
2   Tbsp. taco seasoning
1   cup water
1   pkg. (3 oz.) ramen noodles
¼   cup shredded cheddar or Mexican cheese blend
    Crushed tortilla chips, optional

1. In a small skillet, cook beef and onion over medium heat until meat is no longer pink; drain. Stir in the tomatoes, taco seasoning and water. Bring to a boil. Add ramen noodles (discard seasoning packet or save for another use). Cook and stir until noodles are tender, 3-5 minutes.
2. Spoon into serving bowls; sprinkle with cheese and, if desired, tortilla chips.
1 cup: 480 cal., 21g fat (10g sat. fat), 85mg chol., 1279mg sod., 40g carb. (3g sugars, 2g fiber), 30g pro.

"This is so quick and easy, and it tastes great. It's a good one to make with kids, and also easy for single guys who are not that into cooking."
—PHYLLIS KESLER, TASTEOFHOME.COM

**ASPARAGUS BEEF
CASHEW STIR-FRY**

BRACIOLE

In our family, braciole was served as a special treat for birthdays and holidays. It was my grandma's specialty and the preparation was time-consuming. When the meat and sauce were fully cooked, Grandma called us into the kitchen to watch her lift the big roll from the sauce to the cutting board to slice it. The pinwheels of meat, laid side by side on the platter, topped with Grandma's delicious sauce, made a beautiful picture.
—*Cookie Curci, San Jose, CA*

- -

PREP: 35 min. • **COOK:** 1¼ hours
MAKES: 6 servings

1	beef flank steak (1½ lbs.)
4	Tbsp. olive oil, divided
½	cup soft bread crumbs
½	cup minced fresh parsley
½	cup grated Parmesan cheese
2	garlic cloves, minced
1	tsp. dried oregano
½	tsp. salt, divided
½	tsp. pepper, divided
1	medium onion, chopped
2	cans (15 oz. each) tomato sauce
½	cup water
1	tsp. Italian seasoning
½	tsp. sugar
	Hot cooked spaghetti, optional

1. Flatten steak to ½-in. thickness. Rub with 1 Tbsp. oil. Combine the bread crumbs, parsley, cheese, garlic, oregano, ¼ tsp. salt and ¼ tsp. pepper. Spoon over beef to within 1 in. of edges; press down. Roll up jelly-roll style, starting with a long side; tie with kitchen string.
2. In a Dutch oven, brown meat in remaining oil on all sides. Add the onion and cook until tender. Stir in the tomato sauce, water, Italian seasoning, sugar and the remaining salt and pepper. Bring to a boil. Reduce heat; cover and simmer for 70-80 minutes or until meat is tender.
3. Remove meat from sauce and discard string. Cut into thin slices; serve with sauce and spaghetti if desired.
1 serving: 330 cal., 20g fat (6g sat. fat), 54mg chol., 1028mg sod., 13g carb. (4g sugars, 2g fiber), 25g pro.

ASPARAGUS BEEF CASHEW STIR-FRY

As appetizing to the eye as it is to the palate, this stovetop specialty features plenty of vegetables, beef and crunchy cashews. A local restaurant once handed out asparagus recipes, including this one.
—*Joyce Huebner, Marinette, WI*

- -

PREP: 20 min. • **COOK:** 25 min.
MAKES: 6 servings

2	Tbsp. cornstarch
1	cup beef broth
3	Tbsp. soy sauce
½	tsp. sugar
2	Tbsp. canola oil
2	whole garlic cloves
2	lbs. fresh asparagus, trimmed and cut into 2½-in. pieces
2	medium onions, halved and thinly sliced
1	medium sweet red pepper, julienned
1	large carrot, cut into 2½-in. strips
2½	cups sliced cooked roast beef (2½-in. strips)
1	cup salted cashew halves
	Hot cooked rice

1. In a small bowl, combine cornstarch and broth until smooth. Stir in soy sauce and sugar; set aside. In a wok or large skillet, heat oil; add garlic. Cook and stir until lightly browned, about 1 minute; discard garlic.
2. Stir-fry the asparagus, onions, red pepper and carrot until crisp-tender, 15-20 minutes. Add roast beef; heat through. Stir reserved sauce; add to the pan. Bring to a boil; cook and stir until thickened, about 2 minutes. Sprinkle with cashews. Serve with rice.
¾ cup: 382 cal., 21g fat (4g sat. fat), 54mg chol., 815mg sod., 18g carb. (7g sugars, 4g fiber), 30g pro.

PHILLY CHEESESTEAK
GNOCCHI

TRIPLE-CITRUS STEAKS WITH JICAMA & MANGO

This is a recipe I made up several years ago. It seems to be one of our family favorites. It's colorful to bring to the table and it's easy.
—*Sherry Little, Sherwood, AR*

- -

PREP: 30 min. + marinating • **COOK:** 15 min.
MAKES: 4 servings

- 1 medium orange
- 1 medium lemon
- 1 medium lime
- 4 Tbsp. honey
- 1¼ tsp. salt, divided
- 4 beef flat iron steaks or top sirloin steaks (6 oz. each) and ¾ in. thick
- ½ cup water
- 1 cup julienned peeled jicama
- 1 medium mango, peeled and cubed

1. Cut orange, lemon and lime crosswise in half; squeeze juice from fruits. Stir in honey and salt. Pour ⅓ cup marinade into a bowl or shallow dish. Add steaks and turn to coat. Refrigerate at least 3 hours, turning once. Cover and refrigerate remaining marinade.
2. Drain steaks, discarding marinade. Heat a large skillet over medium heat. Cook steaks until meat reaches desired doneness (for medium-rare, a thermometer should read 135°; medium, 140°; medium-well, 145°), 6-8 minutes on each side. Remove and keep warm.
3. Add water and reserved marinade. Bring to a boil; cook until the liquid is reduced to 3 Tbsp., 10-12 minutes. Add jicama and mango; heat through. Serve with steaks. If desired, garnish with orange, lemon or lime slices.
1 serving: 412 cal., 18g fat (7g sat. fat), 109mg chol., 609mg sod., 29g carb. (24g sugars, 3g fiber), 34g pro.

PHILLY CHEESESTEAK GNOCCHI

My family loves this warm and welcoming meal. It has all the Philly cheesesteak flavor served up in a bowl!
—*Lauren Wyler, Dripping Springs, TX*

- -

TAKES: 30 min. • **MAKES:** 6 servings

- 1 lb. ground beef
- 1 medium green pepper, halved and sliced
- 1 small onion, halved and thinly sliced
- 1 jalapeno pepper, halved, seeded and thinly sliced
- 2 Tbsp. butter
- 2 Tbsp. all-purpose flour
- ½ tsp. pepper
- ¼ tsp. salt
- 1½ cups 2% milk
- 2 Tbsp. Worcestershire sauce
- 2 cups shredded provolone cheese
- 1 pkg. (16 oz.) potato gnocchi

1. In a large skillet, cook and crumble beef with green pepper, onion and jalapeno over medium-high heat until no longer pink, 5-7 minutes. Drain, discarding drippings.

2. In same skillet, melt butter over medium heat. Stir in the flour, pepper and salt until smooth; cook and stir until lightly browned, 2-3 minutes. Gradually whisk in the milk and Worcestershire sauce. Bring to a boil, stirring constantly; cook and stir until thickened, 5-7 minutes. Stir in cheese until melted. Add beef mixture; heat through.
3. Meanwhile, cook gnocchi according to package directions. Drain; add to sauce, stirring gently. Serve immediately.
Note: Wear disposable gloves when cutting hot peppers; the oils can burn skin. Avoid touching your face.
1 cup: 512 cal., 25g fat (14g sat. fat), 93mg chol., 918mg sod., 40g carb. (9g sugars, 2g fiber), 31g pro.

TEST KITCHEN TIP
The Worcestershire sauce may seem odd, but don't leave it out! It adds a savory depth of flavor that balances out this dish.

TRIPLE-CITRUS STEAKS
WITH JICAMA & MANGO

BREADED STEAKS

This homespun, stick-to-your-ribs steak supper was always a favorite with us kids. Mom coated tender steaks with lightly seasoned bread crumbs and fried them in oil until golden brown.
—*Gina Mueller, Converse, TX*

- -

TAKES: 30 min. • **MAKES:** 8 servings

2	lbs. beef top sirloin tip steaks
½	cup all-purpose flour
2	large eggs
1	cup 2% milk
¼	tsp. salt
⅛	tsp. pepper
1	pkg. (15 oz.) seasoned bread crumbs
¼	cup canola oil

1. Flatten steaks to ½-in. thickness. Cut into serving-sized pieces; set aside. Place flour in a shallow bowl. In another shallow bowl, combine eggs, milk, salt and pepper. Place bread crumbs in a third shallow bowl. Coat steaks with flour, then dip into egg mixture and coat with crumbs.
2. In a large skillet over medium-high heat, cook steaks in oil until meat reaches desired doneness (for medium-rare, a thermometer should read 135°, medium, 140°, medium-well, 145°), 2-3 minutes on each side.
1 serving: 478 cal., 18g fat (4g sat. fat), 120mg chol., 968mg sod., 46g carb. (4g sugars, 2g fiber), 32g pro.

TEST KITCHEN TIP
To turn this dish into chicken-fried steak, add flour to some of the pan drippings, milk, salt and lots of pepper to make a classic peppery white gravy. Bring on the biscuits!

QUICK BEEF & NOODLES

QUICK BEEF & NOODLES

My family loves this lighter version of beef Stroganoff. Using roast beef from the deli saves the hours spent cooking a whole roast. I like to serve this entree with a crisp green salad for a home-style meal.
—*Pamela Shank, Parkersburg, WV*

- -

TAKES: 25 min. • **MAKES:** 2 servings

2½	cups uncooked yolk-free noodles
⅓	cup sliced fresh mushrooms
⅓	cup chopped onion
1	Tbsp. olive oil
1¼	cups reduced-sodium beef broth
6	oz. deli roast beef, cubed
⅛	tsp. pepper
	Optional: Sour cream and chopped fresh parsley

1. Cook noodles according to package directions. In a large skillet, saute mushrooms and onion in oil until tender. Add broth, roast beef and pepper. Bring to a boil. Reduce heat; simmer, uncovered, for 10 minutes.
2. Drain noodles; stir into skillet. If desired, top with sour cream and parsley.
1½ cups: 375 cal., 10g fat (2g sat. fat), 50mg chol., 778mg sod., 42g carb. (5g sugars, 3g fiber), 26g pro. **Diabetic exchanges:** 3 starch, 3 lean meat, 1½ fat.

RHUBARB BEEF

My daughter made a trip around the world and brought home this recipe from Iran. I've served it often to many of my friends, and they always seem to savor its different, zingy taste.
—Bertha Davis, Springfield, MO

- -

PREP: 10 min. • **COOK:** 2¼ hours
MAKES: 6 servings

- 2 to 2½ lbs. beef stew meat, cut into 1-in. cubes
- 2 Tbsp. butter
- 2 large onions, chopped
- 1 tsp. saffron
- 1 can (10½ oz.) beef broth
- 1 cup water
- ¼ cup lemon juice
- ¼ cup chopped fresh parsley
- 1½ tsp. dried mint
- 2 tsp. salt
- ¼ tsp. pepper
- 2 to 3 cups sliced fresh or frozen rhubarb
  Hot cooked rice
  Fresh mint leaves, torn

1. In a Dutch oven, brown beef in butter. Remove meat from pan; drain all but 2 Tbsp. drippings. Saute onions until lightly browned.
2. Return meat to pan. Add saffron, broth, water, lemon juice, parsley, mint, salt and pepper; cover and simmer until meat is tender, about 2 hours. Add more water as needed. Add rhubarb during the last 15 minutes of cooking. Serve over rice; top with fresh mint.
1 cup: 287 cal., 15g fat (6g sat. fat), 104mg chol., 1072mg sod., 8g carb. (5g sugars, 2g fiber), 30g pro.

RHUBARB BEEF

BEEF GYROS

Going out to restaurants for gyros can be expensive, so I came up with this homemade version. Usually, I set out the fixings so everyone can assemble their own.
—Sheri Scheerhorn, Hills, MN

- -

TAKES: 30 min. • **MAKES:** 5 servings

- 1 cup ranch salad dressing
- ½ cup chopped seeded peeled cucumber
- 1 lb. beef top sirloin steak, cut into thin strips
- 2 Tbsp. olive oil
- 5 whole pita breads, warmed
- 1 medium tomato, chopped
- 1 can (2¼ oz.) sliced ripe olives, drained
- ½ small onion, thinly sliced
- 1 cup crumbled feta cheese
- 2½ cups shredded lettuce

1. In a small bowl, combine salad dressing and cucumber; set aside. In a large skillet, cook beef in oil over medium heat until no longer pink.
2. Layer half of each pita with steak, tomato, olives, onion, cheese, lettuce and dressing mixture. Fold each pita over filling; secure with toothpicks.
1 serving: 654 cal., 41g fat (9g sat. fat), 57mg chol., 1086mg sod., 41g carb. (4g sugars, 3g fiber), 30g pro.

SPICY CORNED
BEEF TACOS

SPICY CORNED BEEF TACOS

Using leftovers in new and exciting ways is my personal cooking challenge. These fun tacos take my favorite Reuben ingredients and turn them into something totally different—and completely delicious.
—*Fay A. Moreland, Wichita Falls, TX*

TAKES: 30 min. • **MAKES:** 6 servings

- 2 cups coleslaw mix
- 4 green onions, thinly sliced
- 2 jalapeno peppers, seeded and thinly sliced
- 1 cup Thousand Island salad dressing
- 1 to 2 Tbsp. Sriracha chili sauce
- 2 Tbsp. canola oil
- 3 cups chopped cooked corned beef
- 2 cups refrigerated diced potatoes with onion
- 12 flour tortillas (6 in.), warmed

1. In a small bowl, combine the coleslaw mix, green onions and jalapenos. In another small bowl, whisk salad dressing and chili sauce until combined.

2. In a large skillet, heat oil over medium heat. Add corned beef and diced potatoes; cook and stir until heated through, 8-10 minutes. Serve in tortillas with coleslaw mixture and dressing mixture.

Note: Wear disposable gloves when cutting hot peppers; the oils can burn skin. Avoid touching your face.

2 tacos: 621 cal., 39g fat (9g sat. fat), 60mg chol., 1606mg sod., 48g carb. (8g sugars, 4g fiber), 16g pro.

> ### TEST KITCHEN TIP
> Worried that your jalapenos are a little too spicy? After you slice them, toss them in ¼ cup vodka for about 10 minutes. It will remove a lot of the heat, leaving only the great jalapeno flavor.

CAJUN SIRLOIN WITH MUSHROOM LEEK SAUCE

CAJUN SIRLOIN WITH MUSHROOM LEEK SAUCE

In 30 minutes you'll have a restaurant-quality steak with a bold Cajun flair. The best part? You can skip the drive, the wait and the bill!
—*Joshua Keefer, Delaware, OH*

PREP: 15 min. • **COOK:** 15 min.
MAKES: 4 servings

- 1 beef top sirloin steak (1¼ lbs.)
- 2 Tbsp. Cajun seasoning
- 2 Tbsp. olive oil
- ½ lb. sliced assorted fresh mushrooms
- 1 medium leek (white portion only), halved and sliced
- 1 Tbsp. butter
- 1 tsp. minced garlic
- 1½ cups dry red wine or reduced-sodium beef broth
- ¼ tsp. pepper
- ⅛ tsp. salt

1. Rub steak with Cajun seasoning; let stand for 5 minutes.

2. In a large skillet, cook steak in oil over medium-high heat for 7-10 minutes on each side or until meat reaches desired doneness (for medium-rare, a thermometer should read 135°; medium, 140°; medium-well, 145°). Remove and keep warm.

3. In the same skillet, saute mushrooms and leek in butter until tender. Add garlic; cook 1 minute longer. Add the wine, pepper and salt, stirring to loosen browned bits from pan. Bring to a boil; cook until the liquid is reduced by half. Slice the steak; serve with mushroom sauce.

4 oz. cooked beef with ¼ cup sauce: 325 cal., 16g fat (5g sat. fat), 65mg chol., 976mg sod., 7g carb. (2g sugars, 1g fiber), 32g pro.

STEAKS WITH CRAB SAUCE

Here's a simple take on surf and turf that's simple enough for dinner with friends. A creamy crab sauce drapes nicely over New York strip steaks.
—Taste of Home *Test Kitchen*

- -

TAKES: 25 min. • **MAKES:** 4 servings

- 1 tsp. dried rosemary, crushed
- ½ tsp. salt
- ½ tsp. pepper
- 4 boneless beef top loin steaks (8 oz. each)
- 1 Tbsp. canola oil

SAUCE

- 2 tsp. cornstarch
- ¼ cup white wine or chicken broth
- ¾ cup heavy whipping cream
- 1 Tbsp. Dijon mustard
- ½ tsp. prepared horseradish
- ⅛ tsp. salt
- ⅛ tsp. pepper
- 1 pkg. (8 oz.) imitation crabmeat, coarsely chopped

1. Combine the rosemary, salt and pepper; rub over the steaks. In a large skillet over medium-high heat, cook steaks in oil until meat reaches desired doneness (for medium-rare, a thermometer should read 135°; medium, 140°; medium-well, 145°), 5-8 minutes on each side.

2. Meanwhile, in a small saucepan, combine the cornstarch and white wine or broth until smooth. Stir in the cream, Dijon mustard, horseradish, salt and pepper. Bring to a boil; cook and stir 2 minutes or until thickened. Stir in crab; heat through. Serve over steaks.

1 steak with ⅓ cup sauce: 558 cal., 30g fat (14g sat. fat), 157mg chol., 886mg sod., 11g carb. (1g sugars, 0 fiber), 55g pro.

"I used real crabmeat instead of imitation. It was absolutely delicious. My husband said he would give it 6 stars on the 1-to-5 rating system."
—DANCINGFOOL, TASTEOFHOME.COM

KOREAN BEEF & RICE

A friend raved about Korean bulgogi—beef cooked in soy sauce and ginger—so I tried it. It's delicious! Dazzle the table with this tasty version of beef and rice.
—Elizabeth King, Duluth, MN

- -

TAKES: 15 min. • **MAKES:** 4 servings

- 1 lb. lean ground beef (90% lean)
- 3 garlic cloves, minced
- ¼ cup packed brown sugar
- ¼ cup reduced-sodium soy sauce
- 2 tsp. sesame oil
- ¼ tsp. ground ginger
- ¼ tsp. crushed red pepper flakes
- ¼ tsp. pepper
- 2⅔ cups hot cooked brown rice
- 3 green onions, thinly sliced

1. In a large skillet, cook beef and garlic over medium heat 6-8 minutes or until beef is no longer pink, breaking up beef into crumbles. Meanwhile, in a small bowl, mix brown sugar, soy sauce, oil and seasonings.

2. Stir sauce into beef; heat through. Serve with rice. Sprinkle with green onions.

Freeze option: Freeze cooled meat mixture in freezer containers. To use, partially thaw in refrigerator overnight. Heat through in a saucepan, stirring occasionally.

½ cup beef mixture with ⅔ cup rice: 413 cal., 13g fat (4g sat. fat), 71mg chol., 647mg sod., 46g carb. (14g sugars, 3g fiber), 27g pro. **Diabetic exchanges:** 3 starch, 3 lean meat, ½ fat.

KOREAN
BEEF & RICE

ONE-POT DINNER

COCONUT MANGO THAI BEEF CURRY

My recipe provides a lot of sweet heat. The mango and coconut milk taste tropical while the curry paste adds a little fire. It's a great dish to spice up the traditional offerings of the season. To make a milder dish, just reduce the amount of curry paste.
—*Terri Lynn Merritts, Nashville, TN*

PREP: 10 min. • **COOK:** 2¼ hours
MAKES: 6 servings

- 2 Tbsp. peanut oil or canola oil
- 3 Tbsp. red curry paste
- 2½ cups coconut milk
- 2½ lbs. boneless beef chuck roast, cut into 1-in. cubes
- 1 cup dried mango, chopped
- 1 tsp. salt
- ¼ tsp. pepper
  Hot cooked rice, optional

1. In a Dutch oven, heat peanut oil over low heat. Add curry paste; cook and stir 3-5 minutes. Add coconut milk; cook and stir 3-5 minutes longer.
2. Stir in the beef, mango, salt and pepper. Increase heat to medium-high; bring to a boil. Reduce heat; simmer, uncovered, stirring occasionally, until meat is tender, about 2 hours. If desired, serve with rice.
1 cup: 578 cal., 38g fat (23g sat. fat), 123mg chol., 793mg sod., 17g carb. (14g sugars, 1g fiber), 39g pro.

TEST KITCHEN TIP
This recipe was tested with regular (full-fat) coconut milk. Light coconut milk contains less fat.

ONE-POT DINNER

Everyone comes back for seconds when I serve this skillet supper. I like the fact that it's on the table in just 30 minutes.
—*Bonnie Morrow, Spencerport, NY*

TAKES: 30 min. • **MAKES:** 5 servings

- ½ lb. ground beef
- 1 medium onion, chopped
- 1 cup chopped celery
- ¾ cup chopped green pepper
- 2 tsp. Worcestershire sauce
- 1 tsp. salt, optional
- ½ tsp. dried basil
- ¼ tsp. pepper
- 2 cups uncooked medium egg noodles
- 1 can (16 oz.) kidney beans, rinsed and drained
- 1 can (14½ oz.) stewed tomatoes
- ¾ cup water
- 1 beef bouillon cube

1. In a large saucepan or skillet, cook the beef, onion, celery and green pepper over medium heat until the meat is no longer pink and the vegetables are crisp-tender; drain. Add the Worcestershire sauce, salt if desired, basil and pepper. Stir in the noodles, beans, tomatoes, water and bouillon.
2. Bring to a boil. Reduce heat; cover and simmer for 20 minutes or until noodles are tender, stirring occasionally.
1 cup: 263 cal., 6g fat (2g sat. fat), 41mg chol., 535mg sod., 36g carb. (8g sugars, 7g fiber), 17g pro.

CAST-IRON
SKILLET STEAK

GRILLED CHEESE BURGERS WITH SAUTEED ONIONS

My husband loves both my grilled cheese and my iron skillet burgers, so I decided to combine them. He said it was the best burger he ever ate!
—*Lisa Allen, Joppa, AL*

PREP: 35 min. • **COOK:** 25 min.
MAKES: 4 servings

- 1 lb. lean ground beef (90% lean)
- 2 Tbsp. Worcestershire sauce
- 1 tsp. garlic powder
- ½ tsp. salt
- ¼ tsp. pepper
- 1 Tbsp. liquid smoke, optional
- 1 Tbsp. olive oil
- 5 Tbsp. butter, softened, divided
- 1 large onion, thinly sliced
- 16 slices process American cheese
- 16 slices sandwich bread

1. In a large bowl, combine ground beef, Worcestershire sauce, garlic powder, salt, pepper and liquid smoke if desired, mixing lightly but thoroughly. Shape into four 4-in. square patties.
2. In a large nonstick skillet, cook burgers in oil over medium heat until a thermometer reads 160°, 4-5 minutes on each side. Remove and keep warm.
3. In the same skillet, heat 1 Tbsp. butter over medium-high heat. Add onion; cook and stir until tender, 6-8 minutes. Remove and keep warm. Place cheese on 8 bread slices; top with remaining bread. Spread outsides of sandwiches with remaining 4 Tbsp. butter.
4. In the same skillet, toast sandwiches over medium heat until golden brown and cheese is melted, 1-2 minutes on each side. Top 4 sandwiches with burgers and onions. Top with remaining sandwiches.

1 sandwich: 900 cal., 50g fat (27g sat. fat), 129mg chol., 1954mg sod., 56g carb. (12g sugars, 3g fiber), 47g pro.

CAST-IRON SKILLET STEAK

If you've never cooked steak at home before, it can be a little intimidating. That's why I came up with this simple steak recipe that's so easy, you could make it any day of the week.
—*James Schend, Pleasant Prairie, WI*

PREP: 5 min. + standing • **COOK:** 5 min.
MAKES: 2 servings

- 1 Tbsp. kosher salt, divided
- 1 beef NY strip or ribeye steak (1 lb.), 1 in. thick

1. Remove steak from refrigerator and sprinkle with 2 tsp. salt; let stand for 45-60 minutes.
2. Preheat a cast-iron skillet over high heat until extremely hot, 4-5 minutes. Sprinkle remaining 1 tsp. salt in bottom of skillet; pat beef dry with paper towels. Place steak into skillet and cook until steak is easily moved, 1-2 minutes; flip, placing steak in a different section of the skillet. Cook 30 seconds and then begin moving the steak, occasionally pressing slightly to ensure even contact with the skillet.
3. Continue turning and flipping steak until cooked to desired degree of doneness (for medium-rare, a thermometer should read 135°; medium, 140°; medium-well, 145°), 1-2 minutes.

6 oz. cooked beef: 494 cal., 36g fat (15g sat. fat), 134mg chol., 2983mg sod., 0 carb. (0 sugars, 0 fiber), 40g pro.

GRILLED CHEESE BURGERS
WITH SAUTEED ONIONS

TOMATO & PEPPER SIRLOIN

The beefy sauce and zippy peppers in this dish offer an amazing amount of flavor for under 300 calories.

—*Gayle Tarkowski, Traverse City, MI*

PREP: 15 min. • **COOK:** 35 min.
MAKES: 6 servings

- ½ cup all-purpose flour
- ¾ tsp. salt
- ½ tsp. pepper
- 1½ lbs. beef top sirloin steak, thinly sliced
- 3 Tbsp. canola oil
- 1 small onion, chopped
- 1 garlic clove, minced
- 1 can (28 oz.) diced tomatoes, undrained
- 2 large green peppers, cut into strips
- 2 to 3 Tbsp. beef broth
- 1½ tsp. Worcestershire sauce
  Hot cooked rice

1. In a large bowl or shallow dish, combine flour, salt and pepper. Add beef slices, a few pieces at a time. Toss gently to coat.

2. In a Dutch oven, heat oil over medium-high heat. Brown beef in batches. Add onion; cook and stir until tender, 3-4 minutes. Add garlic; cook 1 minute longer. Add tomatoes; bring to a boil. Reduce heat. Simmer, covered, stirring occasionally, until meat is tender, 10-15 minutes.

3. Stir in the green peppers, broth and Worcestershire sauce; simmer, covered, until peppers are tender, 10-15 minutes. Serve with rice.

1 cup pepper steak mixture: 284 cal., 12g fat (2g sat. fat), 46mg chol., 552mg sod., 17g carb. (6g sugars, 4g fiber), 27g pro. **Diabetic exchanges:** 3 lean meat, 2 starch, 1½ fat.

MEAT & POTATO PATTIES

MEAT & POTATO PATTIES

During World War II, when meat was rationed and had to be purchased with tokens, this recipe went a long way in feeding a family. To this day, I reach for it whenever I want something different from regular hamburgers.

—*Gladys Klein, Burlington, WI*

PREP: 10 min. • **COOK:** 25 min.
MAKES: 4 servings

- ¾ lb. lean ground beef (90% lean)
- ¾ cup finely shredded potatoes
- ¼ cup finely chopped onion
- 2 Tbsp. chopped green pepper
- 1 large egg, beaten
- ¼ tsp. salt
- 1 Tbsp. canola oil
- 1 cup tomato juice
- 1 Tbsp. all-purpose flour
- ¼ cup water

1. Combine the first 6 ingredients. Shape into 4 patties; press to flatten slightly. In a large skillet, heat canola oil over medium-high heat. Brown patties on both sides; drain. Add tomato juice. Simmer, covered, until a thermometer inserted into meat reads 160°, 20-25 minutes. Remove patties to a serving platter; keep warm.

2. Whisk flour into water; gradually add to skillet. Reduce heat to medium-low; cook, stirring constantly, until thickened. Spoon over patties. Serve immediately.

1 patty: 237 cal., 12g fat (4g sat. fat), 99mg chol., 373mg sod., 12g carb. (2g sugars, 1g fiber), 20g pro.

ARRABBIATA SAUCE WITH ZUCCHINI NOODLES

This popular Italian dish is spicy and full of flavor. We decided to re-create one of our favorite sauces and serve it over zucchini pasta for a lighter, healthier meal that's naturally gluten-free. The results were simply amazing!
—Courtney Stultz, Weir, KS

PREP: 10 min. • **COOK:** 35 min.
MAKES: 4 servings

- 1 lb. lean ground beef (90% lean)
- ½ cup finely chopped onion
- 2 garlic cloves, minced
- 1 can (14½ oz.) petite diced tomatoes, undrained
- ¼ cup dry red wine or beef broth
- 3 Tbsp. tomato paste
- 2 tsp. honey
- 1 tsp. cider vinegar
- ¾ tsp. dried basil
- ½ to 1 tsp. crushed red pepper flakes
- ½ tsp. salt
- ¼ tsp. dried oregano
- ¼ tsp. dried thyme

ZUCCHINI NOODLES

- 2 large zucchini
- 1 Tbsp. olive oil
- ¼ tsp. salt
  Chopped fresh parsley, optional

1. In a large saucepan, cook and crumble beef with onion and garlic over medium-high heat until no longer pink, 5-7 minutes. Stir in the tomatoes, red wine, tomato paste, honey, cider vinegar and seasonings; bring to a boil. Reduce heat; simmer, uncovered, until the flavors are blended, about 25 minutes, stirring occasionally.

2. For noodles, trim ends of zucchini. Using a spiralizer, cut zucchini into thin strands. In a large cast-iron or other heavy skillet, heat oil over medium-high heat. Add zucchini; cook until slightly softened, 1-2 minutes, tossing constantly with tongs (do not overcook). Sprinkle with salt. Serve noodles with sauce. If desired, sprinkle with parsley.

Freeze option: Freeze cooled sauce in freezer containers. To use, partially thaw in the refrigerator overnight. Heat through in a saucepan, stirring occasionally.

Note: If a spiralizer is not available, zucchini may also be cut into ribbons using a vegetable peeler. Saute as directed, increasing time as necessary.

1 cup sauce with 1 cup zucchini noodles: 287 cal., 13g fat (4g sat. fat), 71mg chol., 708mg sod., 17g carb. (11g sugars, 4g fiber), 26g pro. **Diabetic exchanges:** 3 lean meat, 2 vegetable, ½ starch.

ARRABBIATA SAUCE WITH
ZUCCHINI NOODLES

SWEET HOOSIER
DOG SAUCE

❄ SWEET HOOSIER DOG SAUCE

In our area of Indiana, we love sweet Coney sauce on our hot dogs! Our town still has an old drive-in that is famous for theirs.
—*Jill Thomas, Washington, IN*

TAKES: 30 min. • **MAKES:** 5 cups

- 2 lbs. ground beef
- 1 can (6 oz.) tomato paste
- 1 cup water
- 1 can (8 oz.) tomato sauce
- ½ cup sweet pickle relish
- ¼ cup dried minced onion
- 2 Tbsp. sugar
- 1 Tbsp. chili powder
- 2 tsp. Worcestershire sauce
- 1 tsp. salt
- 1 tsp. cider vinegar
- 1 tsp. yellow mustard
- ½ tsp. celery salt
- ¼ tsp. garlic powder
- ¼ tsp. onion powder
  Hot dogs and buns
  Optional: Diced onion, sliced pickles and shredded cheddar cheese

1. In a Dutch oven, cook beef over medium heat until no longer pink, 8-10 minutes, breaking into crumbles; drain. Stir in tomato paste; cook and stir 3 minutes. Stir in the next 13 ingredients. Bring to a boil; reduce heat. Simmer, uncovered, 15-20 minutes or until thickened, stirring occasionally.
2. Serve sauce over hot dogs in buns. Add optional toppings as desired.
Freeze option: Freeze the cooled sauce in freezer containers. To use, partially thaw in refrigerator overnight. Heat through in a covered saucepan, stirring gently; add water if necessary.
¼ cup: 111 cal., 5g fat (2g sat. fat), 28mg chol., 298mg sod., 7g carb. (4g sugars, 1g fiber), 9g pro.

DID YOU KNOW?
Though it's named after New York's famed amusement park, the Coney dog's roots are actually in the Greek immigrant communities of Michigan and Indiana. Here the idea of smothering hot dogs in savory tomato sauce was born— and is still adored today.

LEMONY GREEK BEEF & VEGETABLES

LEMONY GREEK BEEF & VEGETABLES

I love the lemon in this recipe, which is the latest addition to my collection of quick, healthy dinners. I'm sensitive to cow's milk, so I use goat cheese crumbles on my portion instead of the Parmesan.
—*Alice Neff, Lake Worth, FL*

TAKES: 30 min. • **MAKES:** 4 servings

- 1 bunch baby bok choy
- 1 lb. ground beef
- 1 Tbsp. olive oil
- 5 medium carrots, sliced
- 3 garlic cloves, minced
- ¼ cup plus 2 Tbsp. white wine, divided
- 1 can (15 to 16 oz.) navy beans, rinsed and drained
- 2 Tbsp. minced fresh oregano or 2 tsp. dried oregano
- ¼ tsp. salt
- 2 Tbsp. lemon juice
- ½ cup shredded Parmesan cheese

1. Trim and discard root end of bok choy. Coarsely chop leaves. Cut stalks into 1-in. pieces. Set aside.
2. In a large skillet, cook beef over medium-high heat until no longer pink, breaking into crumbles, 5-7 minutes; drain. Remove from skillet and set aside.
3. In same skillet, heat oil over medium-high heat. Add carrots and bok choy stalks; cook and stir until crisp-tender, 5-7 minutes. Stir in garlic, bok choy leaves and ¼ cup wine; increase heat to medium-high. Cook, stirring to loosen browned bits from pan, until the greens wilt, 3-5 minutes.
4. Stir in ground beef, beans, oregano, salt and enough remaining wine to keep mixture moist. Reduce heat; simmer about 3 minutes. Stir in lemon juice; sprinkle with shredded Parmesan cheese.
1½ cups: 478 cal., 21g fat (7g sat. fat), 77mg chol., 856mg sod., 36g carb. (7g sugars, 10g fiber), 36g pro.

BEEF RAGU WITH RAVIOLI

This sweet, no-stress sauce tastes like it was simmering all day! Serve it over your favorite refrigerated or frozen ravioli for an easy meal.
—Taste of Home *Test Kitchen*

PREP: 15 min. • **COOK:** 40 min.
MAKES: 4 servings

- 1 lb. ground beef
- ½ cup chopped onion
- 1 lb. plum tomatoes, diced
- 1 cup beef broth
- ½ cup red wine or additional beef broth
- 1 can (6 oz.) tomato paste
- 2 tsp. minced fresh rosemary
- 1 tsp. sugar
- 1 tsp. minced garlic
- ½ tsp. salt
- 1 pkg. (20 oz.) refrigerated cheese ravioli
  Grated Parmesan cheese, optional

1. In a large skillet, cook beef and onion over medium heat until meat is no longer pink; drain. Add the tomatoes, broth, wine, tomato paste, rosemary, sugar, garlic and salt. Bring to a boil. Reduce heat; simmer, uncovered, for 30 minutes.
2. Cook ravioli according to the package directions; drain. Serve with meat sauce. If desired, sprinkle with cheese .
1 cup: 672 cal., 21g fat (10g sat. fat), 112mg chol., 1181mg sod., 74g carb. (14g sugars, 7g fiber), 44g pro.

SKILLET NACHOS

My mom gave me a fundraiser cookbook, and the recipe I've used most is for skillet nachos. My whole family's on board. For toppings, think sour cream, tomatoes, jalapeno and red onion.
—*Judy Hughes, Waverly, KS*

TAKES: 30 min. • **MAKES:** 6 servings

- 1 lb. ground beef
- 1 can (14½ oz.) diced tomatoes, undrained
- 1 cup fresh or frozen corn, thawed
- ¾ cup uncooked instant rice
- ½ cup water
- 1 envelope taco seasoning
- ½ tsp. salt
- 1 cup shredded Colby-Monterey Jack cheese
- 1 pkg. (16 oz.) tortilla chips
  Optional toppings: Sour cream, sliced fresh jalapenos, shredded lettuce and lime wedges

1. In a large skillet, cook beef over medium heat until no longer pink, 6-8 minutes, breaking into crumbles; drain. Stir in the tomatoes, corn, rice, water, taco seasoning and salt. Bring to a boil. Reduce heat; simmer, covered, until rice is tender and mixture is slightly thickened, 8-10 minutes.
2. Remove from heat; sprinkle with cheese. Let stand, covered, until cheese is melted, about 5 minutes. Divide tortilla chips among 6 plates; spoon the beef mixture over chips. Serve with toppings as desired.
1 serving: 676 cal., 31g fat (10g sat. fat), 63mg chol., 1293mg sod., 74g carb. (4g sugars, 4g fiber), 25g pro.

SKILLET NACHOS

SLOPPY JOE
STEW

BEEFY TORTELLINI SKILLET

This skillet wonder is a tortellini dish the family craves. From browning beef to cooking the pasta and melting the cheese, everything happens in one pan. You can add basil or chives for a touch of freshness.
—*Juli Meyers, Hinesville, GA*

- -

TAKES: 20 min. • **MAKES:** 4 servings

1   lb. ground beef
½   tsp. Montreal steak seasoning
1   cup water
1   tsp. beef bouillon granules
1   pkg. (19 oz.) frozen cheese tortellini
1   cup shredded Italian cheese blend

1. In a large skillet, cook beef over medium heat 5-6 minutes or until no longer pink, breaking into crumbles; drain. Stir in steak seasoning. Add water and bouillon; bring to a boil. Stir in tortellini; return to a boil. Reduce heat; simmer, covered, 3-4 minutes or until tortellini are tender.
2. Remove from heat; sprinkle with cheese. Let stand, covered, until cheese is melted.
1½ cups: 566 cal., 28g fat (13g sat. fat), 111mg chol., 899mg sod., 37g carb. (2g sugars, 2g fiber), 39g pro.
Beef Tortellini Salad: Cook the beef; add 1 envelope Italian salad dressing mix and ¼ cup water. Simmer as directed. Cook tortellini according to package directions; add to the beef along with 3 chopped plum tomatoes, 1 chopped zucchini, the Italian cheese blend and 2 Tbsp. each olive oil and red wine vinegar.
Pesto Tortellini Salad: Cook tortellini according to package directions; drain and rinse in cold water. Add the cheese blend, a 2¼-oz. can sliced ripe olives, ¼ cup prepared pesto and 5 cooked crumbled bacon strips.

SLOPPY JOE STEW

This old-fashioned stew has a slightly sweet taste from the addition of canned corn. You can make the stew ahead of time and reheat it for a quick meal later.
—*Clair Long, Destrehan, LA*

- -

PTREP: 10 min. • **COOK:** 1¼ hours
MAKES: 6 servings

2   lbs. ground beef
1   medium onion, chopped
1   small green pepper, chopped
2½ cups water
1   can (11 oz.) whole kernel corn, drained
2   cans (10¾ oz. each) condensed tomato soup, undiluted
1   to 2 Tbsp. sugar
1   Tbsp. Worcestershire sauce
1   tsp. hot pepper sauce
    Salt and pepper to taste

1. In a large saucepan, cook the beef, onion and green pepper over medium heat until meat is no longer pink; drain.
2. Stir in the remaining ingredients; bring to a boil. Reduce heat; cover and simmer for 1 hour or until vegetables are tender.
1½ cups: 353 cal., 15g fat (6g sat. fat), 74mg chol., 666mg sod., 25g carb. (15g sugars, 3g fiber), 29g pro.

TEST KITCHEN TIP

Serve additional hot pepper sauce on the side for folks who want a little more of a kick to their Sloppy Joe Stew.

Poultry

QUICK CHICKEN PICCATA

Laced with lemon and simmered in white wine, this stovetop entree is super easy and elegant. Just add sides of bread and veggies to make it into a great meal.
—*Cynthia Heil, Augusta, GA*

TAKES: 30 min. • **MAKES:** 4 servings

- ¼ cup all-purpose flour
- ½ tsp. salt
- ½ tsp. pepper
- 4 boneless skinless chicken breast halves (4 oz. each)
- ¼ cup butter, cubed
- ¼ cup white wine or chicken broth
- 1 Tbsp. lemon juice
  Minced fresh parsley, optional

1. In a shallow bowl, mix the flour, salt and pepper. Pound chicken breasts with a meat mallet to ½-in. thickness. Dip chicken in flour mixture to coat both sides; shake off excess.
2. In a large skillet, heat butter over medium heat. Brown chicken on both sides. Add the wine; bring to a boil. Reduce heat; simmer, uncovered, until chicken is no longer pink, 12-15 minutes. Drizzle with lemon juice. If desired, sprinkle with parsley.

1 chicken breast half with about 1 Tbsp. sauce: 265 cal., 14g fat (8g sat. fat), 93mg chol., 442mg sod., 7g carb. (0 sugars, 0 fiber), 24g pro.

TEST KITCHEN TIP
Unless otherwise specified, *Taste of Home* recipes are tested with lightly salted butter. Unsalted, or sweet, butter is sometimes used to achieve a buttery flavor, such as in shortbread cookies or buttercream frosting. In these recipes, added salt would detract from the buttery taste desired.

QUICK CHICKEN
PICCATA

CHICKEN PARMESAN BURGERS

TURKEY PEA SKILLET

This dish is an all-time favorite. It's a snap to make for a group when time is short. Plus, the recipe is very flexible—you can substitute chicken and use whatever vegetables your family prefers.
—*Barbara Sonsteby, Mesa, AZ*

- -

TAKES: 30 min. • **MAKES:** 6 servings

- 1 small onion, chopped
- 2 Tbsp. butter
- 1¼ cups sliced celery
- 1 can (4 oz.) mushroom stems and pieces, drained
- 1 can (10½ oz.) condensed chicken broth, undiluted
- 1 cup water, divided
- 3 Tbsp. soy sauce
- 2 tsp. chicken bouillon granules
- ¼ cup cornstarch
- 3 cups cubed cooked turkey
- 2 cups frozen peas
- 1 can (8 oz.) pineapple chunks, drained
- 1 can (8 oz.) sliced water chestnuts, drained
  Hot cooked rice or chow mein noodles

1. In a skillet, saute the onion in butter until tender. Stir in celery and mushrooms; cook and stir for 2 minutes. Combine the broth, ¾ cup water, soy sauce and bouillon; stir into skillet. Bring to a boil. Reduce heat; cover and simmer for 3 minutes.

2. Combine cornstarch and remaining water until smooth; stir into skillet. Return to a boil. Cook and stir for 1-2 minutes or until mixture is thickened and bubbly. Stir in the turkey, peas, pineapple and water chestnuts; heat through. Serve over rice.

1 serving: 238 cal., 4g fat (1g sat. fat), 71mg chol., 1245mg sod., 24g carb. (9g sugars, 4g fiber), 27g pro.

CHICKEN PARMESAN BURGERS

A restaurant-quality burger that's topped with marinara and loaded with cheese— what's not to love? Fresh basil adds even more flavor if you'd like.
—*Brooke Petras, Alpine, CA*

- -

TAKES: 30 min. • **MAKES:** 4 servings

- 3 Tbsp. olive oil, divided
- 1 small onion, finely chopped
- 2 garlic cloves, minced
- ¾ cup marinara sauce, divided
- ½ cup finely chopped or shredded part-skim mozzarella cheese
- ½ cup dry bread crumbs
- 1 tsp. Italian seasoning
- 1 tsp. dried oregano
- ½ tsp. salt
- ½ tsp. pepper
- 1 lb. ground chicken
- 4 slices part-skim mozzarella cheese
- 4 hamburger buns, split and toasted
- ¼ cup shredded Parmesan cheese
  Fresh basil leaves, optional

1. In a large skillet, heat 1 Tbsp. oil over medium-high heat. Add onion; cook and stir until tender, about 3 minutes. Add garlic; cook 1 minute longer. Remove from heat; cool slightly.

2. In a large bowl, combine ¼ cup marinara sauce, chopped mozzarella cheese, bread crumbs, seasonings and onion mixture. Add chicken; mix lightly but thoroughly. With wet hands, shape into four ½-in.-thick patties.

3. In the same skillet, heat remaining 2 Tbsp. oil over medium heat. Cook burgers until a thermometer reads 165°, 4-5 minutes on each side. Top with sliced mozzarella cheese; cook, covered, until the cheese is melted, 1-2 minutes.

4. Serve in buns; top with remaining ½ cup marinara sauce, Parmesan cheese and, if desired, basil leaves.

1 burger: 603 cal., 33g fat (10g sat. fat), 108mg chol., 1275mg sod., 41g carb. (8g sugars, 3g fiber), 38g pro.

TURKEY
TOSTADAS

CHICKEN & GARLIC WITH FRESH HERBS

The key to this savory chicken is the combination of garlic with fresh rosemary and thyme. I like to serve it with mashed potatoes or crusty Italian bread.
—Jan Valdez, Lombard, IL

TAKES: 30 min. • **MAKES:** 6 servings

- 6 boneless skinless chicken thighs (about 1½ lbs.)
- ½ tsp. salt
- ¼ tsp. pepper
- 1 Tbsp. olive oil
- 10 garlic cloves, peeled and halved
- 2 Tbsp. brandy or chicken stock
- 1 cup chicken stock
- 1 tsp. minced fresh rosemary or ¼ tsp. dried rosemary, crushed
- ½ tsp. minced fresh thyme or ⅛ tsp. dried thyme
- 1 Tbsp. minced fresh chives

1. Sprinkle chicken with salt and pepper. In a large cast-iron or other heavy skillet, heat oil over medium-high heat. Brown chicken on both sides. Remove from pan.
2. Remove skillet from heat; add halved garlic cloves and brandy. Return to heat; cook and stir over medium heat until liquid is almost evaporated, 1-2 minutes.
3. Stir in stock, rosemary and thyme; return chicken to pan. Bring to a boil. Reduce heat; simmer, uncovered, until a thermometer reads 170°, 6-8 minutes. Sprinkle with chives.
1 chicken thigh with 2 Tbsp. cooking juices: 203 cal., 11g fat (3g sat. fat), 76mg chol., 346mg sod., 2g carb. (0 sugars, 0 fiber), 22g pro. **Diabetic exchanges:** 3 lean meat, ½ fat.

TURKEY TOSTADAS

Have a delicious fiesta in moments with this dish. Made with tostadas, but just as tasty with tortillas, this simple Mexican classic will be requested by your family again and again!
—Taste of Home *Test Kitchen*

TAKES: 25 min. • **MAKES:** 6 servings

- 1 pkg. (20 oz.) lean ground turkey
- ½ cup chopped onion
- ½ cup chopped green pepper
- 1 tsp. canola oil
- ¾ cup water
- 1 envelope taco seasoning
- 1 can (15½ oz.) hominy, rinsed and drained
- 12 tostada shells

- 3 cups shredded lettuce
- 1 cup shredded Mexican cheese blend
- 1 cup chopped tomato
- 1 cup cubed avocado

1. In a large skillet, cook the turkey, onion and green pepper in oil over medium heat for 5 minutes or until meat is no longer pink; drain. Stir in the water, taco seasoning and hominy. Bring to a boil. Reduce heat; simmer, uncovered, for 5 minutes or until heated through.
2. On each tostada shell, layer the lettuce, about ⅓ cup turkey mixture, cheese, tomato and avocado.
2 tostadas: 432 cal., 23g fat (8g sat. fat), 91mg chol., 1185mg sod., 32g carb. (2g sugars, 5g fiber), 24g pro.

CHICKEN & GARLIC
WITH FRESH HERBS

MEDITERRANEAN TURKEY SKILLET

I've always heard that it's important to eat a rainbow of colors to get all of the nutrients we need. Thanks to my garden-grown veggies, this dish is in my regular rotation.
—Nicole Ehlert, Burlington, WI

TAKES: 30 min. • **MAKES:** 6 servings

- 1 Tbsp. olive oil
- 1 pkg. (20 oz.) lean ground turkey
- 2 medium zucchini, quartered lengthwise and cut into ½-in. slices
- 1 medium onion, chopped
- 2 banana peppers, seeded and chopped
- 3 garlic cloves, minced
- ½ tsp. dried oregano
- 1 can (15 oz.) black beans, rinsed and drained
- 1 can (14½ oz.) diced tomatoes, undrained
- 1 Tbsp. balsamic vinegar
- ½ tsp. salt

1. In a large skillet, heat oil over medium-high heat. Add turkey, zucchini, onion, peppers, garlic and oregano; cook 10-12 minutes or until turkey is no longer pink and vegetables are tender, breaking up the turkey into crumbles; drain.
2. Stir in remaining ingredients; heat through, stirring occasionally.

1 cup: 259 cal., 10g fat (2g sat. fat), 65mg chol., 504mg sod., 20g carb. (6g sugars, 6g fiber), 24g pro. **Diabetic exchanges:** 3 lean meat, 1 vegetable, ½ starch, ½ fat.

CHICKEN CHILES RELLENOS ALFREDO

This recipe combines my daughter's love of chiles rellenos and my love of chicken Alfredo! To cut down on the spice level you could substitute Monterey Jack cheese for the pepper jack.
—Jennifer Stowell, Deep River, IA

TAKES: 30 min. • **MAKES:** 8 servings

- 1 pkg. (16 oz.) angel hair pasta
- 1½ to 2 lbs. boneless skinless chicken breasts, cubed
- 1 Tbsp. garlic powder
- 1 Tbsp. dried cilantro
- 1 tsp. ground cumin
- ½ cup butter
- 2 cups heavy whipping cream
- ½ cup cream cheese, softened
- 1½ tsp. grated lime zest
- ½ cup pepper jack cheese
- 2 cans (4 oz. each) chopped green chiles
- 2 Tbsp. lime juice

1. Cook angel hair according to package directions. Drain.
2. Meanwhile, sprinkle chicken with garlic powder, cilantro and cumin. In a large nonstick skillet, cook and stir chicken over medium heat 6-8 minutes or until no longer pink. Remove.
3. In same skillet, melt butter. Stir in heavy cream, cream cheese and lime zest until combined, 4-6 minutes. Stir in pepper jack until melted. Add chiles and lime juice. Return chicken to skillet; heat through. Toss chicken mixture with pasta.

1 cup: 698 cal., 43g fat (26g sat. fat), 167mg chol., 354mg sod., 48g carb. (4g sugars, 3g fiber), 30g pro.

CHICKEN CHILES RELLENOS ALFREDO

**SOUTHERN FRIED
CHICKEN WITH GRAVY**

APRICOT SALSA CHICKEN

Here's an unusual and easy combination: apricots and salsa. They create a sweet and spicy sauce for fried chicken breasts in this simple recipe.
—*Grace Yaskovic, Lake Hiawatha, NJ*

TAKES: 30 min. • **MAKES:** 6 servings

- ½ cup all-purpose flour
- 1 tsp. salt
- ¼ tsp. pepper
- ¼ tsp. paprika
- 6 boneless skinless chicken breast halves (4 oz. each)
- 3 Tbsp. canola oil
- 1 jar (16 oz.) salsa
- 1 jar (12 oz.) apricot preserves
- ½ cup apricot nectar
  Hot cooked rice

1. Combine flour and seasonings in a large bowl; add the chicken in batches and turn to coat.
2. In a large skillet, cook chicken over medium heat in oil until a thermometer reads 165°. Stir in the salsa, preserves and nectar; bring to a boil. Reduce heat; simmer, uncovered, until sauce is thickened, about 2 minutes. Serve with rice.

1 serving: 293 cal., 7g fat (1g sat. fat), 10mg chol., 779mg sod., 50g carb. (40g sugars, 4g fiber), 5g pro.

"Very tasty. My husband liked it, and it was easy to make."
— DVERZIC, TASTEOFHOME.COM

SOUTHERN FRIED CHICKEN WITH GRAVY

Fried chicken may have been perfected in the South, but it is loved everywhere! Seasonings add a little something extra to this recipe, as does a rich gravy.
—Taste of Home *Test Kitchen*

PREP: 25 min. • **COOK:** 45 min.
MAKES: 6 servings

- 1 cup all-purpose flour
- 1 tsp. onion powder
- 1 tsp. paprika
- ¾ tsp. salt
- ½ tsp. rubbed sage
- ½ tsp. pepper
- ¼ tsp. dried thyme
- 1 large egg
- ½ cup whole milk
- 1 broiler/fryer chicken (3 to 3½ lbs.), cut up
  Oil for frying

CREAMY GRAVY

- ⅓ cup all-purpose flour
- ¼ tsp. salt
- ¼ tsp. dried thyme
- ¼ to ½ tsp. pepper
- 2½ cups whole milk
- ½ cup heavy whipping cream

1. In a large shallow dish, combine the first 7 ingredients. In a shallow bowl, beat egg and milk. Dip chicken pieces into egg mixture, then add to flour mixture, a few pieces at a time, and turn to coat.
2. In a large skillet, heat ¼ in. of oil; fry the chicken until browned on all sides. Cover and simmer for 35-40 minutes or until juices run clear and the chicken is tender, turning occasionally. Uncover and cook 5 minutes longer. Drain chicken on paper towels and keep warm. Drain the skillet, reserving 3 Tbsp. drippings.
3. For gravy, in a small bowl, combine the flour, salt, thyme and pepper. Gradually whisk in milk and cream until smooth; add to skillet. Bring to a boil over medium heat; cook and stir for 2 minutes or until thickened. Serve with chicken.

1 serving: 750 cal., 52g fat (14 g sat. fat), 170mg chol., 554mg sod., 28g carb., 1g fiber, 41g pro.

CHICKEN
PAPRIKASH

CHICKEN PAPRIKASH

Some recipes for chicken paprikash include vegetables like bell peppers and celery, but not my grandmother's. Hers was a simple combination of chicken, onions, garlic, paprika and sour cream.

—Lily Julow, Lawrenceville, GA

- -

PREP: 20 min. • **COOK:** 45 min.
MAKES: 12 servings

- 2 broiler/fryer chickens (about 3½ to 4 lbs. each), cut into 8 pieces each
- 2 tsp. kosher salt
- 1 tsp. pepper
- 2 Tbsp. peanut oil or canola oil
- 2 medium onions, halved and sliced
- 2 large garlic cloves, chopped
- 3 Tbsp. all-purpose flour
- 1 Tbsp. sweet Hungarian paprika
- 2 cups hot chicken broth or water
- 1 cup sour cream
   Optional: Minced fresh parsley and additional sweet Hungarian paprika
   Hot cooked noodles or mashed potatoes, optional

1. Season the chicken with kosher salt and pepper. In a Dutch oven, heat peanut oil over medium-high heat. Brown chicken in batches. Remove chicken with a slotted spoon; drain and keep warm.
2. Reduce heat to medium-low. Add onions; cook, stirring to loosen browned bits from pan, 6-8 minutes or until the onions begin to soften. Add garlic; cook 1 minute longer.
3. Stir in flour and paprika; reduce heat to low. Cook 3-5 minutes or until the paprika is fragrant. Add broth; cook, stirring constantly, until smooth, 6-8 minutes. Return chicken to pan; simmer, covered, until a thermometer inserted into deepest part of the thigh reads 170°, about 30 minutes. Transfer chicken to a serving platter.
4. Skim fat. Stir in sour cream; heat just until warmed through, 3-5 minutes (do not allow to boil). If desired, sprinkle with parsley and additional paprika. Serve with hot cooked noodles or mashed potatoes if desired.
1 serving: 422 cal., 26g fat (8g sat. fat), 127mg chol., 596mg sod., 5g carb. (2g sugars, 1g fiber), 40g pro.

SUNSHINE CHICKEN

SUNSHINE CHICKEN

Since it can be easily doubled and takes little time or effort to prepare, this recipe is ideal to serve for large groups. Even my husband, who usually doesn't enjoy cooking, likes to make this dish.

—Karen Gardiner, Eutaw, AL

- -

PREP: 15 min. • **COOK:** 20 min.
MAKES: 6 servings

- 2 to 3 tsp. curry powder
- 1¼ tsp. salt, divided
- ¼ tsp. pepper
- 6 boneless skinless chicken breast halves (5 oz. each)
- 1½ cups orange juice
- 1 cup uncooked long grain rice
- ¾ cup water
- 1 Tbsp. brown sugar
- 1 tsp. ground mustard
   Chopped fresh parsley

1. Combine curry powder, ½ tsp. salt and the pepper; rub over both sides of chicken. In a skillet, combine orange juice, rice, water, brown sugar, mustard and remaining salt. Add chicken pieces; bring to a boil. Reduce heat; cover and simmer until chicken juices run clear, 20-25 minutes.
2. Remove from the heat and let stand, covered, until all liquid is absorbed, about 5 minutes. Sprinkle with parsley.
1 serving: 317 cal., 4g fat (1g sat. fat), 78mg chol., 562mg sod., 36g carb. (8g sugars, 1g fiber), 32g pro. **Diabetic exchanges:** 4 lean meat, 2 starch.

MOM'S CHICKEN & BUTTERMILK DUMPLINGS

I serve this—with a tossed or cucumber salad—to friends dining with us or on visits to our two sons and their families.
—*Ellen Proefrock, Brodhead, WI*

PREP: 45 min. • **COOK:** 2 hours
MAKES: 8 servings

- 1 stewing chicken (about 5 lbs.), cut up
- 10 cups water
- 1 large onion, chopped
- 2 medium carrots, sliced
- 3 celery ribs, chopped
- 4 garlic cloves, minced
- 1 tsp. salt
- ¼ cup butter
- 6 Tbsp. all-purpose flour
- ⅛ tsp. paprika
- ⅛ tsp. pepper
- ½ cup half-and-half cream

DUMPLINGS

- 2 cups all-purpose flour
- 4 tsp. baking powder
- 4 tsp. sugar
- 1 tsp. salt
- 2 large eggs, room temperature
- ½ cup buttermilk
- ¼ cup butter, melted

1. In a Dutch oven, combine the first 7 ingredients. Bring to a boil; skim foam from broth. Reduce heat; cover and simmer until chicken is tender, about 1½ hours. Remove the chicken; when cool enough to handle, debone and dice. Strain, reserving the broth and vegetables.

2. In the same pot, melt butter. Stir in flour, paprika and pepper until smooth. Gradually stir in 6 cups reserved broth (save remaining broth for another use). Bring to a boil; boil and stir 2 minutes. Reduce heat; stir in cream, reserved vegetables and chicken. Cover and bring to a boil; reduce heat to a simmer.

3. For dumplings, combine flour, baking powder, sugar and salt in a bowl. Combine eggs, buttermilk and butter; stir into dry ingredients to form a stiff batter.

4. Drop by tablespoonfuls onto simmering mixture. Cover and simmer until a toothpick inserted in a dumpling comes out clean (do not lift cover while simmering), about 20 minutes. Serve immediately.

1 serving: 614 cal., 32g fat (14g sat. fat), 201mg chol., 1059mg sod., 36g carb. (6g sugars, 2g fiber), 42g pro.

CHICKEN SPARERIBS

CHICKEN SPARERIBS

I love to serve chicken thighs in a zippy sparerib-style sauce.
—*Janice Porterfield, Atlanta, TX*

PREP: 5 min. • **COOK:** 30 min.
MAKES: 4 servings

- 8 bone-in chicken thighs (about 3 lbs.)
- 2 Tbsp. canola oil
- 1 cup water
- ⅔ cup packed brown sugar
- ⅔ cup reduced-sodium soy sauce
- ½ cup apple juice
- ¼ cup ketchup
- 2 Tbsp. cider vinegar
- 2 garlic cloves, minced
- 1 tsp. crushed red pepper flakes
- ½ tsp. ground ginger
- 2 Tbsp. cornstarch
- 2 Tbsp. cold water

1. In a Dutch oven, brown the chicken over medium heat in oil in batches on both sides; drain. Return all of the chicken to the pan.

2. In a large bowl, combine the water, brown sugar, soy sauce, apple juice, ketchup, cider vinegar, garlic, pepper flakes and ginger; pour over chicken. Bring to a boil. Reduce heat; cover and simmer until a thermometer reads 170°-175°, 20-25 minutes.

3. Remove the chicken to a platter and keep warm. Combine cornstarch and water until smooth; stir into the cooking juices. Bring to a boil; cook and stir until thickened, about 2 minutes. Serve with chicken.

2 chicken thighs: 583 cal., 26g fat (6g sat. fat), 116mg chol., 2753mg sod., 48g carb. (41g sugars, 0 fiber), 37g pro.

HONEY MUSTARD APPLE CHICKEN SAUSAGE

I threw this recipe together one day for a fantastic lunch. It's a great way to use up leftover sausage and rice from dinner the night before.
—*Julie Puderbaugh, Berwick, PA*

TAKES: 20 min. • **MAKES:** 4 servings

- ¼ cup honey mustard
- 2 Tbsp. apple jelly
- 1 Tbsp. water
- 1 Tbsp. olive oil
- 2 medium apples, sliced
- 1 pkg. (12 oz.) fully cooked apple chicken sausage links or flavor of your choice, sliced
  Hot cooked rice

1. In a small bowl, whisk honey mustard, jelly and water until blended. In a large skillet, heat oil over medium heat. Add apples; cook and stir 2-3 minutes or until tender. Remove from the pan.

2. Add the sausage to skillet; cook and stir 2-4 minutes or until browned. Return apples to the pan. Add mustard mixture; cook and stir 1-2 minutes or until thickened. Serve with rice.

¾ cup sausage mixture: 288 cal., 12g fat (3g sat. fat), 61mg chol., 609mg sod., 34g carb. (28g sugars, 2g fiber), 15g pro.

OLIVE & FIG CHICKEN

I love green olives and figs, so I put them together with chicken for a salty-sweet combination that's perfect for a special meal.
—*Carol Hull, Hermiston, OR*

TAKES: 25 min. • **MAKES:** 4 servings

- 4 boneless skinless chicken breast halves (5 oz. each)
- ¼ tsp. garlic salt
- ¼ tsp. lemon-pepper seasoning
- 2 Tbsp. olive oil
- 1 jar (6.35 oz.) green olive tapenade
- 2 Tbsp. fig preserves
  Sliced pimiento-stuffed olives, optional

1. Flatten chicken to ½-in. thickness; sprinkle with garlic salt and lemon pepper. In a large skillet, cook chicken in oil over medium heat until a thermometer reads 165°, 4-5 minutes on each side. Remove and keep warm.

2. In the same skillet, cook tapenade and fig preserves over medium heat until heated through, stirring to loosen browned bits from pan. Return chicken to the pan; cook on low heat until it is heated through, 2-3 minutes. If desired, top with olives.

1 chicken breast half with 2 Tbsp. sauce: 360 cal., 22g fat (3g sat. fat), 78mg chol., 899mg sod., 10g carb. (6g sugars, 1g fiber), 30g pro.

TEST KITCHEN TIP
You can use a less expensive olive oil than virgin or extra-virgin for cooking and baking. The higher grades have a more delicate flavor that shines in salads and uncooked foods, but is generally lost in recipes that require cooking. Pure olive oil works fine—and sometimes even better—for cooked recipes.

HONEY MUSTARD APPLE CHICKEN SAUSAGE

LEMON CREAM CHICKEN

ONE-DISH TURKEY DINNER

I'm still settling into married life and learning how to balance our busy schedules. This quick one-dish dinner helps keep us on track throughout the week.
—*Shannon Barden, Alpharetta, GA*

PREP: 10 min. • **COOK:** 20 min.
MAKES: 4 servings

- 1 lb. ground turkey
- 1 medium onion, chopped
- 1 shallot, finely chopped
- 3 garlic cloves, minced
- ¼ cup tomato paste
- 1 medium sweet potato, peeled and cubed
- 1 cup chicken broth
- 2 tsp. smoked paprika
- ½ tsp. salt
- ¼ tsp. pepper
- 3 cups chopped fresh kale
  Dash crushed red pepper flakes
- 1 medium ripe avocado, peeled and sliced
  Minced fresh mint, optional

1. In a large skillet, cook turkey, onion, shallot and garlic over medium heat until the turkey is no longer pink and vegetables are tender, 8-10 minutes, breaking up the turkey into crumbles; drain. Add tomato paste; cook and stir 1 minute longer.
2. Add sweet potato, broth, smoked paprika, salt and pepper. Bring to a boil; reduce heat. Simmer, covered, until the sweet potatoes are tender, about 10 minutes, stirring occasionally. Add kale and red pepper flakes; cook and stir 2 minutes or until kale is wilted. Serve with avocado and, if desired, mint.
Freeze Option: Freeze cooled mixture in freezer containers. To use, partially thaw in the refrigerator overnight. Heat through in a saucepan, stirring occasionally; add broth or water if necessary. Serve with avocado and, if desired, mint.
1⅓ cups: 318 cal., 14g fat (3g sat. fat), 76mg chol., 628mg sod., 24g carb. (8g sugars, 5g fiber), 26g pro. **Diabetic exchanges:** 3 lean meat, 2 fat, 1½ starch.

LEMON CREAM CHICKEN

If you want a dish that's quick, easy and elegant, you can't beat this one. The lemon cream sauce is what makes it irresistible. It goes perfectly with chicken and mushrooms.
—*Mary Anne McWhirter, Pearland, TX*

PREP: 10 min. • **COOK:** 45 min.
MAKES: 6 servings

- ½ cup plus 1 Tbsp. all-purpose flour, divided
- ½ tsp. salt
- ½ tsp. pepper
- 6 boneless skinless chicken breast halves (4 oz. each)
- ¼ cup butter
- 1 cup chicken broth
- 1 cup heavy whipping cream, divided
- 3 Tbsp. lemon juice
- ½ lb. sliced fresh mushrooms

1. In a shallow bowl, mix ½ cup flour, salt and pepper. Dip chicken breasts in flour mixture to coat both sides; shake off excess.
2. In a large cast-iron or other heavy skillet, heat butter over medium heat. Cook chicken in batches until a thermometer reads 165°, 5-7 minutes per side. Remove chicken, reserving drippings in pan.
3. Add broth to skillet; bring to a boil. Simmer, uncovered, until liquid is reduced to ⅓ cup, about 10 minutes. Stir in ¾ cup cream, lemon juice and mushrooms; cook over medium-low heat 5 minutes.
4. In a small bowl, mix the remaining flour and cream until smooth; stir into sauce. Bring to a boil; cook and stir until thickened, 1-2 minutes. Add chicken; heat through.
1 serving: 381 cal., 25g fat (15g sat. fat), 129mg chol., 488mg sod., 12g carb. (2g sugars, 1g fiber), 27g pro.

**ONE-DISH
TURKEY DINNER**

JAMAICAN CHICKEN WITH COUSCOUS

Fantabulous is a word I reserve for only the best dishes like this jerk-seasoned chicken. It's a mouth full of yum.
—Joni Hilton, Rocklin, CA

TAKES: 30 min. • **MAKES:** 6 servings

- 1 can (20 oz.) unsweetened pineapple tidbits, undrained
- 1 tsp. salt, divided
- 1 cup uncooked whole wheat couscous
- ⅓ cup all-purpose flour
- 2 Tbsp. minced fresh cilantro
- 1½ lbs. boneless skinless chicken breasts, cut into ½-in.-thick strips
- 2 tsp. Caribbean jerk seasoning
- 3 Tbsp. olive oil, divided
  Additional minced fresh cilantro, optional

1. In a large saucepan, combine pineapple and ½ tsp. salt; bring to a boil. Stir in the couscous. Remove from heat; let stand, covered, 5 minutes or until liquid is absorbed. Fluff with a fork.

2. Meanwhile, in a shallow bowl, mix flour and 2 Tbsp. cilantro. Toss the chicken with jerk seasoning and remaining salt. Add to flour mixture, a few pieces at a time, and toss to coat lightly; shake off any excess.

3. In a large skillet, heat 1 Tbsp. oil. Add a third of the chicken; cook 1-2 minutes on each side or until no longer pink. Repeat with remaining oil and chicken. Serve with the couscous. If desired, sprinkle with cilantro.

3 oz. cooked chicken with ⅔ cup couscous mixture: 374 cal., 10g fat (2g sat. fat), 63mg chol., 542mg sod., 42g carb. (12g sugars, 5g fiber), 29g pro. **Diabetic exchanges:** 3 starch, 3 lean meat, 1 fat.

MUGHALI CHICKEN

I enjoy cooking for my family and try to incorporate healthy new foods into our menus. This authentic Indian dish is a favorite.
—Aruna Kancharla, Bentonville, AR

TAKES: 30 min. • **MAKES:** 6 servings

- 4 cardamom pods
- 10 garlic cloves, peeled
- 6 whole cloves
- 4½ tsp. chopped fresh gingerroot
- 1 Tbsp. unblanched almonds
- 1 Tbsp. salted cashews
- 1 tsp. ground cinnamon
- 6 small red onions, halved and sliced
- 4 jalapeno peppers, seeded and finely chopped
- ¼ cup canola oil
- 3 Tbsp. water
- 1½ lbs. boneless skinless chicken breasts, cut into ½-in. cubes
- 1 cup coconut milk
- 1 cup plain yogurt
- 1 tsp. ground turmeric
  Fresh cilantro leaves
  Hot cooked basmati rice, optional

1. Remove seeds from cardamom pods; place in a food processor. Add the garlic, cloves, ginger, almonds, cashews and cinnamon; cover and process until blended. Set aside.

2. In a large skillet, saute onions and jalapenos in oil until tender. Stir in water and the garlic mixture. Add the chicken, milk, yogurt and turmeric. Bring to a boil. Reduce the heat; simmer, uncovered, until chicken juices run clear, 8-10 minutes. Sprinkle with cilantro. Serve with rice if desired.

Note: Wear disposable gloves when cutting hot peppers; the oils can burn skin. Avoid touching your face.

1 cup: 367 cal., 23g fat (10g sat. fat), 68mg chol., 93mg sod., 14g carb. (5g sugars, 3g fiber), 27g pro.

MUGHALI CHICKEN

TURKEY CREPES

TURKEY CREPES

This savory crepe recipe has been passed down through many generations in my family. You can also use the turkey filling to make a potpie.

—*Andrea Price, Grafton, WI*

- -

PREP: 30 min. + chilling • **COOK:** 50 min.
MAKES: 6 servings

- 3 large eggs, room temperature
- 3¼ cups 2% milk
- 2 cups all-purpose flour
- 1 tsp. salt
- 1 tsp. baking powder

FILLING

- 3 Tbsp. butter, divided
- 1 cup frozen peas and carrots (about 5 oz.), thawed
- ½ cup chopped onion
- 3 Tbsp. all-purpose flour
- 1 cup 2% milk
- 1 cup chicken broth
- 2 cups chopped cooked turkey
- ½ tsp. salt
- ½ tsp. minced fresh thyme or ¼ tsp. dried thyme
- ⅛ tsp. pepper

1. In a large bowl, whisk eggs and milk. In another bowl, mix flour, salt and baking powder; add to egg mixture and mix well. Refrigerate, covered, 1 hour.

2. Heat a lightly greased 8-in. nonstick skillet over medium heat. Stir batter. Fill a ¼-cup measure with batter; pour into center of pan. Quickly lift and tilt pan to coat bottom evenly. Cook until top appears dry; turn crepe over and cook 15-20 seconds longer or until bottom is cooked. Remove to a wire rack.

Repeat with remaining batter, greasing pan as needed. When cool, stack crepes between pieces of waxed paper or paper towels.

3. For filling, in a large saucepan, heat 2 Tbsp. butter over medium heat. Add the peas and carrots and onion; cook and stir until onion is tender, 8-10 minutes. Stir in the flour until blended; gradually whisk in milk and broth. Bring to a boil, stirring constantly; cook and stir until thickened, 5-8 minutes. Stir in the remaining ingredients; heat through.

4. Spread ¼ cup filling down the center of each crepe; fold sides and ends over filling and roll up. Wipe out skillet. In batches, heat remaining 1 Tbsp. butter over medium heat. Cook crepes until golden brown, 2-4 minutes on each side.

2 filled crepes: 434 cal., 14g fat (7g sat. fat), 170mg chol., 1063mg sod., 47g carb. (9g sugars, 2g fiber), 28g pro.

PINEAPPLE-GLAZED
CHICKEN THIGHS

PINEAPPLE-GLAZED CHICKEN THIGHS

These juicy chicken thighs taste so rich and delicious with a sweet pineapple-maple glaze. I love that I can reach in my pantry for ingredients and end up with this impressive weeknight meal.
—*Trisha Kruse, Eagle, ID*

TAKES: 30 min. • **MAKES:** 4 servings

- 1 can (20 oz.) unsweetened pineapple tidbits
- 4 boneless skinless chicken thighs
- ¾ tsp. salt
- ½ tsp. lemon-pepper seasoning
- 2 tsp. olive oil
- 1 Tbsp. butter
- 2 Tbsp. maple syrup
  Hot cooked brown rice

1. Drain pineapple well, reserving ¼ cup juice. Sprinkle chicken with seasonings. In a large skillet, heat oil over medium-high heat; brown thighs on both sides. Remove from pan.
2. In same skillet, melt butter over medium heat. Add drained pineapple; cook and stir 5 minutes. Stir in maple syrup and reserved pineapple juice. Add chicken; cook, covered, until a thermometer inserted in chicken reads 170°, 5-7 minutes. Remove the chicken to a serving plate; keep warm.
3. Increase heat to medium-high; cook and stir pineapple mixture until slightly thickened. Spoon over chicken; serve with rice.
Freeze Option: Freeze cooled chicken in a freezer container. To use, partially thaw in refrigerator overnight. Reheat in a microwave-safe container, covered, until a thermometer reads at least 165°, stirring occasionally.
1 chicken thigh with ¼ cup pineapple mixture: 328 cal., 14g fat (4g sat. fat), 83mg chol., 571mg sod., 31g carb. (28g sugars, 2g fiber), 22g pro. **Diabetic exchanges:** 3 lean meat, 1 starch, 1 fruit, 1 fat.

SWEET ONION &
SAUSAGE SPAGHETTI

SWEET ONION & SAUSAGE SPAGHETTI

This wholesome pasta dish gets tossed with light cream, basil and tomatoes for a quick, fresh-tasting meal in minutes.
—*Mary Relyea, Canastota, NY*

TAKES: 30 min. • **MAKES:** 4 servings

- 6 oz. uncooked whole wheat spaghetti
- ¾ lb. Italian turkey sausage links, casings removed
- 2 tsp. olive oil
- 1 sweet onion, thinly sliced
- 1 pint cherry tomatoes, halved
- ½ cup loosely packed fresh basil leaves, thinly sliced
- ½ cup half-and-half cream
  Shaved Parmesan cheese, optional

1. Cook spaghetti according to package directions. Meanwhile, in a large nonstick skillet over medium heat, cook sausage in oil for 5 minutes. Add onion; cook 8-10 minutes longer or until meat is no longer pink and onion is tender.
2. Stir in tomatoes and basil; heat through. Add cream; bring to a boil. Drain spaghetti; toss with sausage mixture. Garnish with cheese if desired.
1½ cups: 334 cal., 12g fat (4g sat. fat), 46mg chol., 378mg sod., 41g carb. (8g sugars, 6g fiber), 17g pro. **Diabetic exchanges:** 2½ starch, 2 lean meat, 1 vegetable, 1 fat.

SIMPLE MEDITERRANEAN CHICKEN

I learned to cook with a Mediterranean flair while living in Israel. You'll find this chicken captures that wonderful warm-weather taste.
—*Sally Hinton, Liverpool, PA*

PREP: 15 min. • **COOK:** 50 min.
MAKES: 6 servings

- 1 broiler/fryer chicken (3½ to 4 lbs.), cut up
- 3 Tbsp. canola oil, divided
- 3 medium onions, thinly sliced
- 3 garlic cloves, minced
- ¼ cup minced fresh parsley
- 1 Tbsp. minced fresh tarragon or 1 tsp. dried tarragon
- 1 tsp. salt
- ½ tsp. pepper
- 1 cup chopped pimiento-stuffed olives
  Hot cooked rice or noodles

1. In a large skillet over medium heat, brown chicken in 2 Tbsp. oil. Remove chicken and set aside. Add remaining oil to skillet. Saute onions and garlic until tender. Add parsley, tarragon, salt and pepper; mix well.

2. Return chicken to skillet; cover with onion mixture. Sprinkle with olives. Reduce heat; cover and simmer 40-45 minutes or until chicken is tender and juices run clear. Serve over rice or noodles.

1 cup: 425 cal., 28g fat (5g sat. fat), 102mg chol., 965mg sod., 10g carb. (5g sugars, 2g fiber), 34g pro.

"I used boneless skinless pieces, only four. This was delicious and easy. Definitely different. We served it over gluten-free noodles. You have to love olives, though."
—SHERRYORNDORFF, TASTEOFHOME.COM

TURKEY SCALLOPINI

TURKEY SCALLOPINI

Quick-cooking turkey cutlets make it easy to prepare a satisfying meal in minutes. They are so tasty with a little squeeze of fresh lemon.
—*Karen Adams, Cleveland, TN*

TAKES: 20 min. • **MAKES:** 4 servings

- 1 pkg. (17.6 oz.) turkey breast cutlets
- ¼ cup all-purpose flour
- ⅛ tsp. salt
- ⅛ tsp. pepper
- 1 large egg
- 2 Tbsp. water
- 1 cup soft bread crumbs
- ½ cup grated Parmesan cheese
- ¼ cup butter, cubed
  Minced fresh parsley

1. Flatten turkey to ¼-in. thickness. In a shallow bowl, combine the flour, salt and pepper. In another bowl, beat egg and water. In a third shallow bowl, combine the bread crumbs and cheese.

2. Dredge turkey in flour mixture, then dip in egg mixture and coat with crumbs. Let stand for 5 minutes.

3. Melt butter in a large skillet over medium-high heat; cook turkey for 2-3 minutes on each side or until meat is no longer pink and the coating is golden brown. Sprinkle with parsley.

4 oz. cooked turkey: 358 cal., 17g fat (10g sat. fat), 169mg chol., 463mg sod., 12g carb. (1g sugars, 0 fiber), 38g pro.

Chicken Scallopini: Substitute 4 boneless skinless chicken breast halves for the turkey. Flatten to ¼-in. thickness and proceed as directed.

SKILLET PLUM CHICKEN TENDERS

If you love plums, this recipe is for you! I combine the fruit with chicken tenders for a quick and easy flavorful meal. Serve with brown rice or orzo pasta.

—Nancy Heishman, Las Vegas, NV

PREP: 20 min. • **COOK:** 15 min.
MAKES: 4 servings

- ½ tsp. garlic salt
- ½ tsp. lemon-pepper seasoning
- 1½ lbs. chicken tenderloins
- 1 Tbsp. extra virgin olive oil
- 2 cups sliced fresh plums
- ½ cup diced red onion
- ⅓ cup apple jelly
- 1 Tbsp. grated fresh gingerroot
- 1 Tbsp. balsamic vinegar
- 2 tsp. reduced-sodium soy sauce
- 1 tsp. minced fresh thyme or ½ tsp. dried thyme
- 1 Tbsp. cornstarch
- 2 Tbsp. white wine
- 1 Tbsp. sesame seeds, toasted

1. Combine garlic salt and lemon pepper; sprinkle mixture over chicken. In a large nonstick skillet, heat oil over medium-high heat; brown chicken. Add plums and red onion; cook and stir 1-2 minutes.
2. Reduce heat. Stir in next 5 ingredients. Mix cornstarch and wine until smooth; gradually stir into pan. Cook, covered, until chicken juices run clear and plums are tender, about 10 minutes. Just before serving, sprinkle with toasted sesame seeds.

1 serving: 343 cal., 6g fat (1g sat. fat), 83mg chol., 483mg sod., 33g carb. (26g sugars, 2g fiber), 41g pro.

SKILLET PLUM CHICKEN TENDERS

BREADED CHICKEN WITH AVOCADO

A tasty topping of avocado, Monterey Jack and sour cream gives this crispy chicken a little taste of California. To round out the meal, serve a steamed veggie or green salad.

—Taste of Home *Test Kitchen*

TAKES: 30 min. • **MAKES:** 2 servings

- 3 Tbsp. cornmeal
- 1 Tbsp. cornstarch
- ½ tsp. garlic salt
- ½ tsp. ground cumin
- 1 large egg
- 1 Tbsp. water
- 2 boneless skinless chicken breast halves (4 oz. each)
- 4 tsp. canola oil
- ½ cup shredded Monterey Jack cheese
- 6 slices ripe avocado
- ¼ cup sour cream
- 2 Tbsp. sliced green onion

1. In a large large shallow dish, combine the cornmeal, cornstarch, garlic salt and cumin. In a shallow bowl, beat the egg and water. Flatten chicken to ¼-in. thickness; dip into egg mixture, then place in the cornmeal mixture and turn to coat.
2. In a large skillet, heat oil. Cook chicken until a thermometer reads 165°, about 4 minutes on each side. Top with cheese and avocado; cover and cook until cheese is melted, about 1 minute. Top with sour cream and onion.

1 serving: 548 cal., 36g fat (13g sat. fat), 214mg chol., 713mg sod., 19g carb. (2g sugars, 3g fiber), 36g pro.

TURKEY SALISBURY STEAKS

TURKEY LO MEIN

I substituted turkey for pork in this classic Chinese recipe. It was a hit at our church potluck, and my husband and two children love it, too.
—*Leigh Lundy, York, NE*

- -

TAKES: 30 min. • **MAKES:** 6 servings

- 1 **lb. lean ground turkey**
- 2 **medium carrots, thinly sliced**
- 1 **medium onion, chopped**
- ½ **tsp. garlic powder**
- 2 **pkg. (3 oz. each) ramen noodles**
- 1½ **cups water**
- 6 **cups shredded cabbage**
- 1 **cup frozen peas, thawed**
- ¼ **cup reduced-sodium soy sauce**

1. In a large skillet, cook and crumble turkey with carrots, onion and garlic powder over medium-high heat meat is until no longer pink, 5-7 minutes.
2. Break up noodles and add to skillet; stir in contents of seasoning packets and water. Bring to a boil. Reduce heat; simmer, covered, 3-5 minutes. Add the remaining ingredients; cook and stir until cabbage is crisp-tender, 1-3 minutes.

1⅓ cups: 294 cal., 11g fat (4g sat. fat), 52mg chol., 1024mg sod., 28g carb. (3g sugars, 4g fiber), 21g pro.

TEST KITCHEN TIP
Easily upgrade instant ramen by stirring in some peanut butter, chopped green onion or sliced boiled egg. Or, stir a raw beaten egg into the ramen during the last 30 seconds of cooking. Cook and stir until egg is firm.

TURKEY SALISBURY STEAKS

My mother always made Salisbury steak. My own recipe is one of my husband's favorites.
—*Leann Doyle, Patchogue, NY*

- -

PREP: 20 min. • **COOK:** 15 min.
MAKES: 4 servings

- ⅔ **cup seasoned bread crumbs, divided**
- ⅓ **cup finely chopped onion**
- 2 **tsp. low-sodium Worcestershire sauce**
- 2 **tsp. A.1. steak sauce**
- 1 **garlic clove, minced**
- ½ **tsp. dried basil**
- ½ **tsp. dried oregano**
- ¼ **tsp. garlic powder**
- ¼ **tsp. pepper**
- 1 **lb. extra-lean ground turkey**
- 1½ **tsp. olive oil**

SAUCE
- 2 **Tbsp. olive oil**
- 2 **Tbsp. all-purpose flour**
- 1½ **cups reduced-sodium beef broth**
- 1 **Tbsp. low-sodium Worcestershire sauce**
- 1 **Tbsp. A.1. steak sauce**
- 1 **can (4 oz.) sliced mushrooms, drained**

1. In a large bowl, combine ⅓ cup bread crumbs, onion, Worcestershire sauce, steak sauce, garlic and seasonings. Add turkey; mix lightly but thoroughly. Shape into four ½-in.-thick oval patties. Place remaining bread crumbs in a shallow bowl. Press patties into crumbs, patting to help coating adhere.
2. In a large nonstick skillet, heat 1½ tsp. oil over medium heat. Add patties; cook until a thermometer reads 165°, 3-4 minutes on each side. Remove from pan.
3. In same pan, heat 2 Tbsp. oil over medium heat. Stir in flour until smooth; gradually whisk in the broth, Worcestershire sauce and steak sauce. Bring to a boil, stirring constantly; cook and stir 1-2 minutes or until thickened. Stir in mushrooms. Return patties to pan. Reduce the heat; simmer, covered, 2-3 minutes or until heated through.

1 patty with ⅓ cup sauce: 291 cal., 11g fat (1g sat. fat), 47mg chol., 703mg sod., 18g carb. (5g sugars, 2g fiber), 32g pro. **Diabetic exchanges:** 3 lean meat, 2 fat, 1 starch.

TURKEY
LO MEIN

BACON-FETA STUFFED CHICKEN

My son and I love feta cheese, so we tucked some into quick-cooking chicken breasts to create this dish. I think feta cheese is so underrated. You can buy feta in so many different flavors—basil and tomato is one of our favorites.
—Vicki Smith, Okeechobee, FL

- -

PREP: 15 min. • **COOK:** 25 min.
MAKES: 4 servings

- 4 boneless skinless chicken breasts (4 oz. each)
- ¼ cup crumbled cooked bacon
- ¼ cup crumbled feta cheese
- ½ tsp. salt
- ¼ tsp. pepper
- 1 Tbsp. canola oil
- 2 cans (14½ oz. each) diced tomatoes
- 1 Tbsp. dried basil

1. Carefully cut a slit in the deepest part of each chicken breast. Fill with the bacon and cheese; secure with toothpicks. Sprinkle with salt and pepper. In a large skillet, brown chicken in oil.

2. Drain one can of tomatoes; add to skillet. Stir in the remaining tomatoes; sprinkle with basil. Cover and simmer for 10 minutes. Simmer, uncovered, until a thermometer reads 165°, and the tomato mixture is thickened, about 5 minutes longer. Discard the toothpicks.

1 stuffed chicken breast half with ⅔ cup tomatoes: 237 calories, 9g fat (2g saturated fat), 68mg cholesterol, 766mg sodium, 10g carbohydrate (7g sugars, 4g fiber), 29g protein. Diabetic Exchanges: 4 lean meat, 1 vegetable, 1 fat..

"I used salsa instead of diced tomatoes and sprinkled a tablespoon of feta cheese into the salsa while cooking. Hubby said it was awesome!"
— CYOUNG55, TASTEOFHOME.COM

BALSAMIC CHICKEN & PEARS

Pears and dried cherries go amazingly well with chicken and a kiss of balsamic vinegar. We use them to make a clean-your-plate meal that's great for company.
—Marcia Whitney, Gainesville, FL

- -

TAKES: 30 min. • **MAKES:** 4 servings

- 4 boneless skinless chicken breast halves (6 oz. each)
- ¾ tsp. salt
- ½ tsp. pepper
- 1 Tbsp. canola oil
- 1 cup reduced-sodium chicken broth
- 3 Tbsp. white balsamic vinegar
- ½ tsp. minced fresh rosemary
- 2 tsp. cornstarch
- 1½ tsp. sugar
- 2 medium unpeeled pears, each cut into 8 wedges
- ⅓ cup dried cherries or dried cranberries

1. Sprinkle chicken breasts with salt and pepper. In a large nonstick skillet, heat oil over medium-high heat. Add chicken; cook until a thermometer reads 165°, 8-10 minutes. Remove.

2. Meanwhile, stir together the next 5 ingredients until blended. Pour into skillet; add pears and dried cherries. Bring to a boil over medium-high heat; reduce heat and simmer, covered, until pears are tender, about 5 minutes. Return chicken to skillet; simmer, uncovered, until heated through, 3-5 minutes. If desired, sprinkle with additional minced rosemary.

1 chicken breast half with ⅓ cup sauce and 4 pear wedges: 335 cal., 8g fat (1g sat. fat), 94mg chol., 670mg sod., 30g carb. (22g sugars, 3g fiber), 36g pro. **Diabetic exchanges:** 3 lean meat, 1½ starch, ½ fruit.

BALSAMIC CHICKEN & PEARS

**SAUSAGE PASTA
WITH VEGETABLES**

DOWN-HOME CHICKEN

Mom served the thick, tangy sauce that coats this tender chicken as a gravy over rice or mashed potatoes. It makes a welcome centerpiece for any meal.
—*Donna Sasser Hinds, Milwaukie, OR*

PREP: 10 min. • **COOK:** 50 min.
MAKES: 6 servings

- ½ cup all-purpose flour
- 1 tsp. salt
- ½ tsp. pepper
- 1 broiler/fryer chicken (3 to 4 lbs.), cut up
- ¼ cup canola oil
SAUCE
- ⅔ cup lemon juice
- ⅔ cup ketchup
- ⅔ cup molasses
- ⅓ cup canola oil
- ¼ cup Worcestershire sauce
- 1 tsp. ground cloves
- ½ tsp. salt
- ¼ tsp. pepper
   Hot cooked rice

1. In a large shallow dish, combine the flour, salt and pepper. Add chicken, a few pieces at a time, and turn to coat.
2. In a large skillet, heat oil. Brown chicken in oil on all sides; remove to paper towels. Drain drippings and return chicken to the pan.
3. In a bowl, combine lemon juice, ketchup, molasses, oil, Worcestershire sauce, cloves, salt and pepper. Pour over chicken. Bring to a boil. Reduce heat; simmer, uncovered, for 35-40 minutes or until chicken juices run clear. Serve with rice.
1 serving: 612 cal., 36g fat (7g sat. fat), 88mg chol., 1108mg sod., 45g carb. (26g sugars, 1g fiber), 29g pro.

🍎 SAUSAGE PASTA WITH VEGETABLES

I made this for our pastor one night. He loved it so much we nicknamed it Jason's Pasta. It's a sneaky way to get our children to eat more veggies.
—*Suzie Foutty, Mansfield, OH*

- -

TAKES: 25 min. • **MAKES:** 4 servings

- 2 cups uncooked whole wheat penne pasta
- 1 lb. Italian turkey sausage links, casings removed
- 1¾ cups sliced fresh mushrooms
- 1 can (14½ oz.) fire-roasted diced tomatoes with garlic, undrained
- 6 oz. fresh baby spinach (about 8 cups)
- ¼ cup shredded part-skim mozzarella cheese

1. In a 6-qt. stockpot, cook pasta according to package directions; drain and return to the pot.
2. Meanwhile, in a large skillet, cook and crumble sausage with mushrooms over medium-high heat until no longer pink, 5-7 minutes. Stir in tomatoes; bring to a boil. Stir in spinach until wilted.
3. Add to pasta; heat through. Sprinkle with cheese; remove from heat. Let stand, covered, until cheese is melted.
1½ cups: 392 cal., 10g fat (3g sat. fat), 46mg chol., 825mg sod., 51g carb. (4g sugars, 8g fiber), 26g pro.

Pork

TORTELLINI WITH SAUSAGE & MASCARPONE

TORTELLINI WITH SAUSAGE & MASCARPONE

When I crave Italian comfort food on a busy night and don't have a lot of time to cook, this dish is fast and yummy. You can have it on the table in less time than a takeout order.
—*Gerry Vance, Millbrae, CA*

- -

TAKES: 20 min. • **MAKES:** 6 servings

- 1 pkg. (20 oz.) refrigerated cheese tortellini
- 8 oz. bulk Italian sausage
- 1 jar (24 oz.) pasta sauce with mushrooms
- ½ cup shredded Parmesan cheese
- 1 carton (8 oz.) mascarpone cheese
  Crushed red pepper flakes, optional

1. Prepare tortellini according to package directions. Meanwhile, in a large skillet, cook sausage over medium heat until no longer pink, 6-8 minutes, breaking into crumbles; drain. Stir in pasta sauce; heat through.
2. Drain tortellini, reserving 1 cup cooking water. Add tortellini to sauce and enough reserved cooking water to reach desired consistency; toss to coat.
3. Stir in the Parmesan cheese; dollop with mascarpone cheese. Sprinkle with crushed red pepper flakes if desired.
1 cup: 637 cal., 37g fat (17g sat. fat), 113mg chol., 1040mg sod., 57g carb. (11g sugars, 4g fiber), 24g pro.

SAUSAGE COBB SALAD
LETTUCE WRAPS

CAULIFLOWER PORK SOUP

This recipe was given to me by a friend several years ago. Even my husband enjoys it, and he typically doesn't care for cauliflower.
—*Loretta Wohlenhaus, Cumberland, IA*

TAKES: 30 min. • **MAKES:** 6-8 servings (2 qt.)

- 1   lb. ground pork
- 1   small head cauliflower, broken into florets
- 2   cups water
- ½   cup chopped onion
- 2   cups whole milk, divided
- ¼   cup all-purpose flour
- 2   cups shredded sharp cheddar cheese
- ½   tsp. salt
- ⅛   tsp. pepper
    Chopped chives, optional

1. In a large skillet, cook pork until no longer pink; drain and set aside.

2. In a Dutch oven, cook cauliflower in water 10 minutes or until tender. Do not drain. Add pork, onion and 1¼ cups milk to cauliflower.

3. In a small bowl, combine the flour and remaining milk until smooth; stir into the cauliflower mixture. Bring to a boil; cook and stir for 2 minutes. Remove from the heat; add cheese, salt and pepper, stirring until cheese is melted. If desired, sprinkle with chives.

1 cup: 283 cal., 19g fat (10g sat. fat), 76mg chol., 387mg sod., 9g carb. (4g sugars, 1g fiber), 20g pro.

SAUSAGE COBB SALAD LETTUCE WRAPS

I substituted sausage for the bacon to make this lettuce roll-up. Your family and friends will adore the dish. It's flavorful, crunchy and pretty on the plate.
—*Devon Delaney, Westport, CT*

TAKES: 25 min. • **MAKES:** 6 servings

- ¾   cup ranch salad dressing
- ⅓   cup crumbled blue cheese
- ¼   cup watercress, chopped
- 1   lb. bulk pork sausage
- 2   Tbsp. minced fresh chives
- 6   large iceberg lettuce leaves, edges trimmed
- 1   medium ripe avocado, peeled and diced
- 4   hard-boiled large eggs, chopped
- 1   medium tomato, chopped

1. Mix dressing, blue cheese and watercress. In a large skillet, cook and crumble sausage over medium heat until no longer pink, 5-7 minutes; drain. Stir in chives.

2. To serve, spoon the sausage into lettuce leaves. Top with avocado, eggs and tomato. Drizzle with dressing mixture.

1 serving: 433 cal., 38g fat (10g sat. fat), 174mg chol., 887mg sod., 7g carb. (3g sugars, 3g fiber), 15g pro.

TEST KITCHEN TIP

Sharp cheddar cheese has been aged longer than regular cheddar. As cheese ages, its flavor becomes more pronounced. Using aged cheese in a recipe can add complexity and rich flavor, even to humble favorites like soup and mac 'n' cheese.

**MEAT LOVER'S PIZZA
RICE SKILLET**

OPEN-FACED BRATWURST SANDWICHES WITH BEER GRAVY

A nod to my Volga German heritage, this classic diner fare comes together in a snap and can be made all in one skillet! I serve it with a green vegetable and french fries or mashed potatoes on the side. Cook the sausages in lager or stout beer for a deeper flavor profile.
—*Allison Ochoa, Hays, KS*

- -

TAKES: 30 min. • **MAKES:** 5 servings

- ¼   cup butter, divided
- 1   pkg. uncooked bratwurst links (20 oz.)
- 1   medium onion, thinly sliced
- 1   bottle (12 oz.) beer or nonalcoholic beer
- 2   Tbsp. all-purpose flour
- ⅛   tsp. dill weed
- ⅛   tsp. pepper
- 5   slices thick bread

1. In a Dutch oven, heat 2 Tbsp. butter over medium-high heat. Add bratwurst and onion; cook and stir until bratwurst starts to brown and onion softens. Stir in beer. Bring to a boil. Reduce the heat; simmer, covered, turning occasionally, until a thermometer inserted in bratwurst reads 165° and brats are no longer pink, 12-14 minutes.
2. Remove brats and onions; keep warm. Add remaining butter to pan; whisk in flour, dill weed and pepper. Bring to a boil, stirring constantly until thickened, 3-5 minutes. To serve, place 1 brat on each slice of bread; top with onions and gravy.

1 bratwurst sandwich with ¼ cup gravy:
567 cal., 43g fat (17g sat. fat), 108mg chol., 1176mg sod., 23g carb. (3g sugars, 1g fiber), 19g pro.

> **TEST KITCHEN TIP**
> Using a dark beer will give the gravy a deeper, richer flavor, but watch out for intense dark beers; you don't want to make the gravy bitter.

MEAT LOVER'S PIZZA RICE SKILLET

I threw this together for a quick dinner from what I had in the fridge and pantry. Add any other pizza toppings you desire. I often add black olive slices or mushrooms. My son loves it and calls it "pizza rice."
—*Teri Rasey, Cadillac, MI*

- -

TAKES: 25 min. • **MAKES:** 6 servings

- 1   lb. bulk Italian sausage
- 1   can (14½ oz.) diced tomatoes with basil, oregano and garlic
- 1   can (15½ oz.) cannellini beans, rinsed and drained
- 1½   cups water
- 1½   cups uncooked instant rice
- ¼   cup grated Parmesan cheese
- ½   cup (2 oz.) sliced mini pepperoni
    Additional grated Parmesan cheese, optional
    Chopped fresh basil, optional

1. In a large skillet, cook the sausage over medium heat 5-7 minutes or until no longer pink, breaking into crumbles; drain. Return to skillet with next 4 ingredients. Bring to a boil; cover and remove from heat. Let stand for 5 minutes.
2. Fluff with a fork; stir in cheese. Top with pepperoni and, if desired, additional grated Parmesan cheese and basil.

1¼ cups: 390 cal., 20g fat (6g sat. fat), 48mg chol., 906mg sod., 35g carb. (2g sugars, 4g fiber), 15g pro.

OPEN-FACED BRATWURST
SANDWICHES WITH
BEER GRAVY

VEGGIE PORK SAUTE

When time is of the essence, try this quick meal. We love the lightly sauced combination of pork, mushrooms, zucchini and tomato over a bed of cooked rice.
—*Audra LeGay, Grand Junction, CO*

TAKES: 30 min. • **MAKES:** 4 servings

5	Tbsp. all-purpose flour, divided
1	tsp. Italian seasoning
½	tsp. salt
¼	tsp. pepper
1	lb. boneless pork, cubed
5	Tbsp. butter, divided
1	Tbsp. olive oil
1	medium onion, halved and sliced
2	celery ribs, sliced
½	cup sliced fresh mushrooms
1	medium zucchini, halved and sliced
1	medium tomato, diced
1½	cups chicken broth
1	Tbsp. balsamic vinegar
	Hot cooked rice

1. In a large shallow dish, combine 3 Tbsp. flour, Italian seasoning, salt and pepper. Add the pork; toss to coat. In a large skillet over medium-high heat, brown pork in 3 Tbsp. butter and oil; remove and keep warm.
2. In the same skillet, saute the onion, celery and mushrooms in remaining butter for 5 minutes. Add pork and zucchini; saute until meat is tender and vegetables are crisp-tender.
3. Stir in the tomato. Place the remaining flour in a small bowl; stir in chicken broth and vinegar until smooth. Add to skillet. Bring to a boil; cook and stir until thickened, 2 minutes. Serve with rice.
1½ cups: 390 cal., 25g fat (12g sat. fat), 107mg chol., 848mg sod., 15g carb. (5g sugars, 2g fiber), 26g pro.

OPEN-FACED BREAKFAST BANH MI

I love banh mi sandwiches and their delicious pickled veggies. I also love naan, so I decided to combine the two for an easy brunch dish!
—*Lori McLain, Denton, TX*

PREP: 25 min. + standing • **COOK:** 15 min.
MAKES: 4 servings

1	cup rice vinegar
½	cup water
¼	cup sugar
½	tsp. salt
¼	tsp. pepper
⅓	cup thinly sliced radishes
⅓	cup julienned carrot
⅓	cup julienned sweet red pepper
½	lb. smoked sausage, thinly sliced
4	large eggs
4	naan flatbreads, warmed
¼	cup zesty bell pepper relish
½	cup thinly sliced cucumber
½	cup thinly sliced red onion
	Fresh cilantro leaves

1. In a large bowl, whisk the first 5 ingredients until the sugar is dissolved. Add the radishes, carrot and red pepper; let stand until serving. Meanwhile, in a large nonstick skillet, cook and stir sausage over medium-high heat until browned, 6-8 minutes. Remove and keep warm. Reduce heat to low. In same pan, cook eggs until whites are set and yolks begin to thicken, turning once if desired. Keep warm.
2. Drain the vegetable mixture. Spread naan with relish. Top with sausage, eggs, pickled vegetables, cucumber, red onion and cilantro.
Note: This recipe was tested with Mezzetta brand bell pepper relish.
1 open-faced sandwich: 459 cal., 24g fat (9g sat. fat), 229mg chol., 1370mg sod., 42g carb. (12g sugars, 2g fiber), 19g pro.

OPEN-FACED
BREAKFAST
BANH MI

SPAGHETTI SQUASH &
SAUSAGE EASY MEAL

PORK STEW WITH CORNBREAD DUMPLINGS

Cornbread dumplings add a delectable down-home flavor to this country meal. I frequently make a double batch of this stew on Sunday so we can have leftovers all week.
—*Shelly Gresham, Dawson, IL*

PREP: 20 min. • **COOK:** 80 min.
MAKES: 6 servings

- 2   lbs. boneless pork, trimmed and cut into ¾-in. cubes
- 2   Tbsp. canola oil
- 1   can (28 oz.) stewed tomatoes
- 1¼ cups chicken broth, divided
- 1   medium onion, quartered
- 2   bay leaves
- 1   tsp. Worcestershire sauce
- 1   tsp. dried thyme
- ¾   tsp. sugar
- ¾   tsp. salt
- ¼   tsp. pepper
- ¼   tsp. garlic powder
- ⅛   tsp. ground nutmeg
- 2   Tbsp. all-purpose flour

DUMPLINGS
- ½   cup all-purpose flour
- ⅓   cup yellow cornmeal
- 1½ tsp. baking powder
- ¼   tsp. salt
      Dash pepper
- 1   large egg, room temperature
- 3   Tbsp. 2% milk
- 2   Tbsp. canola oil
- 1   can (8¾ oz.) whole kernel corn, drained

1. In a large skillet over medium heat, brown pork in oil; drain. Stir in the tomatoes, 1 cup broth, onion and seasonings; bring to a boil. Reduce heat; cover and simmer until pork is tender, 60-70 minutes.
2. Combine flour and remaining broth until smooth; gradually add to the stew, stirring constantly. Bring to a boil; boil and stir for 2 minutes. Remove bay leaves.
3. For dumplings, in a bowl, combine flour, cornmeal, baking powder, salt and pepper. Beat egg, milk and oil; stir into flour mixture just until moistened. Fold in corn. Drop by rounded tablespoonfuls into simmering stew. Cover and cook until dumplings are tender and cooked through, 10-12 minutes.
1 cup: 461 cal., 20g fat (5g sat. fat), 121mg chol., 1166mg sod., 34g carb. (11g sugars, 3g fiber), 37g pro.

SPAGHETTI SQUASH & SAUSAGE EASY MEAL

My son's favorite dish uses homegrown spaghetti squash, kielbasa and pico de gallo or salsa. It only uses a few ingredients, so what could be easier?
—*Pam Mascarenas, Taylorsville, UT*

TAKES: 30 min. • **MAKES:** 6 servings

- 1   medium spaghetti squash
- 1   Tbsp. olive oil
- 1   pkg. (14 oz.) smoked sausage, halved lengthwise and sliced
- 1   cup pico de gallo
- ¼   tsp. salt
- ⅛   tsp. pepper

1. Cut squash lengthwise in half; discard seeds. Place halves on a microwave-safe plate, cut side down. Microwave, uncovered, on high 15-20 minutes or until tender.
2. Meanwhile, in a large skillet, heat oil over medium heat. Add sausage; cook and stir for 4-5 minutes or until lightly browned.
3. When squash is cool enough to handle, use a fork to separate strands. Add squash, pico de gallo, salt and pepper to sausage; heat through, tossing to combine.
1 cup: 326 cal., 22g fat (8g sat. fat), 44mg chol., 901mg sod., 24g carb. (2g sugars, 5g fiber), 12g pro.

TEST KITCHEN TIP
Eating lower-carb, but still want a homey, satisfying dinner? One cup cooked spaghetti squash has about 10 grams of carbs, versus 45 grams for regular spaghetti.

❄ THREE-MEAT SPAGHETTI SAUCE

I simmer this hearty sauce in large batches, freeze it and use it for spaghetti, lasagna, mostaccioli and pizza. I experimented with the original recipe until I came up with the perfect sauce. I've received many compliments on it.

—Ellen Stringer, Bourbonnais, IL

PREP: 15 min. • **COOK:** 1 hour
MAKES: 11½ cups

- 1 lb. ground beef
- 1 lb. bulk Italian sausage
- 1 cup chopped onion
- 1 can (28 oz.) crushed tomatoes
- 3 cups water
- 2 cans (6 oz. each) tomato paste
- 2 jars (4½ oz. each) sliced mushrooms, drained
- 1 cup chopped pepperoni
- 2 Tbsp. grated Parmesan cheese
- 2 Tbsp. Italian seasoning
- 1 Tbsp. sugar
- 2 tsp. garlic salt
- 1 tsp. dried parsley flakes
- 1 tsp. pepper
    Hot cooked spaghetti and additional Parmesan cheese

1. In a Dutch oven, cook the beef, sausage and onion over medium heat until meat is no longer pink; drain. Stir in the tomatoes, water, tomato paste, sliced mushrooms, pepperoni, cheese, Italian seasoning, sugar, garlic salt, parsley and pepper. Bring to a boil. Reduce heat; cover and simmer for 30 minutes.
2. Serve with spaghetti and sprinkle with additional cheese.

Freeze Option: Cool the sauce. Freeze in serving-sized portions in freezer containers for up to 3 months. To use frozen sauce, thaw in refrigerator overnight. Place in a saucepan; heat through, stirring occasionally. Serve over spaghetti and sprinkle with Parmesan cheese.
½ cup: 121 cal., 8g fat (3g sat. fat), 23mg chol., 467mg sod., 6g carb. (2g sugars, 1g fiber), 8g pro.

MAPLE SAUSAGE SKILLET

MAPLE SAUSAGE SKILLET

Maple syrup adds a welcome hint of sweetness to this stovetop supper. If I'm looking for more green, I stir in a little broccoli, too.

—Dottie Tarlton, Malvern, AR

TAKES: 25 min. • **MAKES:** 2 servings

- 1 tsp. canola oil
- ½ lb. fully cooked kielbasa or Polish sausage, sliced
- 1½ cups sliced fresh mushrooms
- 1 medium green pepper, thinly sliced
- 1 small onion, halved and sliced
- 1 celery rib, sliced
- 2 Tbsp. maple syrup
- ¼ tsp. pepper
    Hot cooked rice

In a large skillet, heat oil over medium-high heat. Add sausage; cook and stir 3-4 minutes or until lightly browned. Add the vegetables; cook and stir 3-4 minutes longer or until vegetables are crisp-tender. Stir in syrup and pepper; heat through. Serve with rice.
1½ cups: 472 cal., 34g fat (11g sat. fat), 76mg chol., 1244mg sod., 26g carb. (0 sugars, 3g fiber), 17g pro.

HAM STEAKS WITH GRUYERE, BACON & MUSHROOMS

This meat lover's ham steak has a big wow factor. The Gruyere, bacon and fresh mushrooms in the topping are a great combination.
—*Lisa Speer, Palm Beach, FL*

- -

TAKES: 25 min. • **MAKES:** 4 servings

- 2   Tbsp. butter
- ½   lb. sliced fresh mushrooms
- 1   shallot, finely chopped
- 2   garlic cloves, minced
- ⅛   tsp. coarsely ground pepper
- 1   fully cooked boneless ham steak (about 1 lb.), cut into 4 pieces
- 1   cup shredded Gruyere cheese
- 4   bacon strips, cooked and crumbled
- 1   Tbsp. minced fresh parsley, optional

1. In a large nonstick skillet, heat butter over medium-high heat. Add mushrooms and shallot; cook and stir 4-6 minutes or until tender. Add garlic and pepper; cook 1 minute longer. Remove from pan; keep warm. Wipe skillet clean.

2. In same skillet, cook ham over medium heat 3 minutes. Turn; sprinkle with cheese and bacon. Cook, covered, 2-4 minutes longer or until cheese is melted and ham is heated through. Serve with mushroom mixture. If desired, sprinkle with parsley.

1 serving: 352 cal., 22g fat (11g sat. fat), 113mg chol., 1576mg sod., 5g carb. (2g sugars, 1g fiber), 34g pro.

SAUSAGE & SQUASH PENNE

I love using frozen cooked winter squash because the hard work—peeling, chopping and cooking—is all done for me.
—*Jennifer Roberts, South Burlington, VT*

- -

TAKES: 30 min. • **MAKES:** 4 servings

- 2   cups uncooked penne pasta
- 1   pkg. (12 oz.) frozen cooked winter squash
- 2   Tbsp. olive oil
- 3   cooked Italian sausage links (4 oz. each), sliced
- 1   medium onion, chopped
- ¼   cup grated Parmesan cheese
- ¼   tsp. salt
- ¼   tsp. dried parsley flakes
- ¼   tsp. pepper
    Optional: Additional grated Parmesan cheese and minced fresh parsley

1. Cook pasta and squash according to package directions. Meanwhile, in a large skillet, heat oil over medium heat. Add sausage and onion; cook and stir until sausage is browned and onion is tender; keep warm.

2. In a small bowl, mix the cooked squash, cheese, salt, parsley and pepper until blended. Drain pasta; transfer to a serving plate. Spoon squash mixture over pasta; top with sausage mixture. Sprinkle with additional cheese and parsley if desired.

¾ cup pasta with ½ cup sausage and ¼ cup squash: 468 cal., 26g fat (8g sat. fat), 40mg chol., 705mg sod., 41g carb. (4g sugars, 4g fiber), 19g pro.

HAM STEAKS WITH GRUYERE, BACON & MUSHROOMS

SODA POP CHOPS WITH SMASHED POTATOES

Root beer gives this family-friendly recipe a tangy taste kids will love. Served alongside the smashed potatoes, this makes a scrumptious stick-to-the-ribs meal any weeknight.
—Taste of Home *Test Kitchen*

PREP: 25 min. • **COOK:** 15 min.
MAKES: 4 servings

- 1½ lbs. small red potatoes, halved
- 1 cup root beer
- 1 cup ketchup
- 1 Tbsp. brown sugar
- 2 tsp. chili powder
- 2 tsp. Worcestershire sauce
- ½ tsp. garlic powder, divided
- 2 Tbsp. all-purpose flour
- ¾ tsp. pepper, divided
- ½ tsp. salt, divided
- 4 bone-in pork loin chops (7 oz. each)
- 2 Tbsp. olive oil
- 2 Tbsp. butter

1. Place potatoes in a large saucepan and cover with water. Bring to a boil over high heat. Reduce heat to medium; cover and cook until tender, 15-20 minutes.
2. Meanwhile, in a small bowl, combine the root beer, ketchup, brown sugar, chili powder, Worcestershire sauce and ¼ tsp. garlic powder; set aside. In a large shallow dish, combine the flour, ½ tsp. pepper and ¼ tsp. salt. Add pork chops, 1 at a time, and turn to coat.
3. In a large skillet, cook chops in oil over medium heat until chops are lightly browned, 2-3 minutes on each side. Drain. Add root beer mixture; bring to a boil. Reduce heat; cover and simmer until a thermometer reads 145°, 6-8 minutes. Remove pork and keep warm. Let pork chops stand for 5 minutes before serving.
4. Bring sauce to a boil; cook until liquid is reduced by half. Meanwhile, drain potatoes; mash with butter, remaining garlic powder and remaining salt and pepper. Serve with pork chops and sauce.
1 pork chop with ½ cup potatoes and ⅓ cup sauce: 637 cal., 29g fat (11g sat. fat), 112mg chol., 1222mg sod., 59g carb. (29g sugars, 4g fiber), 36g pro.

KOREAN SAUSAGE BOWL

When we hosted a student from South Korea, she shared some of her favorite Korean dishes. We especially like bibimbap. I created a variation on the dish that uses Italian sausage.
—Michal Riege, Cedarburg, WI

PREP: 15 min. + marinating • **COOK:** 25 min.
MAKES: 4 servings

- 1 pkg. (19 oz.) Italian sausage links, cut into 1-in. pieces
- ¾ cup Korean barbecue sauce, divided
- 1 tsp. plus 1 Tbsp. canola oil, divided
- 1 large egg
- 2 medium carrots, julienned
- 1 medium sweet red pepper, julienned
- 3 green onions, thinly sliced
- 2 garlic cloves, minced
- ½ tsp. salt
- ¼ tsp. crushed red pepper flakes
- ¼ tsp. pepper
- 8 oz. uncooked angel hair pasta
  Additional sliced green onions, optional

1. In a large bowl, toss sausage pieces with ½ cup barbecue sauce; refrigerate, covered, 4 hours.
2. In a large skillet, heat 1 tsp. canola oil over medium heat. Break egg into pan; cook until yolk is set, turning once. Remove from pan; cut into thin strips.
3. In the same pan, heat remaining oil over medium-high heat. Add the carrots and red pepper; cook and stir until crisp-tender. Stir in green onions, garlic and seasonings; cook 1 minute longer. Remove from pan.
4. Drain sausage, discarding marinade. In same pan, cook and stir sausage until no longer pink, 12-15 minutes.
5. Cook pasta according to the package directions; drain, reserving ¼ cup pasta water. Add pasta, pasta water, carrot mixture and remaining barbecue sauce to sausage. Toss to combine. Divide among 4 bowls; top with egg strips and, if desired, additional green onions.
1¾ cups: 672 cal., 39g fat (10g sat. fat), 119mg chol., 1620mg sod., 56g carb. (9g sugars, 4g fiber), 25g pro.

SODA POP CHOPS WITH
SMASHED POTATOES

PASTA WITH CHORIZO & SPINACH

This zippy entree looks and tastes special, but it's a cinch to make. When I get home from work, I like to prepare quick dishes, and this is one of my family's favorites.
—*Athena Russell, Greenville, SC*

TAKES: 20 min. • **MAKES:** 2 servings

1¼ cups uncooked penne pasta
4 tsp. olive oil
⅓ lb. uncooked chorizo or bulk spicy pork sausage
1 small onion, thinly sliced
4 oz. sliced fresh mushrooms
⅓ cup water-packed artichoke hearts, rinsed, drained and quartered
⅓ cup chopped oil-packed sun-dried tomatoes, drained
1 garlic clove, minced
¼ tsp. dried oregano
⅛ tsp. salt
⅛ tsp. pepper
3 cups chopped fresh spinach
2 Tbsp. grated Parmesan cheese

1. Cook pasta according to the package directions. Meanwhile, heat oil in a large skillet; crumble chorizo into the pan. Add the onion, mushrooms, artichokes, tomatoes, garlic, oregano, salt and pepper. Cook and stir over medium heat until chorizo is fully cooked and vegetables are tender.
2. Add spinach; cook and stir for 1-2 minutes or until wilted. Drain pasta; top with chorizo mixture. Sprinkle with cheese.
1 cup: 635 cal., 37g fat (11g sat. fat), 71mg chol., 1333mg sod., 47g carb. (5g sugars, 5g fiber), 29g pro.

"Love this recipe. I've made it several times. I used chorizo-flavored ground chicken. I also drizzle some of the oil from the tomatoes over the top. YUMMY!"
—LKIMK77, TASTEOFHOME.COM

PORK PIPERADE

I like to spice up my meat dishes with peppers, and this Basque piperade—adapted from a Spanish recipe—is a family favorite.
—*Hyacinth Rizzo, Buffalo, NY*

TAKES: 30 min. • **MAKES:** 4 servings

¼ cup all-purpose flour
1 envelope (1¼ oz.) reduced-sodium taco seasoning, divided
1 lb. boneless pork, cut into 1½x⅛-in. strips
2 Tbsp. canola oil

PIPERADE

3 Tbsp. olive oil
1 medium Spanish onion, thinly sliced
2 medium sweet red peppers, julienned
2 cups canned plum tomatoes, drained (reserve juices)

1. In a shallow bowl, combine flour and half of seasoning mix. Add pork, a few pieces at a time, and toss to coat; shake off excess.
2. In a large skillet, heat the canola oil over medium-high heat. Add pork; stir-fry until browned, 3-4 minutes. Remove with a slotted spoon; cover and keep warm.
3. In same skillet, heat olive oil. Stir-fry onion and peppers until crisp-tender. Chop the tomatoes; add to skillet. In a small bowl, combine remaining taco seasoning and reserved tomato juices. Add to the skillet. Bring to a boil; cook and stir until thickened. Reduce heat to medium-low. Return pork to skillet; heat through.
1 serving: 414 cal., 24g fat (4g sat. fat), 67mg chol., 720mg sod., 23g carb. (10g sugars, 4g fiber), 26g pro.

PORK PIPERADE

SAUSAGE & ASPARAGUS PASTA WITH CAJUN CREAM SAUCE

GROUND PORK TACO SALAD

Even with my family's busy schedule, I enjoy cooking from scratch. We love this easy taco salad made with ground pork. If I don't fix it often enough, they ask for it.
—*Sherry Duval, Baltimore, MD*

- -

TAKES: 30 min. • **MAKES:** 6 servings

- 1 lb. ground pork or beef
- 1 envelope taco seasoning
- 1 can (16 oz.) kidney beans, rinsed and drained
- ¾ cup water
- 10 cups torn romaine
- 2 medium tomatoes, chopped
- ⅓ cup chopped onion
- 2 cups shredded cheddar cheese
- ½ to ¾ cup Western salad dressing
  Tortilla chips, crushed
  Optional: Sour cream and guacamole

1. In a large skillet, cook pork over medium heat until no longer pink; drain. Stir in the taco seasoning, beans and water. Bring to a boil. Reduce heat; simmer, uncovered, for 5 minutes, stirring occasionally. Remove from the heat; cool for 10 minutes.
2. In a large bowl, combine the romaine, tomatoes, onion and cheese. Stir in pork mixture. Drizzle with salad dressing and toss to coat. Sprinkle with chips. Serve immediately. Top with sour cream and guacamole if desired.

2 cups: 493 cal., 30g fat (13g sat. fat), 90mg chol., 1106mg sod., 29g carb. (9g sugars, 6g fiber), 28g pro.

SAUSAGE & ASPARAGUS PASTA WITH CAJUN CREAM SAUCE

I needed to use up some ingredients in my refrigerator, so I threw together this dish. It's delicious and everyone loved it. I only use Tony Chachere's Creole seasoning mix.
—*Angela Lively, Conroe, TX*

- -

TAKES: 25 min. • **MAKES:** 8 servings

- 1 pkg. (16 oz.) spiral pasta
- 1 lb. fresh asparagus, trimmed and cut into 2-in. pieces
- 1 pkg. (14 oz.) smoked sausage, sliced
- 2 garlic cloves, minced
- 1 cup heavy whipping cream
- ½ cup shredded Parmesan cheese
- 1 Tbsp. Creole seasoning
- ¼ tsp. pepper

1. In a Dutch oven, cook pasta according to package directions, adding asparagus during the last 4 minutes of cooking. Meanwhile, in a large nonstick skillet, cook sausage over medium heat until browned. Add garlic; cook 1 minute longer. Stir in cream, Parmesan cheese, Creole seasoning and pepper; cook and stir until slightly thickened, about 3 minutes.
2. Drain pasta mixture, reserving ½ cup cooking water; add to sausage mixture. Toss to coat, gradually adding enough reserved cooking water to reach desired consistency.

1¼ cups: 496 cal., 26g fat (14g sat. fat), 71mg chol., 909mg sod., 46g carb. (4g sugars, 2g fiber), 18g pro.

KIMCHI CAULIFLOWER
FRIED RICE

KIMCHI CAULIFLOWER FRIED RICE

This is one of my favorite recipes because it is customizable. If there's a vegetarian in the family, leave out the bacon. You can also add your favorite veggies.
—*Stefanie Schaldenbrand, Los Angeles, CA*

TAKES: 30 min. • **MAKES:** 2 servings

- 2 bacon strips, chopped
- 1 green onion, chopped
- 2 garlic cloves, minced
- 1 cup kimchi, chopped
- 3 cups frozen riced cauliflower
- 2 large eggs
- 1 to 3 Tbsp. kimchi juice
  Optional: Sesame oil and sesame seeds

1. In a large skillet, cook bacon over medium heat until partially cooked but not crisp, stirring occasionally. Add the green onion and garlic, cook 1 minute longer. Add the kimchi; cook and stir until heated through, 2-3 minutes. Add cauliflower; cook and stir until tender, 8-10 minutes.

2. Meanwhile, heat a large nonstick skillet over medium-high heat. Break eggs, 1 at a time, into pan; reduce heat to low. Cook until whites are set and yolks begin to thicken, turning once if desired. Stir enough kimchi juice into cauliflower mixture to moisten. Divide among 2 serving bowls. Top with fried eggs, additional green onions and if desired, sesame seeds and oil.

1 serving: 254 cal., 17g fat (5g sat. fat), 204mg chol., 715mg sod., 13g carb. (6g sugars, 6g fiber), 15g pro. **Diabetic exchanges:** 2 high-fat meat, 2 vegetable.

CHICKPEA SAUSAGE SKILLET

CHICKPEA SAUSAGE SKILLET

This quick dish is perfect for weeknight meals! It comes together quickly with only a few ingredients.
—*Phyllis Schwartz, Arcadia, FL*

TAKES: 30 min. • **MAKES:** 8 servings

- 1 lb. Italian sausage links, cut into 1-in. slices
- 1 cup chopped onion
- 1 cup chopped green pepper
- ⅔ cup chopped celery
- ½ cup chopped carrot
- 1½ tsp. minced garlic
- 2 Tbsp. olive oil
- 1 can (28 oz.) stewed tomatoes
- 1 can (15 oz.) chickpeas or garbanzo beans, rinsed and drained
- 1 can (6 oz.) tomato paste
- 1 tsp. sugar
- 1 tsp. Italian seasoning
- ⅛ tsp. crushed red pepper flakes
  Hot cooked rice or pasta, optional

1. In a large skillet, cook sausage until no longer pink; drain. Remove and keep warm. In the same skillet, saute the onion, green pepper, celery, carrot and garlic in olive oil for until vegetables are tender, 3-4 minutes. Stir in the tomatoes, chickpeas, tomato paste, sugar, Italian seasoning, pepper flakes and sausage.

2. Bring to a boil. Reduce heat; simmer, uncovered until heated through, 4-6 minutes.

1 cup: 284 cal., 17g fat (4g sat. fat), 31mg chol., 619mg sod., 25g carb. (10g sugars, 5g fiber), 11g pro. **Diabetic exchanges:** 2 starch, 1 medium-fat meat, 1 fat.

Fish & Seafood

EAST COAST SHRIMP & LENTIL BOWLS

If you have frozen shrimp, a few seasoning ingredients, bagged spinach and lentils on hand, you can make this dish in no time. It's so delicious, nobody needs to know that it's also healthy!

—Mary Kay LaBrie, Clermont, FL

PREP: 10 min. • **COOK:** 25 min.
MAKES: 4 servings

- ½ cup dried brown lentils, rinsed
- 1 Tbsp. olive oil
- ⅛ tsp. salt
- 1¾ cups water
- 2 Tbsp. garlic powder, divided
- 1 lb. uncooked shrimp (26-30 per lb.), peeled and deveined
- 2 tsp. seafood seasoning
- 2 Tbsp. butter
- ½ tsp. crushed red pepper flakes
- 2 tsp. lemon juice
- 3 cups fresh baby spinach
- ¼ tsp. ground nutmeg
- ¼ cup finely chopped sweet onion
  Lemon wedges

1. Place first 4 ingredients and 1 Tbsp. garlic powder in a small saucepan; bring to a boil. Reduce heat; simmer, covered, until lentils are tender, 17-20 minutes.
2. Toss shrimp with seafood seasoning. In a large skillet, melt butter over medium-high heat. Add pepper flakes and remaining garlic powder; cook and stir 30 seconds. Add the shrimp; cook and stir until shrimp turn pink, 3-4 minutes. Stir in lemon juice; remove from pan and keep warm.
3. Add spinach and nutmeg to pan; cook and stir over medium-high heat until spinach is wilted. Remove from heat.
4. To serve, divide lentils among 4 bowls. Top with shrimp, spinach and onion. Serve with lemon wedges.
1 serving: 289 cal., 11g fat (5g sat. fat), 153mg chol., 645mg sod., 22g carb. (1g sugars, 4g fiber), 26g pro. **Diabetic exchanges:** 3 lean meat, 1½ starch, 1 fat.

EAST COAST SHRIMP & LENTIL BOWLS

SALMON WITH TOMATO-GOAT CHEESE COUSCOUS

SALMON WITH TOMATO-GOAT CHEESE COUSCOUS

Rich with goat cheese and tomato, this recipe works for a weeknight supper or an elegant company dinner—and is adjustable for any number of people.

—*Toni Roberts, La Canada, CA*

- -

TAKES: 30 min. • **MAKES:** 4 servings

4	salmon fillets (5 oz. each)
¼	tsp. salt
¼	tsp. garlic salt
¼	tsp. pepper
1	Tbsp. olive oil
1	cup chicken stock
¾	cup uncooked whole wheat couscous
2	plum tomatoes, chopped
4	green onions, chopped
¼	cup crumbled goat cheese

1. Sprinkle the salmon with salt, garlic salt and pepper. Heat oil in a large skillet over medium-high heat; add salmon skin side up and cook 3 minutes. Turn fish and cook an additional 4 minutes or until fish flakes easily with a fork. Remove salmon from heat and keep warm.

2. In a large saucepan, bring stock to a boil. Stir in the couscous. Remove from heat; let stand, covered, until stock is absorbed, about 5 minutes. Stir in tomatoes, green onions and goat cheese. Serve with salmon.

1 fillet with 1 cup couscous mixture: 414 cal., 19g fat (4g sat. fat), 80mg chol., 506mg sod., 31g carb. (2g sugars, 6g fiber), 32g pro. **Diabetic exchanges:** 4 lean meat, 2 starch, 1 fat.

DID YOU KNOW?

Wild salmon is 20% leaner than farm-raised fish, while being higher in heart-healthy omega-3 fatty acids. Some people prefer its flavor over farm-raised fish, too. Fresh wild salmon is available from May through October, as the different species travel upstream to spawn.

BACON-WRAPPED SCALLOPS WITH PINEAPPLE QUINOA

This is the first recipe I developed using quinoa as an ingredient. My husband thoroughly enjoyed helping me test it. We both loved that it can be easily prepared in just 30 minutes.

—*Laura Greenberg, Lake Balboa, CA*

- -

TAKES: 30 min. • **MAKES:** 4 servings

1	can (14½ oz.) vegetable broth
1	cup quinoa, rinsed
¼	tsp. salt
⅛	tsp. plus ¼ tsp. pepper, divided
10	bacon strips
16	sea scallops (about 2 lbs.), side muscles removed
1	cup drained canned pineapple tidbits

1. In a small saucepan, bring broth to a boil. Add quinoa, salt and ⅛ tsp. pepper. Reduce heat; simmer, covered, 12-15 minutes or until liquid is absorbed.

2. Meanwhile, place bacon in a large nonstick skillet. Cook over medium heat, removing 8 of the strips when partially cooked but not crisp. Continue cooking remaining strips until crisp. Remove to paper towels to drain. Finely chop crisp bacon strips. Cut remaining bacon strips lengthwise in half.

3. Wrap a halved bacon strip around each scallop; secure with a toothpick. Sprinkle with remaining pepper.

4. Wipe the pan clean, if necessary; heat over medium-high heat. Add scallops; cook for 3-4 minutes on each side or until firm and opaque.

5. Remove quinoa from heat; fluff with a fork. Stir in pineapple and chopped bacon. Serve with scallops.

4 scallops with ¾ cup quinoa: 468 cal., 11g fat (3g sat. fat), 89mg chol., 1364mg sod., 43g carb. (7g sugars, 3g fiber), 48g pro.

HONEY WALLEYE

Our state is known as the Land of 10,000 Lakes, so fishing is a favorite recreational activity here. This recipe is a quick way to prepare all the fresh walleye hooked by the anglers in our family.
—*Kitty McCue, St. Louis Park, MN*

TAKES: 20 min. • **MAKES:** 6 servings

- 1 large egg
- 2 tsp. honey
- 2 cups crushed Ritz crackers (about 45 to 50)
- ½ tsp. salt
- 1½ lbs. walleye fillets
- ⅓ to ½ cup canola oil
   Optional: Minced fresh parsley and lemon wedges

1. In a shallow bowl, beat egg; add honey. In a shallow dish, combine crackers and salt. Dip fish in egg mixture, then in cracker mixture; turn until coated.

2. In a cast-iron or other heavy skillet, cook fillets in oil over medium heat until golden and fish flakes easily with a fork, 3-5 minutes on each side. If desired, top with parsley and serve with lemon wedges.

3 oz. cooked fish: 389 cal., 22g fat (3g sat. fat), 133mg chol., 514mg sod., 23g carb. (5g sugars, 1g fiber), 25g pro.

"This recipe has delicious flavor and a crispy crust. The breading also tastes great with skinless chicken breasts."
—REMENIC, TASTEOFHOME.COM

MODERN TUNA CASSEROLE

I loved tuna casserole as a kid and found myself craving it as an adult. However, the amounts of fat and salt in the traditional recipe were a turnoff healthwise, and it just didn't taste as good as I remembered. I reconfigured the recipe to include more vegetables, and the result was delicious.
—*Rebecca Blanton, St. Helena, CA*

PREP: 20 min. • **COOK:** 20 min.
MAKES: 6 servings

- 3 Tbsp. butter, divided
- 4 medium carrots, chopped
- 1 medium onion, chopped
- 1 medium sweet red pepper, chopped
- 1 cup sliced baby portobello mushrooms
- 2 cans (5 oz. each) albacore white tuna in water, drained and flaked
- 2 cups fresh baby spinach
- 1 cup frozen peas
- 3 cups uncooked spiral pasta
- 1 Tbsp. all-purpose flour
- ⅔ cup reduced-sodium chicken broth
- ⅓ cup half-and-half cream
- ½ cup shredded Parmesan cheese
- ¾ tsp. salt
- ¼ tsp. pepper

1. In a large skillet, heat 1 Tbsp. butter over medium-high heat. Add carrots, onion, red pepper and mushrooms. Cook and stir until tender, 8-10 minutes. Add the tuna, spinach and peas; cook until spinach is just wilted, 2-3 minutes.

2. Meanwhile, cook pasta according to the package directions for al dente. Drain pasta, reserving 1 cup pasta water. In a large bowl, place the pasta and tuna mixture; toss to combine. Wipe skillet clean.

3. In the same skillet, melt remaining butter over medium heat. Stir in flour until smooth; gradually whisk in broth and cream. Bring to a boil, stirring constantly; cook and stir until thickened, adding reserved pasta water if needed, 1-2 minutes. Stir in cheese, salt and pepper. Pour over pasta; toss to coat.

1¾ cups: 372 cal., 11g fat (6g sat. fat), 47mg chol., 767mg sod., 44g carb. (7g sugars, 5g fiber), 23g pro. **Diabetic exchanges:** 3 lean meat, 2½ starch, 1½ fat, 1 vegetable.

HONEY
WALLEYE

FAJITA-STYLE SHRIMP & GRITS

I combined two of my favorite dishes—shrimp with cheesy grits, and fajitas—into this spicy meal. For more heat, use pepper jack cheese instead of the shredded Mexican cheese blend.

—*Arlene Erlbach, Morton Grove, IL*

TAKES: 30 min. • **MAKES:** 4 servings

- 1   lb. uncooked shrimp (16-20 per lb.), peeled and deveined
- 2   Tbsp. fajita seasoning mix
- 1   cup quick-cooking grits
- 4   cups boiling water
- 1½ cups shredded Mexican cheese blend
- 3   Tbsp. 2% milk
- 2   Tbsp. canola oil
- 3   medium sweet peppers, seeded and cut into 1-in. strips
- 1   medium sweet onion, cut into 1-in. strips
- 1   jar (15½ to 16 oz.) chunky medium salsa
- ¼   cup orange juice
- ¼   cup plus 1 Tbsp. fresh cilantro leaves, divided

1. Sprinkle shrimp with fajita seasoning; toss to coat. Set aside.

2. Slowly stir grits into boiling water. Reduce heat to medium; cook, covered, stirring occasionally, until thickened, 5-7 minutes. Remove from heat. Stir in cheese until melted; stir in milk. Keep warm.

3. In a large skillet, heat oil over medium-high heat. Add peppers and onion; cook and stir until tender and pepper edges are slightly charred. Add salsa, orange juice and shrimp. Cook, stirring constantly, until shrimp turn pink, 4-6 minutes. Stir in ¼ cup cilantro. Remove from heat.

4. Spoon the grits into serving bowls; top the with shrimp mixture. Sprinkle with the remaining cilantro.

1 serving: 561 cal., 23g fat (8g sat. fat), 176mg chol., 1324mg sod., 55g carb. (12g sugars, 4g fiber), 33g pro.

SEARED SALMON WITH BALSAMIC SAUCE

A friend gave me this quick and easy approach to salmon. It has a mildly sweet sauce and is such a hit, I've passed it to other fish fans.

—*Trish Horton, Colorado Springs, CO*

TAKES: 30 min. • **MAKES:** 4 servings

- 4   salmon fillets (4 oz. each)
- ½   tsp. salt
- 2   tsp. canola oil
- ¼   cup water
- ¼   cup balsamic vinegar
- 4   tsp. lemon juice
- 4   tsp. brown sugar
     Coarsely ground pepper

1. Sprinkle the salmon with salt. In a large nonstick skillet, heat oil over medium heat. Place salmon in skillet, skin side up; cook until fish just begins to flake easily with a fork, 4-5 minutes on each side. Remove from pan; keep warm.

2. In same skillet, combine water, vinegar, lemon juice and brown sugar. Bring to a boil; cook until liquid is reduced to about ⅓ cup, stirring occasionally. Serve salmon with sauce; sprinkle with pepper.

1 fillet with about 1 Tbsp. sauce: 231 cal., 13g fat (2g sat. fat), 57mg chol., 353mg sod., 9g carb. (9g sugars, 0 fiber), 19g pro.
Diabetic exchanges: 3 lean meat, ½ starch, ½ fat.

FAJITA-STYLE SHRIMP & GRITS

COMFORTING
TUNA PATTIES

ARTICHOKE TUNA TOSS

I do volunteer work one evening a week and leave a meal behind for my family. On one occasion, I left this easy dinner. When I came home, my husband said it was the best pasta dish I'd ever made!

—Emily Perez, Alexandria, VA

TAKES: 30 min. • **MAKES:** 6 servings

3½ cups water
¼ cup butter, cubed
2 pkg. (4.6 oz. each) garlic and olive oil vermicelli mix
1 can (14 oz.) water-packed artichoke hearts, rinsed, drained and quartered
2 cans (5 oz. each) light tuna in water, drained
1 pkg. (10 oz.) frozen peas
1 Tbsp. olive oil
1 Tbsp. red wine vinegar
4 to 6 garlic cloves, minced

1. In a saucepan, bring water and butter to a boil. Stir in the vermicelli with contents of seasoning packets, artichokes, tuna, peas, oil, vinegar and garlic.
2. Return to a boil; cook, uncovered, until vermicelli is tender, 8-10 minutes. Let stand for 5 minutes.

1 cup: 266 cal., 11g fat (5g sat. fat), 29mg chol., 687mg sod., 27g carb. (3g sugars, 3g fiber), 14g pro.

TEST KITCHEN TIP
If you're concerned about mercury, look for skipjack light tuna. It's a species of small tuna, and smaller fish contain less mercury than very large ones.

COMFORTING TUNA PATTIES

My grandmother and mother made these tuna patties on Fridays during Lent. I'm not the biggest fan of tuna, but it's perfect in this dish. These patties are even good cold the next day, if there are any leftovers.

—Ann Marie Eberhart, Gig Harbor, WA

PREP: 25 min. + chilling
COOK: 5 min./batch • **MAKES:** 6 servings

2 Tbsp. butter
3 Tbsp. all-purpose flour
1 cup evaporated milk
1 pouch (6.4 oz.) light tuna in water
⅓ cup plus ½ cup dry bread crumbs, divided
1 green onion, finely chopped
2 Tbsp. lemon juice
½ tsp. salt
¼ tsp. pepper
Oil for frying

1. In a small saucepan, melt the butter over medium heat. Stir in the flour until smooth; gradually whisk in milk. Bring to a boil, stirring constantly; cook and stir until thickened, 2-3 minutes. Remove from heat. Transfer to a small bowl; cool.
2. Stir in tuna, ⅓ cup bread crumbs, green onion, lemon juice, salt and pepper. Refrigerate, covered, at least 30 minutes.
3. Place remaining ½ cup bread crumbs in a shallow bowl. Drop ⅓ cup tuna mixture into the crumbs. Gently coat and shape into a ½-in.-thick patty. Repeat. In a large skillet, heat oil over medium heat. Add the tuna patties in batches; cook until golden brown, 2-3 minutes per side. Drain on paper towels.
Freeze option: Freeze cooled tuna patties in freezer containers, separating layers with waxed paper. To use, reheat tuna patties on a baking sheet in a preheated 325° oven until heated through.

1 tuna patty: 255 cal., 17g fat (5g sat. fat), 34mg chol., 419mg sod., 15g carb. (5g sugars, 1g fiber), 10g pro.

LAUREN'S
BOUILLABAISSE

LAUREN'S BOUILLABAISSE

This golden-colored soup is brimming with an assortment of seafood and is topped with savory and colorful sourdough croutons.
—*Lauren Covas, New Brunswick, NJ*

PREP: 30 min. • **COOK:** 20 min.
MAKES: 12 servings (5 qt.)

- ⅔ cup chopped roasted sweet red pepper, drained
- ¼ cup reduced-fat mayonnaise

TOASTS

- 6 slices sourdough bread
- 1 garlic clove, halved

BOUILLABAISSE

- 1 medium onion, chopped
- 1 Tbsp. olive oil
- 2 garlic cloves, minced
- 2 plum tomatoes, chopped
- ½ tsp. saffron threads or 2 tsp. ground turmeric
- 3½ cups cubed red potatoes
- 2½ cups thinly sliced fennel bulb
- 1 carton (32 oz.) reduced-sodium chicken broth
- 3 cups clam juice
- 2 tsp. dried tarragon
- 24 fresh littleneck clams
- 24 fresh mussels, scrubbed and beards removed
- 1 lb. red snapper fillet, cut into 2-in. pieces
- ¾ lb. uncooked large shrimp, peeled and deveined
- ¼ cup minced fresh parsley

1. Place red pepper and mayonnaise in a food processor; cover and process until smooth. Refrigerate until serving.
2. For toasts, rub 1 side of each bread slice with garlic; discard garlic. Cut bread slices in half. Place on an ungreased baking sheet. Bake at 400 for 4-5 minutes on each side or until lightly browned.
3. In a stockpot, saute onion in oil until tender. Add garlic; cook 1 minute longer. Reduce heat; stir in tomatoes and saffron. Add the potatoes, fennel, broth, clam juice and tarragon. Bring to a boil. Reduce heat; simmer, uncovered, for 10-12 minutes or until potatoes are almost tender.
4. Add the clams, mussels, snapper and shrimp. Cook, stirring occasionally, until clams and mussels open and the fish flakes easily with a fork, 10-15 minutes. Discard any unopened clams or mussels. Spoon into bowls; sprinkle with parsley. Spread pepper mayo over toasts; serve with bouillabaisse.

1⅔ cups with 2 tsp. spread on ½ slice of bread: 239 cal., 5g fat (1g sat. fat), 70mg chol., 684mg sod., 23g carb. (3g sugars, 2g fiber), 24g pro. **Diabetic exchanges:** 3 lean meat, 1½ starch, ½ fat.

CRAB EGG FOO YONG

Enjoy a classic Chinese takeout dish without leaving your home. This makes a quick dinner and is as delicious as what you would get in any restaurant.
—*Beverly Preston, Fond du Lac, WI*

TAKES: 30 min. • **MAKES:** 4 servings

- 4 tsp. cornstarch
- 2 tsp. sugar
- 1 can (14½ oz.) reduced-sodium chicken broth
- 2 Tbsp. reduced-sodium soy sauce
- 1 Tbsp. white vinegar

EGG FOO YONG

- 2 Tbsp. all-purpose flour
- 4 large eggs
- 1 can (14 oz.) bean sprouts, drained
- 2 cans (6 oz. each) lump crabmeat, drained
- ⅓ cup thinly sliced green onions
- ⅛ tsp. garlic powder
- ⅛ tsp. pepper
- 3 Tbsp. canola oil

1. In a small saucepan, combine cornstarch and sugar. Stir in the broth, soy sauce and vinegar until smooth. Bring to a boil; cook and stir for 2 minutes or until thickened. Set aside and keep warm.
2. In a large bowl, whisk flour and eggs until smooth. Stir in bean sprouts, crab, onions, garlic powder and pepper. In a large skillet, heat oil. Drop crab mixture by ⅓ cupfuls into oil. Cook until for 2 minutes on each side or until golden brown. Serve with sauce.

2 pieces: 297 cal., 16g fat (3g sat. fat), 269mg chol., 1159mg sod., 12g carb. (3g sugars, 2g fiber), 25g pro.

CRAB EGG FOO YONG

BATTER-FRIED FISH

Whether I'm fixing cod fillets or my husband's catch of the day, this fish fry batter makes the fish golden and crispy. Club soda gives it a different twist, and the sweet and zippy sauce complements the fish nicely.
—*Nancy Johnson, Connersville, IN*

TAKES: 15 min. • **MAKES:** 2 servings

- ½ lb. cod fillet
- 2 Tbsp. all-purpose flour
- 2 to 3 Tbsp. cornstarch
- ¼ tsp. garlic powder
- ¼ tsp. onion powder
- ¼ tsp. salt
- ¼ tsp. cayenne pepper
- ¼ tsp. paprika
- ⅛ tsp. dried oregano
- ⅛ tsp. dried thyme
- ⅓ cup club soda
- Oil for frying
- ¼ cup orange marmalade
- 1 to 2 Tbsp. prepared horseradish

1. Rinse fillets in cold water; pat dry. In a large shallow dish, toss flour and fish, 1 piece at a time. Combine next 9 ingredients.

2. In a cast-iron or other heavy skillet, heat 1 in. of oil. Dip floured fillets in cornstarch batter; fry over medium heat until fish just begins to flake easily with a fork, 2-3 minutes on each side. Combine the marmalade and horseradish; serve with fish.

1 serving: 346 cal., 12g fat (1g sat. fat), 43mg chol., 420mg sod., 42g carb. (25g sugars, 1g fiber), 19g pro.

FETA SHRIMP SKILLET

FETA SHRIMP SKILLET

My husband and I tried a dish similar to this one on our honeymoon in Greece. I re-created the flavors in this recipe when we got home. When I make it now, it brings back wonderful memories.
—*Sonali Ruder, New York, NY*

TAKES: 30 min. • **MAKES:** 4 servings

- 1 Tbsp. olive oil
- 1 medium onion, finely chopped
- 3 garlic cloves, minced
- 1 tsp. dried oregano
- ½ tsp. pepper
- ¼ tsp. salt
- 2 cans (14½ oz. each) diced tomatoes, undrained
- ¼ cup white wine, optional
- 1 lb. uncooked medium shrimp, peeled and deveined
- 2 Tbsp. minced fresh parsley
- ¾ cup crumbled feta cheese

1. In a large nonstick skillet, heat oil over medium-high heat. Add onion; cook and stir 4-6 minutes or until tender. Add garlic and seasonings; cook 1 minute longer. Stir in tomatoes and, if desired, wine. Bring to a boil. Reduce heat; simmer, uncovered, 5-7 minutes or until sauce is slightly thickened.

2. Add shrimp and parsley; cook 5-6 minutes or until shrimp turn pink, stirring occasionally. Remove from heat; sprinkle with cheese. Let stand, covered, until cheese is softened.

1¼ cups: 240 cal., 8g fat (3g sat. fat), 149mg chol., 748mg sod., 16g carb. (9g sugars, 5g fiber), 25g pro. **Diabetic exchanges:** 3 lean meat, 1 starch, 1 fat.

TEST KITCHEN TIP

For even more Mediterranean flavor, try adding ¼ cup of chopped kalamata olives wiith the tomatoes.

SALMON CROQUETTE BAGEL SANDWICH

I'm obsessed with smoked salmon on bagels with all the accoutrements! I could seriously eat it every day for breakfast! But smoked salmon can get pricey, so I found a cheaper alternative without sacrificing the flavor!
—*Jessi Hampton, Richmond Hill, GA*

PREP: 25 min. • **COOK:** 10 min.
MAKES: 2 servings

- 1 large egg, lightly beaten
- ¼ cup dry bread crumbs
- 1 tsp. garlic powder
- 1 tsp. smoked paprika
- 1 pouch (6 oz.) boneless skinless pink salmon
- 1 Tbsp. olive oil
- 2 everything bagels, split and toasted
- 4 Tbsp. cream cheese, softened
- 1 Tbsp. capers, drained
- 1 medium tomato, sliced
- ½ medium red onion, thinly sliced into rings
  Snipped fresh dill, optional

1. In a small bowl, combine egg, bread crumbs, garlic powder and smoked paprika. Add the salmon and mix well. Shape into 2 patties.

2. In a large skillet, cook patties in oil over medium heat until browned, 5-6 minutes on each side. Spread bagels with cream cheese; sprinkle with capers. Serve burgers on bagels with tomato, red onion and, if desired, dill.

1 sandwich: 656 cal., 25g fat (10g sat. fat), 152mg chol., 1205mg sod., 75g carb. (14g sugars, 4g fiber), 34g pro.

SALMON CROQUETTE BAGEL SANDWICH

SOUTHERN SEAFOOD GUMBO

A local restaurant serves a terrific gumbo, and I duplicated it pretty closely with this recipe. I did lighten it up a bit, but no one in my family seems to mind.
—*Susan Wright, Champaign, IL*

PREP: 25 min. • **COOK:** 35 min.
MAKES: 12 servings

- 1 medium onion, chopped
- 2 celery ribs with leaves, chopped
- 1 medium green pepper, chopped
- 1 Tbsp. olive oil
- 3 garlic cloves, minced
- 1 bottle (46 oz.) spicy hot V8 juice
- 1 can (14½ oz.) diced tomatoes, undrained
- ¼ tsp. cayenne pepper
- 1 pkg. (16 oz.) frozen sliced okra, thawed
- 1 lb. catfish fillets, cut into ¾-in. cubes
- ¾ lb. uncooked medium shrimp, peeled and deveined
- 3 cups cooked long grain rice

1. In a Dutch oven, saute the onion, celery and green pepper in oil until tender. Add garlic; cook 1 minute longer. Stir in the V8 juice, tomatoes and cayenne; bring to a boil. Reduce heat; cover and simmer for 10 minutes.

2. Stir in okra and catfish; cook 8 minutes longer. Add the shrimp; cook 7 minutes longer or until shrimp turn pink. Place ¼ cup rice in a serving bowl; top with gumbo.

1 cup: 180 cal., 5g fat (1g sat. fat), 60mg chol., 512mg sod., 22g carb. (7g sugars, 3g fiber), 14g pro. **Diabetic exchanges:** 2 vegetable, 2 lean meat, 1 starch.

TOMATO-POACHED HALIBUT

Halibut can be a pricey fish, so it makes sense to save it for special occasions. This simple and elegant preparation with a burst of lemon comes together in one pan. For a delicious and unusual holiday meal, pair it with polenta, angel hair pasta or crusty bread—and break out the good wine!
—*Danna Rogers, Westport, CT*

TAKES: 30 min. • **MAKES:** 4 servings

1 Tbsp. olive oil
2 poblano peppers, finely chopped
1 small onion, finely chopped
1 can (14½ oz.) fire-roasted diced tomatoes, undrained
1 can (14½ oz.) no-salt-added diced tomatoes, undrained
¼ cup chopped pitted green olives
3 garlic cloves, minced
¼ tsp. pepper
⅛ tsp. salt
4 halibut fillets (4 oz. each)
⅓ cup chopped fresh cilantro
4 lemon wedges
Crusty whole grain bread, optional

1. In a large nonstick skillet, heat oil over medium-high heat. Add poblano peppers and onion; cook and stir 4-6 minutes or until tender.
2. Stir in tomatoes, olives, garlic, pepper and salt. Bring to a boil. Adjust heat to maintain a gentle simmer. Add fillets. Cook, covered, 8-10 minutes or until fish just begins to flake easily with a fork. Sprinkle with cilantro. Serve with lemon wedges and, if desired, bread.
1 fillet with 1 cup sauce: 224 cal., 7g fat (1g sat. fat), 56mg chol., 651mg sod., 17g carb. (8g sugars, 4g fiber), 24g pro. **Diabetic exchanges:** 3 lean meat, 1 starch, ½ fat.

NAKED FISH TACOS

NAKED FISH TACOS

This is one of my husband's all-time favorite meals. I've even converted some friends to fish after eating this. I serve it with fresh melon when it's in season to balance the subtle heat of the cabbage mixture.
—*Elizabeth Bramkamp, Gig Harbor, WA*

TAKES: 25 min. • **MAKES:** 2 servings

1 cup coleslaw mix
¼ cup chopped fresh cilantro
1 green onion, sliced
1 tsp. chopped seeded jalapeno pepper
4 tsp. canola oil, divided
2 tsp. lime juice
½ tsp. ground cumin
½ tsp. salt, divided
¼ tsp. pepper, divided
2 tilapia fillets (6 oz. each)
½ medium ripe avocado, peeled and sliced

1. Place the first 4 ingredients in a bowl; toss with 2 tsp. oil, lime juice, cumin, ¼ tsp. salt and ⅛ tsp. pepper. Refrigerate until serving.
2. Pat fillets dry with paper towels; sprinkle with the remaining salt and pepper. In a large nonstick skillet, heat the remaining oil over medium-high heat; cook tilapia until fish just begins to flake easily with a fork, 3-4 minutes per side. Top with slaw and avocado.
Note: Wear disposable gloves when cutting hot peppers; the oils can burn skin. Avoid touching your face.
1 serving: 293 cal., 16g fat (2g sat. fat), 83mg chol., 663mg sod., 6g carb. (1g sugars, 3g fiber), 33g pro. **Diabetic exchanges:** 5 lean meat, 3 fat, 1 vegetable.

TEST KITCHEN TIP
If you're following a low-carb diet, this dish is for you! If not, pair it up with a whole grain side like brown rice pilaf or corn and pepper saute.

TOMATO-POACHED
HALIBUT

THAI SCALLOP SAUTE

Just open a bottle of Thai peanut sauce to give this easy seafood stir-fry some serious authenticity.

—Taste of Home *Test Kitchen*

PREP: 15 min. • **COOK:** 20 min.
MAKES: 4 servings

- 3 tsp. olive oil, divided
- 1½ lbs. sea scallops
- 2 cups fresh broccoli florets
- 2 medium onions, halved and sliced
- 1 medium zucchini, sliced
- 4 small carrots, sliced
- ¼ cup Thai peanut sauce
- ¼ tsp. salt
  Hot cooked rice
  Lime wedges, optional

1. In a large skillet, heat 1 tsp. oil over medium-high heat. Add half the scallops; stir-fry until firm and opaque. Remove from pan. Repeat with an additional 1 tsp. oil and remaining scallops.

2. In same skillet, heat remaining oil over medium-high heat. Add vegetables; stir-fry until crisp-tender, 7-9 minutes. Stir in peanut sauce and salt. Return scallops to pan; heat through. Serve with hot cooked rice and, if desired, lime wedges.

1½ cups: 268 cal., 8g fat (1g sat. fat), 41mg chol., 1000mg sod., 24g carb. (10g sugars, 4g fiber), 25g pro.

THAI SCALLOP
SAUTE

TILAPIA WITH CITRUS SAUCE

The lemon, lime and orange sauce adds zest to this flaky, delicate-flavored fish.

—Francis Garland, Anniston, AL

TAKES: 30 min. • **MAKES:** 4 servings

- ½ cup 2% milk
- ½ cup all-purpose flour
- ½ tsp. salt
- ½ tsp. pepper
- 4 tilapia fillets (4 oz. each)
  Olive oil-flavored cooking spray
- 3 garlic cloves, minced
- 1 Tbsp. butter
- 2 tsp. olive oil
- ½ small lemon, sliced
- ½ medium lime, sliced
- ½ small navel orange, sliced
- 3 Tbsp. lemon juice
- 3 Tbsp. lime juice
- 2 Tbsp. orange juice
- 2 green onions, finely chopped

1. Place milk in a shallow bowl. In another shallow bowl, combine the flour, salt and pepper. Dip fish in milk, then coat with the flour mixture.

2. Spray fillets with cooking spray. In a large nonstick skillet, cook fish over medium-high heat for 3-4 minutes on each side or until the fish flakes easily with a fork. Remove and keep warm.

3. In the same pan, saute garlic in butter and oil for 1 minute. Add the lemon, lime and orange slices, juices and onions; cook 1 minute longer. Serve with fish.

1 fillet with ¼ cup sauce: 197 cal., 8g fat (3g sat. fat), 63mg chol., 142mg sod., 11g carb. (3g sugars, 1g fiber), 22g pro. **Diabetic exchanges:** 3 lean meat, 1 fat, ½ fruit.

SPICY SHRIMP FETTUCCINE ALFREDO

GOLDEN SEAFOOD CHOWDER

Flavored with crab, shrimp and cheddar cheese, this chowder is so good that I make it weekly. Sometimes I substitute chicken or ham for the seafood and leave out the Clamato juice. Either way, this pretty soup is a winner.
—*Ami Paton, Waconia, MN*

PREP: 25 min. • **COOK:** 25 min.
MAKES: 4 servings (1½ qt.)

- ½ cup finely chopped onion
- ¼ cup butter, cubed
- 1 can (14½ oz.) chicken broth
- 1 cup cubed peeled potato
- 2 celery ribs, chopped
- 2 medium carrots, chopped
- ¼ cup Clamato juice
- ¼ tsp. lemon-pepper seasoning
- ¼ cup all-purpose flour
- 2 cups 2% milk
- 2 cups shredded sharp cheddar cheese
- 1 can (6 oz.) crabmeat, drained, flaked and cartilage removed
- 1 cup chopped cooked shrimp

1. In a large saucepan, saute onion in butter until tender. Stir in the broth, potato, celery, carrots, Clamato juice and lemon pepper. Bring to a boil. Reduce heat; cover and simmer for 15-20 minutes or until vegetables are tender.

2. In a small bowl, whisk flour and milk until smooth; add to soup. Bring to a boil; cook and stir for 2 minutes or until thickened. Reduce heat. Add the cheese, crab and shrimp; cook and stir until cheese is melted.

1½ cups: 550 cal., 33g fat (22g sat. fat), 198mg chol., 1233mg sod., 28g carb. (10g sugars, 2g fiber), 35g pro.

"This recipe is delicious. I usually double it as my family is big, but it doesn't require any other adjusting. My only comment would be that you can use V8 if Clamato isn't available."
—JOERICESGIRL, TASTEOFHOME.COM

SPICY SHRIMP FETTUCCINE ALFREDO

I make this pasta a lot because it's a something my family never seems to get tired of. The sauce is so fast to make, I can get it done while the pasta is cooking. In the past, I have also added red peppers and spinach. And who's to say you couldn't add mushrooms?
—*Stephanie Beluk, Sharpsburg, GA*

PREP: 20 min. • **COOK:** 15 min.
MAKES: 8 servings

- 1 pkg. (16 oz.) fettuccine
- 5 garlic cloves, minced
- 1 red serrano pepper, chopped
- 3 Tbsp. butter
- 1 Tbsp. olive oil
- 2 lbs. uncooked medium shrimp, peeled and deveined
- 1 tsp. garlic powder
- 1 tsp. dried rosemary, crushed
- 1 tsp. dried oregano
- ¼ tsp. coarsely ground pepper
- 1 jar (15 oz.) Alfredo sauce
- ¾ cup chicken broth

1. Cook fettuccine according to package directions. Meanwhile, saute garlic and serrano pepper in butter and oil in a large skillet. Add shrimp and seasonings; cook and stir until shrimp turn pink, 4-6 minutes.

2. Stir in Alfredo sauce and broth; heat through. Drain fettuccine. Serve with the shrimp mixture.

Note: Wear disposable gloves when cutting hot peppers; the oils can burn skin. Avoid touching your face.

1 serving: 427 cal., 14g fat (7g sat. fat), 165mg chol., 491mg sod., 46g carb. (2g sugars, 3g fiber), 29g pro.

MIMOSA ROASTED
CHICKEN, PAGE 195

172

193

200

221

Oven Entrees

Everybody adores the simplicity of sizzling dinners from the oven. Here, you will find more than 90 ways to treat the family to fresh-from-the-oven casseroles, roasts, seafood meals, muffin-tin entrees and more. These are the dishes you'll turn to for everyday suppers and special occasions alike.

BEEF & GROUND BEEF » 162

POULTRY » 178

PORK » 200

FISH & SEAFOOD » 214

Beef & Gound Beef

BEEF & BISCUIT BAKE

BEEF & BISCUIT BAKE

My satisfying dish is perfect—great flavor and it's quick and easy. With the combo of beef, corn and biscuits, I think it's a fine example of Midwest cuisine.
—*Erin Schneider, St. Peters, MO*

- -

TAKES: 30 min. • **MAKES:** 8 servings

- 1   **lb. ground beef**
- 1   **can (16 oz.) kidney beans, rinsed and drained**
- 1   **can (15¼ oz.) whole kernel corn, drained**
- 1   **can (10¾ oz.) condensed tomato soup, undiluted**
- ¼   **cup 2% milk**
- 2   **Tbsp. finely chopped onion**
- ½   **tsp. chili powder**
- ¼   **tsp. salt**
- 1   **cup cubed Velveeta**
- 1   **tube (12 oz.) refrigerated biscuits**
- 2   **to 3 Tbsp. butter, melted**
- ⅓   **cup yellow cornmeal**

1. Preheat oven to 375°. In a saucepan over medium heat, cook beef until no longer pink; drain. Add beans, corn, soup, milk, onion, chili powder and salt; bring to a boil. Remove from heat; stir in cheese until melted. Spoon into a greased 2½-qt. baking dish. Bake, uncovered, 10 minutes.

2. Meanwhile, brush all sides of biscuits with butter; roll in cornmeal. Place on top of bubbling meat mixture. Return to oven for 10-12 minutes or until biscuits are lightly browned and cooked through.

1 serving: 439 cal., 19g fat (8g sat. fat), 46mg chol., 1180mg sod., 44g carb. (10g sugars, 5g fiber), 21g pro.

"Very easy and yummy dish. I substituted grated cheddar for the Velveeta."
—JACQUELINE, TASTEOFHOME.COM

STEAKHOUSE PIZZA

OSSO BUCO

This dish can be assembled several hours ahead and put in the oven while you relax. I try to get veal shanks that are similar in size so they'll cook evenly, and usually plan on serving two shanks per person.
—*Karen Jaffe, Short Hills, NJ*

PREP: 30 min. • **BAKE:** 2 hours
MAKES: 6 servings

- ⅓ cup all-purpose flour
- 1 tsp. salt
- ½ tsp. pepper
- 6 veal shanks
- 5 Tbsp. olive oil
- 1 tsp. Italian seasoning
- ½ tsp. rubbed sage
- 2 medium carrots, sliced
- 1 medium onion, chopped
- 1 celery rib, cut in ½-in. slices
- 1 garlic clove, minced
- 1½ cups dry white wine or chicken broth
- 1 can (10½ oz.) condensed chicken broth, undiluted
- 2 Tbsp. tomato paste

GREMOLATA

- 2 garlic cloves, minced
- 1 to 2 Tbsp. minced fresh parsley
- 1 Tbsp. grated lemon zest

1. Combine flour, salt and pepper; dredge meat. In a large skillet, brown meat in oil on all sides. Place shanks in a single layer in a Dutch oven or oblong baking dish; sprinkle with Italian seasoning and sage. Combine the carrots, onion, celery and garlic; sprinkle over meat. In a small bowl, whisk together wine, broth and tomato paste. Pour over the vegetables.
2. Cover and bake at 325° for 2 hours or until fork-tender. Just before serving, combine gremolata ingredients; sprinkle over each shank. Serve immediately.
1 serving: 413 cal., 22g fat (6g sat. fat), 111mg chol., 804mg sod., 13g carb. (3g sugars, 2g fiber), 30g pro.

STEAKHOUSE PIZZA

One of my first jobs was in a steakhouse. This recipe gives me a chance to celebrate two of my favorite foods: steak and pizza. I love the addition of eggs baked onto the pizza to make a "steak and eggs" breakfast pizza.
—*Lisa Benoit, Cookeville, TN*

PREP: 35 min. • **BAKE:** 10 min. + standing
MAKES: 8 servings

- 1 loaf (1 lb.) frozen pizza dough, thawed
- 1 pkg. (8 oz.) frozen spinach and artichoke cheese dip, thawed
- ¾ cup grape tomatoes, halved
- 1 boneless beef top loin steak (1 lb.), thinly sliced
- 1½ tsp. Montreal steak seasoning
- ⅓ cup torn fresh basil
- 3 Tbsp. pine nuts
- 2 bacon strips, cooked and crumbled
- ⅓ cup prepared ranch salad dressing
- 1 Tbsp. prepared horseradish

1. Preheat oven to 400°. Press dough to fit a greased 14-in. pizza pan. Pinch edges to form a rim. Bake until edges are lightly browned, 10-12 minutes. Let cool 10 minutes.
2. Spread with dip; top with tomatoes. Toss the steak with steak seasoning; place over tomatoes. Bake on a lower oven rack until steak reaches desired doneness and crust is golden brown, 10-12 minutes. Let stand 10 minutes. Sprinkle with basil, pine nuts and bacon. Combine dressing and horseradish; serve with pizza.
1 slice: 290 cal., 12g fat (2g sat. fat), 28mg chol., 434mg sod., 27g carb. (2g sugars, 1g fiber), 18g pro.

BUTTERNUT SQUASH,
CAULIFLOWER & BEEF
SHEPHERD'S PIE

REUBEN BREAD PUDDING

Our Aunt Renee always brought this casserole to family picnics in Chicago. It became so popular that she started bringing two or three. I have also made it using dark rye bread or marbled rye, and ham instead of corned beef—all the variations are delicious!
—*Johnna Johnson, Scottsdale, AZ*

PREP: 20 min. • **BAKE:** 35 min.
MAKES: 6 servings

    4   cups cubed rye bread (about 6 slices)
    2   Tbsp. butter, melted
    2   cups cubed or shredded cooked
        corned beef (about ½ lb.)
    1   can (14 oz.) sauerkraut,
        rinsed and well drained
    1   cup shredded Swiss cheese, divided
    3   large eggs
    1   cup 2% milk
    ⅓   cup prepared Thousand Island
        salad dressing
    1½ tsp. prepared mustard
    ¼   tsp. pepper

1. Preheat oven to 350°. In a large bowl, toss bread cubes with butter. Stir in corned beef, sauerkraut and ½ cup cheese; transfer to a greased 11x7-in. baking dish.
2. In same bowl, whisk eggs, milk, salad dressing, mustard and pepper; pour over top. Bake, uncovered, 30 minutes. Sprinkle with remaining cheese. Bake until top is golden and a knife inserted in the center comes out clean, 5-7 minutes longer.
1 piece: 390 cal., 25g fat (10g sat. fat), 165mg chol., 1295mg sod., 21g carb. (7g sugars, 3g fiber), 19g pro.

DID YOU KNOW?

New York City or Omaha? The debate rages hot over where the tasty Reuben got its start. One thing on which we all can agree: It's always a combination of corned beef, kraut and Swiss on rye, with either a Russian dressing or Thousand Island.

BUTTERNUT SQUASH, CAULIFLOWER & BEEF SHEPHERD'S PIE

I love to get creative with classic dishes, such as this colorful version of shepherd's pie. Adding squash and cauliflower boosts the nutritional value and cuts calories.
—*Jenn Tidwell, Fair Oaks, CA*

PREP: 50 min. • **BAKE:** 35 min. + standing
MAKES: 6 servings

    4   Tbsp. butter, divided, melted
    2   Tbsp. maple syrup
         Dash pepper
    1   medium butternut squash
         (about 2½ lbs.), peeled and cubed
    1   Tbsp. minced fresh thyme or 1 tsp.
         dried thyme
    1¼   lbs. ground beef
    1   envelope onion soup mix
    1   cup water
    1   medium head cauliflower, broken
         into small florets
    4   garlic cloves, minced
    1   cup freshly grated Parmesan cheese

1. Preheat oven to 350°. Combine 2 Tbsp. melted butter, syrup and pepper; toss with squash to coat. Roast squash in a greased 15x10x1-in. baking pan until tender, 40-45 minutes. Transfer to a large bowl; mash until smooth, stirring in thyme.
2. In a large skillet over medium heat, cook and stir beef, crumbling meat, until no longer pink, 6-8 minutes; drain. Stir in soup mix and water; bring to a boil. Reduce heat; simmer, uncovered, until slightly thickened, 4-6 minutes. Transfer to a greased 13x9-in. baking dish.
3. Top evenly with cauliflower. Sprinkle with garlic; drizzle with remaining melted butter. Spread squash mixture over top. Bake, uncovered, until the cauliflower is tender, 35-40 minutes. Sprinkle with cheese. Let stand 10 minutes before serving.
1½ cups: 438 cal., 23g fat (11g sat. fat), 90mg chol., 798mg sod., 37g carb. (11g sugars, 9g fiber), 25g pro.

REUBEN BREAD
PUDDING

❄ ALL-AMERICAN MEAT LOAF

There are many variations on meat loaf, but my family loves this stick-to-your-ribs version.
—*Margie Williams, Mount Juliet, TN*

PREP: 30 min. • **BAKE:** 50 min. + standing
MAKES: 2 loaves (8 servings each)

1	large green pepper, chopped
1	large onion, chopped
2	tsp. olive oil
4	garlic cloves, minced
2	large eggs, lightly beaten
1	cup 2% milk
6	slices bread, cubed
1½	cups shredded cheddar cheese
2¼	tsp. dried rosemary, crushed
2	tsp. salt
1	tsp. pepper
2	lbs. lean ground beef (90% lean)
1	lb. ground pork
1½	cups ketchup
¼	cup packed brown sugar
2	tsp. cider vinegar

1. Saute green pepper and onion in oil in a large skillet until tender. Add garlic; cook 1 minute longer. Transfer to a large bowl; cool to room temperature.
2. Preheat oven to 350°. Add the eggs, milk, bread, cheese, rosemary, salt and pepper to sauteed vegetables. Crumble beef and pork over mixture and mix well.
3. Pat into 2 greased 9x5-in. loaf pans. Combine ketchup, brown sugar and vinegar in a small bowl. Spread over tops.
4. Bake, uncovered, 50-55 minutes or until no pink remains and a thermometer reads 160°. Let stand 10 minutes before slicing.
Freeze option: Shape the meat loaves in plastic wrap-lined loaf pans; top with ketchup mixture. Cover and freeze until firm. Remove from pan and wrap securely in foil; return to freezer. Freeze up to 3 months. To use, partially thaw in refrigerator overnight. Preheat oven to 350°. Unwrap meat loaf and place in pan. Bake, uncovered, 1¼-1½ hours, or until a thermometer reads 160°.
1 slice: 286 cal., 14g fat (6g sat. fat), 89mg chol., 765mg sod., 18g carb. (11g sugars, 1g fiber), 21g pro.

SLOPPY JOE BISCUIT CUPS

I'm a busy teacher and mom, so weekday meals with shortcuts are a huge help. I always have to share the recipe when I take these to events at school.
—*Julie Ahern, Waukegan, IL*

TAKES: 30 min. • **MAKES:** 10 biscuit cups

1	lb. lean ground beef (90% lean)
¼	cup each finely chopped celery, onion and green pepper
½	cup barbecue sauce
1	tube (12 oz.) refrigerated flaky biscuits (10 count)
½	cup shredded cheddar cheese

1. Heat oven to 400°. In a large skillet, cook beef and vegetables over medium heat until beef is no longer pink, 5-7 minutes, breaking up beef into crumbles; drain. Stir in barbecue sauce; bring to a boil. Reduce heat; simmer, uncovered, 2 minutes, stirring occasionally.
2. Separate dough into 10 biscuits; flatten to 5-in. circles. Press onto bottoms and up sides of greased muffin cups. Fill with beef mixture.
3. Bake until the biscuits are golden brown, 9-11 minutes. Sprinkle with cheese; bake until cheese is melted, 1-2 minutes longer.
2 biscuit cups: 463 cal., 22g fat (8g sat. fat), 68mg chol., 1050mg sod., 41g carb. (16g sugars, 1g fiber), 25g pro.

SLOPPY JOE BISCUIT CUPS

ROAST BEEF
CARIBBEAN STYLE

BROILED STEAK FAJITAS

I make these hearty fajitas all the time. Sometimes I like to add portobello mushrooms to the onion and pepper mixture. The whole family loves them.
—*Amber Jensen, Whispering Pines, NC*

PREP: 30 min. + marinating • **BROIL:** 10 min.
MAKES: 6 servings

- ½ cup plus 2 Tbsp. olive oil, divided
- ½ cup red wine vinegar
- 2 Tbsp. minced fresh oregano or 2 tsp. dried oregano
- 2 tsp. sugar
- 2 tsp. chili powder
- 1 tsp. salt
- 1 tsp. garlic powder
- ½ tsp. pepper
- 1½ lbs. beef top sirloin steak
- 2 large onions, sliced
- 1 large green pepper, cut into strips
- 1 large sweet red pepper, cut into strips
- 12 flour tortillas (10 in.), warmed
  Optional toppings: Picante sauce, shredded cheese, guacamole and sour cream

1. In a small bowl, combine ½ cup oil, vinegar, oregano, sugar, chili powder, salt, garlic powder and pepper. Pour ½ cup marinade into a shallow dish. Add the beef and turn to coat. Cover; refrigerate for at least 8 hours or overnight. Cover and refrigerate the remaining marinade.
2. Drain steak and discard marinade. Broil 4 in. from the heat for 5-7 minutes on each side or until meat reaches desired doneness (for medium-rare, a thermometer should read 135°; medium, 140°; medium-well, 145°), basting occasionally with reserved marinade. Let steak stand for 5 minutes before slicing.
3. Meanwhile, in a large skillet, saute onions and peppers in oil until tender. Serve on tortillas with beef and toppings.
2 fajitas: 788 cal., 34g fat (9g sat. fat), 46mg chol., 1430mg sod., 82g carb. (10g sugars, 8g fiber), 37g pro.

ROAST BEEF CARIBBEAN STYLE

This recipe took first place in the 2011 South Dakota Beef Cook-Off. Cooking the roast uncovered for the first 30 minutes gives it a crusty exterior similar to barbecued brisket, and the flavorful sauce adds just a hint of heat.
—*Susan Patrick, Watertown, SD*

PREP: 35 min. • **BAKE:** 3½ hours + standing
MAKES: 8 servings

- 6 green onions, thinly sliced
- ½ cup lime juice
- ½ cup soy sauce
- ½ cup olive oil
- 2 to 3 habanero peppers, seeded and finely chopped
- 2 Tbsp. minced fresh gingerroot or ½ tsp. ground ginger
- 2 Tbsp. dark brown sugar
- 1 Tbsp. minced fresh thyme
- 2 to 3 garlic cloves, minced
- 2 tsp. freshly ground pepper
- 1 tsp. ground allspice
- 1 tsp. ground cinnamon
- ¾ tsp. ground nutmeg

ROAST
- 1 boneless beef chuck roast (2½ lbs.)
- 4 garlic cloves, halved
- 3 Tbsp. olive oil, divided
- 1 garlic clove, minced
- ½ tsp. seasoned salt
- ½ tsp. pepper
  Lime wedges

1. Preheat oven to 300°. For sauce, mix first 13 ingredients.
2. Cut 8 small slits in roast; fill with garlic halves. Mix 2 Tbsp. oil, minced garlic, seasoned salt and pepper; rub onto roast.
3. In a Dutch oven, heat remaining oil over medium heat; brown roast on all sides. Spoon 3 Tbsp. sauce over roast, spreading evenly. Add 1 cup sauce to pan. Bake, uncovered, 30 minutes.
4. Reduce oven setting to 250°. Top roast with an additional 3 Tbsp. sauce. Cover pan; bake until beef is tender, 3-3½ hours. Remove from oven; let stand 15 minutes.
5. If desired, remove garlic halves before slicing. Serve roast with remaining sauce and lime wedges.
Note: Wear disposable gloves when cutting hot peppers; the oils can burn skin. Avoid touching your face.
3 oz. cooked beef with 4 tsp. sauce: 449 cal., 32g fat (8g sat. fat), 92mg chol., 1078mg sod., 9g carb. (5g sugars, 1g fiber), 31g pro.

GAME-NIGHT
NACHO PIZZA

GAME-NIGHT NACHO PIZZA

Some like it hot with jalapenos; others like it cool with a dollop of sour cream. But one thing's for sure: This is nacho ordinary pizza night.
—*Jamie Jones, Madison, GA*

TAKES: 20 min. • **MAKES:** 6 servings

- 1   prebaked 12-in. pizza crust
- 1   Tbsp. olive oil
- 1   cup refried beans
- 1   cup refrigerated fully cooked barbecued shredded beef
- ½   cup chopped seeded tomatoes
- ½   cup pickled jalapeno slices
- 1   cup shredded Colby-Monterey Jack cheese
     Optional toppings: Shredded lettuce, sour cream and salsa

1. Place crust on an ungreased pizza pan. Brush with oil. Spread beans over crust. Top with beef, tomatoes, jalapenos and cheese.
2. Bake at 450° until cheese is melted, 10-15 minutes. Serve with lettuce, sour cream and salsa if desired.
1 serving: 370 cal., 13g fat (5g sat. fat), 30mg chol., 1103mg sod., 46g carb. (6g sugars, 3g fiber), 18g pro.

TEST KITCHEN TIP
This recipe was tested with Lloyd's seasoned shredded barbecued beef, but feel free to use your favorite brand or leftover homemade barbecued beef.

PRIME RIB WITH HORSERADISH CREAM

PRIME RIB WITH HORSERADISH CREAM

This recipe makes wonderful, special dinners. Mouths will water over this juicy prime rib.
—*Margaret Dady, Grand Island, NE*

PREP: 30 min. • **BAKE:** 3 hours + standing
MAKES: 12 servings (1½ cups cream)

- 1   bone-in beef rib roast (6 to 8 lbs.)
- 3   garlic cloves, sliced
- 1   tsp. pepper

HORSERADISH CREAM
- 1   cup heavy whipping cream
- 2   Tbsp. prepared horseradish
- 2   tsp. red wine vinegar
- 1   tsp. ground mustard
- ¼   tsp. sugar
- ⅛   tsp. salt
     Dash pepper

1. Place roast fat side up in a shallow roasting pan. Cut slits into roast; insert garlic slices. Sprinkle with pepper. Bake, uncovered, at 450° for 15 minutes. Reduce heat to 325°; bake 2¾-3¼ hours longer or until meat reaches desired doneness (for medium-rare, a thermometer should read 135°; medium, 140°; medium-well, 145°).
2. Meanwhile, in a small bowl, beat cream until soft peaks form. Fold in the horseradish, vinegar, ground mustard, sugar, salt and pepper. Cover and refrigerate for 1 hour.
3. Remove roast to a serving platter and keep warm; let stand for 15 minutes. Serve with horseradish cream.
6 oz. cooked beef with 2 Tbsp. cream: 336 cal., 22g fat (10g sat. fat), 27mg chol., 121mg sod., 1g carb., trace fiber, 31g pro.

OLD-FASHIONED BEEF BRISKET

Tender slices of beef smothered in onions in a sweet tomato sauce give this entree an old-fashioned feel. Simple to prepare, it's delicious comfort food.
—*Gerry Thorpe, East Falmouth, MA*

PREP: 20 min. • **BAKE:** 3 hours
MAKES: 12 servings

- 1   fresh beef brisket (4 lbs.)
- 2   Tbsp. canola oil
- 2   large sweet onions, sliced
- 2   cups ketchup
- 2   cups water
- ½   cup dry red wine or beef broth

1. In an oven-proof Dutch oven, brown meat in oil on all sides; drain. Top with the onions. Combine the ketchup, water and wine; pour over meat and onions.

2. Cover and bake at 350° for 3-3½ hours or until meat is tender. Let stand 5 minutes. Thinly slice brisket across the grain. Thicken sauce if desired; serve with beef.

Freeze option: Place individual portions of sliced brisket in freezer containers; top with cooking sauce. Cool and freeze. To use, partially thaw in refrigerator overnight. Heat through in a covered saucepan, gently stirring and adding a little water if necessary.

4 oz. cooked beef: 277 cal., 9g fat (3g sat. fat), 64mg chol., 562mg sod., 15g carb. (13g sugars, 0 fiber), 31g pro. **Diabetic exchanges:** 4 lean meat, 1 starch.

EASY BEEF PIES

EASY BEEF PIES

We make a lot of French dips and always have leftover roast beef. Here's how I put it to good use. For these pies, use any vegetables you like. They're extra awesome drenched in cheese sauce.
—*Jennie Weber, Palmer, AK*

TAKES: 30 min. • **MAKES:** 4 servings

- 1   pkg. (15 oz.) refrigerated beef roast au jus
- 1   Tbsp. canola oil
- ¼   cup finely chopped onion
- ¼   cup finely chopped green pepper
- 1   garlic clove, minced
- 2   sheets refrigerated pie crust
- 1   cup shredded Mexican cheese blend
     Salsa con queso dip, optional

1. Preheat oven to 425°. Drain beef, reserving ¼ cup juices; shred meat with 2 forks. In a large skillet, heat oil over medium-high heat. Add onion and pepper; cook and stir until tender, 1-2 minutes. Add garlic; cook for 30 seconds longer. Remove from heat; stir in beef and reserved juices.

2. Unroll 1 pie crust; cut in half. Layer ¼ cup shredded cheese and about ⅓ cup beef mixture over half of each crust to within ½ in. of edge. Fold crust over filling; press edges with a fork to seal. Place on a greased baking sheet. Repeat with remaining crust and filling.

3. Bake until golden brown, 15-18 minutes. If desired, serve with queso dip.

Freeze option: Freeze cooled pies in a freezer container. To use, reheat pies on a greased baking sheet in a preheated 350° oven until heated through.

1 pie: 752 cal., 46g fat (19g sat. fat), 108mg chol., 921mg sod., 53g carb. (7g sugars, 0 fiber), 31g pro.

MAKE-AHEAD CABBAGE ROLLS

I've relied on this recipe for years, and my cabbage rolls never fail to impress. My guests have come to expect these at holiday parties.
—*Nancy Foust, Stoneboro, PA*

PREP: 1 hour + chilling • **BAKE:** 50 min.
MAKES: 12 rolls

- 12 cabbage leaves
- 2 lbs. ground beef
- ¾ tsp. salt
- ¼ tsp. pepper
- 2 cups cooked long grain rice
- 2 large eggs, lightly beaten

SAUCE
- ¼ cup butter, cubed
- 1 large onion, halved and thinly sliced
- 2 celery ribs, chopped
- 2½ cups water
- 2 cans (one 15 oz., one 8 oz.) tomato sauce
- 2 Tbsp. lemon juice
- 2 tsp. sugar
- 2 tsp. dried parsley flakes
- 1 tsp. salt
- ¼ tsp. pepper

1. In batches, cook cabbage leaves in boiling water until crisp-tender, 3-5 minutes. Drain; cool slightly. Trim the thick vein from the bottom of each cabbage leaf, making a V-shaped cut.

2. Meanwhile, in a large skillet, cook beef, salt and pepper over medium heat until no longer pink, 8-10 minutes, breaking into crumbles; drain. Stir in rice and eggs.

3. In another skillet, heat the butter over medium-high heat. Add onion and celery; cook and stir until tender, 6-8 minutes. Stir in water, tomato sauce, lemon juice, sugar, parsley, salt and pepper. Bring to a boil. Reduce heat; simmer, uncovered, until thickened, 15-20 minutes.

4. Spoon about ½ cup meat mixture onto each cabbage leaf. Pull together cut edges of leaf to overlap; fold over filling. Fold in sides and roll up. Transfer to a greased 13x9-in. baking dish. Pour sauce over the rolls. Refrigerate, covered, overnight.

5. Remove from refrigerator 30 minutes before baking. Preheat oven to 350°. Bake, covered, until rolls are heated through, 50-60 minutes.

Freeze option: Cover and freeze unbaked cabbage rolls. To use, partially thaw in refrigerator overnight. Remove from refrigerator 30 minutes before baking. Preheat oven to 350°. Bake casserole as directed, increasing time as necessary to heat through and for a thermometer inserted in center to read 165°.

2 cabbage rolls: 492 cal., 28g fat (12g sat. fat), 176mg chol., 1376mg sod., 28g carb. (6g sugars, 4g fiber), 33g pro.

MAKE-AHEAD
CABBAGE ROLLS

**TACO BAKED
POTATOES**

ITALIAN STUFFED BEEF ROLLS

The combination of spinach, artichoke and cream cheese is always a crowd-pleaser. Add basil and a roasted red pepper sauce, and you have perfection on a fork! To save time, the filling can be made ahead and chilled. You can also make the sauce ahead and reheat it when you are ready to serve.
—*Noelle Myers, Grand Forks, ND*

- -

PREP: 30 min. • **BAKE:** 20 min.
MAKES: 6 servings

- 1   beef top sirloin steak (2 lbs.)
- 2   jars (8 oz. each) roasted sweet red peppers, drained and chopped, divided
- 1   pkg. (10 oz.) frozen chopped spinach, thawed and squeezed dry
- 1   carton (8 oz.) spreadable chive and onion cream cheese
- 1   jar (7½ oz.) marinated quartered artichoke hearts, drained and finely chopped
- 2   Tbsp. minced fresh basil or 2 tsp. dried basil
- ¼   tsp. salt
- ¼   tsp. pepper
- 1   jar (24 oz.) pasta sauce
- 1   Tbsp. tomato paste

1. Preheat oven to 425°. Cut steak into 6 serving-size pieces; pound with a meat mallet to ¼-in. thickness. In a large bowl, combine ¼ cup roasted peppers, spinach, cream cheese, artichokes and basil; spread over steaks. Roll up jelly-roll style, starting with a short side. Place seam side down in a greased 13x9-in. baking dish; sprinkle with salt and pepper.
2. Bake until meat reaches desired doneness (for medium-rare, a thermometer should read 135°; medium, 140°; medium-well, 145°), 30-35 minutes.
3. Meanwhile, place the pasta sauce and remaining roasted peppers in a blender; cover and process until smooth. Transfer to a large saucepan; stir in tomato paste. Bring to a boil; reduce heat. Simmer, uncovered, until slightly thickened, 15-20 minutes. Let steaks stand 5 minutes before cutting into 1-in.-thick slices. Serve with sauce.
1 serving: 438 cal., 21g fat (9g sat. fat), 86mg chol., 1326mg sod., 21g carb. (13g sugars, 6g fiber), 38g pro.

TACO BAKED POTATOES

Stuffed with your favorite fixin's, this taco baked potato is an easy meal. Make it vegetarian by using smashed black beans instead of ground beef.
—*Anne Ormond, Dover, NH*

- -

PREP: 10 min. • **BAKE:** 50 min
MAKES: 4 servings

- 4   large baking potatoes
     Olive oil, optional
- 1   lb. lean ground beef (90% lean)
- 1   envelope reduced-sodium taco seasoning
- ⅔   cup water
     Dash salt
     Dash pepper
     Toppings: Salsa, sour cream, Cotija cheese, cubed avocado and chopped green onions

1. Preheat oven to 400°. Scrub potatoes; pierce several times with a fork. If desired, rub with oil. Bake until tender, 50-75 minutes.
2. Meanwhile, in a large skillet, cook beef over medium heat until no longer pink, 6-8 minutes, breaking into crumbles; drain. Stir in taco seasoning and water; bring to a boil. Reduce heat; simmer, uncovered, until thickened, 3-4 minutes, stirring occasionally.
3. With a sharp knife, cut an X in each potato. Fluff pulp with a fork; season with salt and pepper. Spoon beef mixture over top. Serve with toppings.
1 stuffed potato: 484 cal., 10g fat (4g sat. fat), 71mg chol., 600mg sod., 70g carb. (6g sugars, 8g fiber), 29g pro.

**ITALIAN STUFFED
BEEF ROLLS**

BROILED STEAKS WITH PARMESAN-SAGE POTATOES

This five-star meal would likely cost you around $25 in a restaurant, and that's without the tip! Serve this to guests, and they're sure to personally thank the chef.
—Taste of Home *Test Kitchen*

PREP: 20 min. • **BROIL:** 15 min.
MAKES: 4 servings

- 1 tsp. paprika
- 1 tsp. pepper
- 1 tsp. salt, divided
- ½ tsp. sugar
- ½ tsp. garlic powder
- ½ tsp. dried sage leaves, divided
- 4 beef tenderloin steaks (6 oz. each)
- 1 large onion, halved and thinly sliced
- 2 Tbsp. butter
- 2 tsp. brown sugar
- 1 pkg. (24 oz.) refrigerated mashed potatoes
- ½ cup shredded Parmesan cheese

1. Combine the paprika, pepper, ½ tsp. salt, sugar, garlic powder and ¼ tsp. sage; sprinkle onto steaks on both sides.
2. Broil steaks 4 in. from the heat for 7-9 minutes on each side or until meat reaches desired doneness (for medium-rare, a thermometer should read 135°; medium, 140°; medium-well, 145°).
3. Meanwhile, in a large skillet, saute onion in butter until tender. Add brown sugar and remaining salt; saute 1 minute longer.
4. In a small microwave-safe bowl, combine the potatoes, cheese and remaining sage. Microwave, uncovered, on high 2-3 minutes or until heated through. Serve with steaks and onion.
1 serving: 596 cal., 29g fat (19g sat. fat), 115mg chol., 1355mg sod., 38g carb. (7g sugars, 5g fiber), 44g pro.

> ### TEST KITCHEN TIP
> It doesn't take much: Just a tiny amount of sugar and salt in the spice mix helps create a crisp and delicious crust on the outsides of the steaks. Try the same technique with seared chicken breasts, substituting Old Bay seasoning for the pepper.

PHILLY CHEESESTEAK ROLLS

My light take on cheesesteak gets straight to the tender meat, creamy cheese, and sweet and tangy veggies.
—*Paige Day, North Augusta, SC*

PREP: 30 min. • **BAKE:** 15 min.
MAKES: 4 servings

- ½ lb. sliced fresh mushrooms
- 1 medium onion, halved and sliced
- 1 small green pepper, cut into thin strips
- 1 beef top round steak (1 lb.)
- 4 wedges The Laughing Cow light Swiss cheese
- ¼ tsp. pepper
- 3 cups hot mashed potatoes

1. Preheat oven to 450°. Place a large cast-iron or other heavy skillet over medium-high heat. Add mushrooms, onion and green pepper; cook and stir until tender, 8-10 minutes. Remove vegetables from skillet; cool slightly.
2. Cut steak into 4 pieces; pound with a meat mallet to ¼-in. thickness. Spread with cheese. Sprinkle with pepper; top with mushroom mixture. Roll up from a short side; secure with toothpicks. Place back in skillet.
3. Bake until meat reaches desired doneness (for medium-rare, a thermometer should read 135°; medium, 140°, medium-well, 145°), 12-17 minutes. Let stand 5 minutes before serving. Serve with mashed potatoes.
1 roll with ¾ cup mashed potatoes: 364 cal., 10g fat (3g sat. fat), 68mg chol., 822mg sod., 34g carb. (5g sugars, 4g fiber), 33g pro.
Diabetic exchanges: 4 lean meat, 2 starch, 1 vegetable.

PHILLY CHEESESTEAK ROLLS

DELUXE PIZZA CASSEROLE

MEXICAN PIE

This recipe combines a ground beef main dish with a rice side dish to make a hearty, satisfying meal. I prepare this pie often because my husband loves it—and he always asks for second helpings!

—*Denise Simeth, Greendale, WI*

- -

PREP: 25 min. + cooling • **BAKE:** 30 min.
MAKES: 6 servings

RICE CRUST
- 2 cups beef broth
- 1 cup uncooked long grain rice
- 1 Tbsp. butter
- 1 tsp. salt
- 2 large eggs, beaten
- 2 Tbsp. diced pimientos, drained

FILLING
- 1 lb. ground beef
- 1 garlic clove, minced
- 1 tsp. ground cumin
- ½ cup taco sauce
- 1 large egg, beaten

TOPPINGS
- 1 large avocado
- 1 Tbsp. chopped onion
- 1 Tbsp. taco sauce
- ½ tsp. lemon juice
- 1 cup sour cream

1. In a large saucepan, combine beef broth, rice, butter and salt. Cover and cook rice according to package directions. Remove from heat; cool slightly. Stir in eggs and pimientos.
2. Press onto the bottom and up the sides of a greased 10-in. pie plate; set aside. For filling, cook beef until no longer pink; drain. Stir in garlic and cumin; cook for 2 minutes. Remove from heat; stir in taco sauce and egg. Spoon filling into crust. Bake at 350° for 25 minutes.
3. Meanwhile, for guacamole, mash avocado with a fork in a small bowl. Stir in the onion, taco sauce and lemon juice; cover and set aside. Remove pie from oven; spread the guacamole over meat. Top with sour cream. Bake 5 minutes longer.
1 piece: 438 cal., 23g fat (9g sat. fat), 149mg chol., 875mg sod., 32g carb. (3g sugars, 2g fiber), 22g pro.

DELUXE PIZZA CASSEROLE

This is the family's favorite dish for special occasions, and we always make it for my granddaughter's birthday. Mushrooms are a wonderful addition if you like them.

—*Vickie Oldham, Dubuque, IA*

- -

PREP: 30 min. • **BAKE:** 20 min.
MAKES: 12 servings

- 3 cups uncooked spiral pasta
- 1 lb. ground beef
- ½ lb. bulk pork sausage
- 1 medium onion, chopped
- 1 medium green pepper, chopped
- 1 jar (24 oz.) meatless pasta sauce
- 1 can (15 oz.) pizza sauce
- 1 tsp. brown sugar
- 2 cups shredded part-skim mozzarella cheese
- 1 pkg. (3½ oz.) sliced pepperoni
- ¼ cup grated Parmesan cheese

1. Preheat oven to 350°. Cook the pasta according to package directions for al dente; drain. Meanwhile, in a Dutch oven, cook and crumble beef and sausage with onion and pepper over medium-high heat until meat is no longer pink and vegetables are tender, 6-8 minutes; drain.
2. Stir in pasta sauce, pizza sauce and brown sugar. Bring to a boil. Reduce heat; simmer, uncovered, 10 minutes, stirring occasionally. Stir in pasta. Transfer to a greased 13x9-in. baking dish. Top with mozzarella cheese and pepperoni. Sprinkle with Parmesan cheese.
3. Bake, uncovered, until lightly browned and cheese is melted, 20-25 minutes.
1 serving: 346 cal., 17g fat (7g sat. fat), 55mg chol., 797mg sod., 27g carb. (7g sugars, 3g fiber), 20g pro.

CHEESEBURGER
CRESCENT RING

CHEESEBURGER CRESCENT RING

This is an easy entree that can be put together quickly after a long day at work. I guarantee that adults will enjoy it as much as kids do.
—*Stephanie Hurd, Oxford, AL*

TAKES: 45 min. • **MAKES:** 8 servings

- ¾ lb. ground beef
- ½ cup ketchup
- 2 Tbsp. yellow mustard
- 4 slices American cheese, quartered
- ¾ cup dill pickle slices, blotted dry
- 2 tubes (8 oz. each) refrigerated crescent rolls
  Thousand Island salad dressing, optional

1. Preheat oven to 375°. Unroll crescent dough and separate into triangles. On an ungreased 12-in. pizza pan, arrange triangles in a ring with points toward the outside and wide ends overlapping. Press overlapping dough to seal.

2. In a large skillet, cook beef over medium heat until no longer pink, 6-8 minutes, breaking into crumbles; drain. Stir in ketchup and mustard. Remove from the heat.

3. Spoon beef mixture across wide end of triangles. Top with cheese and pickles. Fold pointed end of triangles over filling, tucking points under to form a ring (filling will be visible). Bake 25-30 minutes or until golden brown. If desired, serve with Thousand Island dressing.

1 serving: 333 cal., 18g fat (3g sat. fat), 29mg chol., 899mg sod., 29g carb. (11g sugars, 0 fiber), 14g pro.

DEEP-DISH BEEF & BEAN TACO PIZZA

DEEP-DISH BEEF & BEAN TACO PIZZA

My whole family enjoys this dish that tastes like a taco and looks like deep-dish pizza. The thick, tasty crust can handle lots of toppings, so load it up for a fun meal.
—*Nancy Circle, Perkins, OK*

PREP: 15 min. + resting
BAKE: 15 min. **MAKES:** 8 servings

- 3 cups all-purpose flour
- ½ cup cornmeal
- 1 tsp. salt
- 1 pkg. (¼ oz.) quick-rise yeast
- 2 cups warm water (120° to 130°), divided
- 1 Tbsp. honey
- 1 lb. ground beef
- 1 envelope taco seasoning
- 1 cup refried beans
- ⅓ cup taco sauce
- 2 cups shredded Colby-Monterey Jack cheese

OPTIONAL TOPPINGS
- Shredded lettuce
- Chopped tomatoes
- Crushed tortilla chips
- Sliced ripe olives, drained
- Diced avocado
- Sour cream
- Salsa

1. Preheat oven to 400°. Combine 2½ cups flour, cornmeal, salt and yeast. In another bowl, combine 1¼ cups warm water and honey. Gradually add dry ingredients; beat just until moistened. Stir in enough remaining flour to form a soft dough. Do not knead. Cover; let rest 20 minutes.

2. Meanwhile, in a small skillet over medium heat, cook and stir beef, crumbling meat, until no longer pink; drain. Add the taco seasoning and remaining water. Cook and stir until thickened, about 2 minutes.

3. Press dough to fit a greased 13x9-in. baking pan. Combine beans and taco sauce; spread over dough. Top with beef mixture and cheese. Bake on a lower oven rack until crust is golden and the cheese is melted, 15-18 minutes. Let stand 5 minutes. If desired, serve with optional toppings.

1 piece: 469 cal., 16g fat (9g sat. fat), 60mg chol., 1050mg sod., 55g carb. (3g sugars, 3g fiber), 23g pro.

Poultry

SHEET-PAN TANDOORI CHICKEN

SHEET-PAN TANDOORI CHICKEN

This tandoori chicken recipe is easy for weeknights since it uses just one pan, but it's also special enough for company. The best part is there isn't much to clean up when dinner is over!
—*Anwar Khan, Iriving, TX*

- -

PREP: 20 min. + marinating • **BAKE:** 25 min.
MAKES: 4 servings

- 1 cup plain Greek yogurt
- 3 Tbsp. tandoori masala seasoning
- ⅛ to ¼ tsp. crushed red pepper flakes, optional
- 8 bone-in chicken thighs (about 3 lbs.), skin removed
- 2 medium sweet potatoes, peeled and cut into ½-in. wedges
- 16 cherry tomatoes
- 1 Tbsp. olive oil
  Lemon slices
  Optional: Minced fresh cilantro and naan flatbreads

1. In a large bowl, whisk yogurt, tandoori seasoning and, if desired, pepper flakes until blended. Add the chicken and turn to coat. Cover and refrigerate chicken for 6-8 hours, turning occasionally.

2. Preheat oven to 450°. Drain chicken, discarding marinade in bowl. Place chicken in a greased 15x10x1-in. baking pan. Add sweet potatoes; drizzle with oil. Bake 15 minutes. Add tomatoes and lemon slices. Bake until a thermometer inserted into chicken reads 170°-175°, 10-15 minutes longer. Broil 4-5 in. from the heat until browned, 4-5 minutes. If desired, serve with naan and cilantro.

2 chicken thighs with 1 cup sweet potatoes and 4 tomatoes: 589 cal., 27g fat (9g sat. fat), 186mg chol., 187mg sod., 29g carb. (13g sugars, 6g fiber), 52g pro.

CHICKEN POTPIE

Chicken potpie was a favorite childhood food, but my mother never wrote the recipe down. After some trial and error, I came up with this version. I'm happy to say it tastes just like hers.
—Brenda Sawatzky, Niverville, MB

PREP: 20 min. • **BAKE:** 45 min.
MAKES: 6 servings

- 1 cup chopped celery
- ¼ cup chopped onion
- 2 Tbsp. butter
- 2¼ cups water, divided
- 1½ cups diced cooked chicken
- 1 cup frozen mixed vegetables
- ¾ cup uncooked thin egg noodles
- 1 Tbsp. chicken bouillon granules
- ¼ tsp. pepper
- 2 Tbsp. cornstarch
  Pastry for single-crust pie

1. In a medium saucepan, saute celery and onion in butter until tender. Add 2 cups water, chicken, vegetables, noodles, bouillon and pepper. Cook, uncovered, over medium heat for 5 minutes or just until noodles are tender, stirring occasionally. Combine the cornstarch and remaining water; add to saucepan. Bring to a boil. Reduce the heat; cook and stir for 2 minutes or until thickened and bubbly.

2. Pour into an ungreased 10-in. pie plate. Roll out dough to fit plate; place over filling. Cut several 1-in. slits in the top.

3. Bake at 350° for 45-55 minutes or until lightly browned. Let stand for 5 minutes before serving.

1 piece: 315 cal., 16g fat (7g sat. fat), 53mg chol., 651mg sod., 29g carb. (3g sugars, 2g fiber), 13g pro.

"Really good! I used broken-up angel hair pasta. And instead of pie pastry, I used biscuits from a can."
—JOHNSEN, TASTEOFHOME.COM

GARLIC-GINGER TURKEY TENDERLOINS

GARLIC-GINGER TURKEY TENDERLOINS

This good-for-you entree can be on your family's plates quicker than Chinese takeout—and for less money! Ginger and brown sugar flavor the sauce the turkey while it bakes.
—Taste of Home *Test Kitchen*

TAKES: 30 min. • **MAKES:** 4 servings

- 3 Tbsp. brown sugar, divided
- 2 Tbsp. plus 2 tsp. reduced-sodium soy sauce, divided
- 2 Tbsp. minced fresh gingerroot
- 6 garlic cloves, minced
- ½ tsp. pepper
- 1 pkg. (20 oz.) turkey breast tenderloins
- 1 Tbsp. cornstarch
- 1 cup reduced-sodium chicken broth

1. Preheat oven to 375°. In a small saucepan, mix 2 Tbsp. brown sugar, 2 Tbsp. soy sauce, ginger, garlic and pepper.

2. Place the turkey in a 13x9-in. baking dish coated with cooking spray; drizzle with half of the soy sauce mixture. Bake, uncovered, until a thermometer reads 165°, 25-30 minutes.

3. Meanwhile, add the cornstarch and the remaining brown sugar and soy sauce to the remaining mixture in saucepan; stir until smooth. Stir in broth. Bring to a boil; cook and stir until thickened, 1-2 minutes. Cut turkey into slices; serve with sauce.

4 oz. cooked turkey with 2 Tbsp. sauce: 212 cal., 2g fat (1g sat. fat), 69mg chol., 639mg sod., 14g carb. (10g sugars, 0 fiber), 35g pro. **Diabetic exchanges:** 4 lean meat, 1 starch.

CORNMEAL
OVEN-FRIED
CHICKEN

BUFFALO CHICKEN BISCUITS

These spicy, savory muffins are always a hit at parties. We love them as a simple snack on game day, too.
—*Jasmin Baron, Livonia, NY*

PREP: 20 min. • **BAKE:** 25 min.
MAKES: 1 dozen

- 3 cups chopped rotisserie chicken
- ¼ cup Louisiana-style hot sauce
- 2 cups biscuit/baking mix
- ¼ tsp. celery seed
- ⅛ tsp. pepper
- 1 large egg, room temperature
- ½ cup 2% milk
- ¼ cup ranch salad dressing
- 1½ cups shredded Colby-Monterey Jack cheese, divided
- 2 green onions, thinly sliced
  Optional: Additional ranch dressing and hot sauce

1. Preheat oven to 400°. Toss chicken with hot sauce. In large bowl, whisk together the baking mix, celery seed and pepper. In another bowl, whisk together egg, milk and dressing; add to dry ingredients, stirring just until moistened. Fold in 1 cup cheese, green onions and chicken mixture.

2. Spoon into 12 greased muffin cups. Sprinkle with remaining cheese. Bake until a toothpick inserted in center comes out clean, 25-30 minutes.

3. Cool 5 minutes before removing from pan to a wire rack. Serve warm. If desired, serve biscuits with additional dressing and hot sauce. Refrigerate leftovers.

2 biscuits: 461 cal., 24g fat (10g sat. fat), 121mg chol., 1180mg sod., 29g carb. (3g sugars, 1g fiber), 31g pro.

CORNMEAL OVEN-FRIED CHICKEN

This cornmeal fried chicken dish perks up the dinner table. Its flavorful coating is a good variation from the usual.
—*Deborah Williams, Peoria, AZ*

PREP: 20 min. • **BAKE:** 40 min.
MAKES: 6 servings

- ½ cup dry bread crumbs
- ½ cup cornmeal
- ⅓ cup grated Parmesan cheese
- ¼ cup minced fresh parsley or 4 tsp. dried parsley flakes
- ¾ tsp. garlic powder
- ½ tsp. salt
- ½ tsp. onion powder
- ½ tsp. dried thyme
- ½ tsp. pepper
- ½ cup buttermilk
- 1 broiler/fryer chicken (3 to 4 lbs.), cut up and skin removed
- 1 Tbsp. butter, melted

1. In a large shallow dish, combine the first 9 ingredients. Place buttermilk in a shallow bowl. Dip chicken in buttermilk, then dip in bread crumb mixture, a few pieces at a time, and turn to coat.

2. Place in a 13x9-in. baking pan coated with cooking spray. Bake at 375° for 10 minutes; drizzle with butter. Bake until juices run clear, 30-40 minutes longer.

3 oz. cooked chicken: 244 cal., 9g fat (3g sat. fat), 82mg chol., 303mg sod., 11g carb. (1g sugars, 1g fiber), 27g pro. **Diabetic exchanges:** 3 lean meat, 1 starch, ½ fat.

TEST KITCHEN TIP

Instead of buying buttermilk, you can place 1½ tsp. of white vinegar or lemon juice in a liquid measuring cup and add enough milk to measure ½ cup. Stir, then let stand for 5 minutes.

BUFFALO CHICKEN
BISCUITS

MEXICAN TURKEY HASH BROWN BAKE

Here's a hearty, easy dinner casserole that really delivers on nutrition and flavor!
—*Tim Ash, Salem, IN*

PREP: 20 min. • **BAKE:** 35 min.
MAKES: 6 servings

1	lb. lean ground turkey
¼	cup chopped onion
3	garlic cloves, minced
1	pkg. (32 oz.) frozen cubed hash brown potatoes, thawed
1	can (10 oz.) enchilada sauce
1	can (8 oz.) tomato sauce
1	can (4 oz.) chopped green chiles
1	Tbsp. reduced-sodium taco seasoning
1	cup shredded cheddar cheese Reduced-fat sour cream, optional

1. In a large skillet, cook the turkey, onion and garlic over medium heat until the meat is no longer pink. Add the hash browns, enchilada sauce, tomato sauce, green chiles and taco seasoning; heat through.
2. Transfer to a 13x9-in. baking dish coated with cooking spray.
3. Cover and bake at 375° for 30 minutes. Sprinkle with cheese; bake, uncovered, until cheese is melted, 5-10 minutes longer. Serve with sour cream if desired.

1⅓ cups: 330 cal., 12g fat (6g sat. fat), 80mg chol., 799mg sod., 35g carb. (3g sugars, 4g fiber), 23g pro. **Diabetic exchanges:** 3 lean meat, 2 starch, 1 fat.

CHICKEN DINNER POPPERS

I could eat jalapeno poppers all day long, but who wants to say they had seven stuffed peppers for dinner? For this tasty meal, I use poblanos for my husband and son, and hotter peppers for my daughter and me.
—*Sherri Jerzyk, Somerville, TX*

PREP: 20 min. • **BAKE:** 25 min.
MAKES: 4 servings

4	bacon strips
4	chicken tenderloins
¼	tsp. salt
⅛	tsp. pepper
2	tsp. canola oil
4	poblano peppers
1½	cups shredded cheddar cheese, divided
4	oz. cream cheese, cut into 4 strips

1. Preheat oven to 350°. In a large skillet, cook bacon over medium heat until partially cooked but not crisp. Remove to paper towels to drain.
2. Sprinkle chicken with salt and pepper. In a skillet, heat oil over medium-high heat; brown tenderloins on both sides. Cool slightly.
3. Carefully cut a slit down the side of each pepper and remove seeds. Fill each with one tenderloin; top each with 2 Tbsp. cheese and a strip of cream cheese. Close peppers; wrap with bacon and secure with toothpicks.
4. Place on a foil-lined baking sheet, slit side up. Top with the remaining cheddar cheese; bake until browned and the peppers are tender, 25-30 minutes. Remove toothpicks before serving.

1 serving: 389 cal., 30g fat (15g sat. fat), 96mg chol., 682mg sod., 9g carb. (4g sugars, 2g fiber), 23g pro.

CHICKEN DINNER POPPERS

CHICKEN & SWEET
POTATO POTPIE

CHICKEN & SWEET POTATO POTPIE

Chicken potpie is a top-10 comfort food for me. To save time, I use ready-made phyllo dough and rotisserie chicken. For nutrition, I add sweet potatoes and red peppers.
—*Jacyn Siebert, San Francisco, CA*

- -

PREP: 40 min. • **BAKE:** 10 min.
MAKES: 6 servings

- 2 tsp. olive oil
- ½ lb. sliced fresh mushrooms
- 1 small onion, chopped
- 1 large sweet potato, cubed
- 1 cup chopped sweet red pepper
- ½ cup chopped celery
- 2 cups reduced-sodium chicken broth, divided
- ⅓ cup all-purpose flour
- ½ cup 2% milk
- 1 skinned rotisserie chicken, shredded
- 2 Tbsp. sherry or reduced-sodium chicken broth

- ¾ tsp. minced fresh rosemary
- ½ tsp. salt
- ½ tsp. dried thyme
- ¼ tsp. pepper
- 5 sheets phyllo dough (14x9-in. size)
     Butter-flavored cooking spray

1. Preheat oven to 425°. In a large skillet, heat oil over medium-high heat. Add the mushrooms and onion; cook and stir until tender, 3-4 minutes. Stir in sweet potato, red pepper and celery; cook 5 minutes longer. Add ¼ cup chicken broth. Reduce the heat; cook, covered, over medium-low heat until vegetables are tender, 6-8 minutes.

2. Sprinkle flour over vegetables; cook and stir 1 minute. Gradually add milk and the remaining broth. Bring to a boil; cook and stir until thickened, 1-2 minutes. Stir in chicken, sherry or broth and seasonings. Transfer to an 11x7-in. baking dish coated with cooking spray. Bake, uncovered, until heated through, 10-15 minutes.

3. Meanwhile, stack all 5 sheets of phyllo dough. Roll up lengthwise; cut crosswise into

½-in.-wide strips. In a bowl, toss strips to separate; spritz with butter-flavored spray. Place on an ungreased baking sheet; spritz again. Bake until golden brown, 4-5 minutes. Arrange over chicken mixture.

1 cup: 329 cal., 10g fat (2g sat. fat), 75mg chol., 517mg sod., 30g carb. (10g sugars, 3g fiber), 30g pro. **Diabetic exchanges:** 4 lean meat, 2 starch, ½ fat.

TEST KITCHEN TIP

To shred chicken fast, just reach for your mixer. Place chicken in the bowl and use the stand mixer's paddle attachment to quickly break up the meat for casseroles and other recipes.

CHINESE CASHEW
CHICKEN PIZZA

CHINESE CASHEW CHICKEN PIZZA

I make this quick weeknight dinner recipe when I'm craving takeout pizza and Chinese food. I like using shortcuts like premade pizza crust and rotisserie chicken to cut down on my time in the kitchen.
—*Joseph A. Sciascia, San Mateo, CA*

TAKES: 30 min. • **MAKES:** 8 servings

- 1 prebaked 12-in. pizza crust or flatbread
- 1 Tbsp. sesame oil
- ¾ cup hoisin sauce
- 2 tsp. chili garlic sauce
- 1½ cups shredded cooked chicken
- 4 green onions, chopped, divided
- ½ cup chopped sweet red pepper
- ⅓ cup shredded carrots
- ½ cup chopped cashews
- 3 Tbsp. chopped fresh cilantro
- 1¼ cups shredded mozzarella cheese

1. Preheat oven to 425°. Place pizza crust on a pizza pan; brush with sesame oil. In small bowl, combine hoisin sauce and chili garlic sauce; brush ⅓ cup over crust. Toss the remaining mixture with chicken; sprinkle over crust. Top with 2 green onions, red pepper, carrots, cashews and cilantro. Sprinkle mozzarella over top.
2. Bake pizza until cheese is lightly browned, 12-15 minutes. Let stand 5 minutes; sprinkle with remaining 2 green onions.
1 slice: 357 cal., 15g fat (5g sat. fat), 38mg chol., 876mg sod., 37g carb. (9g sugars, 2g fiber), 19g pro.

SOUTHWEST-STYLE SHEPHERD'S PIE

SOUTHWEST-STYLE SHEPHERD'S PIE

I was born in Montreal and lived in New England and the Southwest, so I've merged these influences into recipes like this shepherd's pie with turkey, corn and green chiles.
—*Lynn Price, Millville, MA*

PREP: 20 min. • **BAKE:** 25 min.
MAKES: 6 servings

- 1¼ lbs. lean ground turkey
- 1 small onion, chopped
- 2 garlic cloves, minced
- ½ tsp. salt, divided
- 1 can (14¾ oz.) cream-style corn
- 1 can (4 oz.) chopped green chiles
- 1 to 2 Tbsp. chipotle hot pepper sauce, optional
- 2⅔ cups water
- 2 Tbsp. butter
- 2 Tbsp. half-and-half cream
- ½ tsp. pepper
- 2 cups mashed potato flakes

1. Preheat oven to 425°. In a large skillet, cook turkey, onion, garlic and ¼ tsp. salt over medium heat 8-10 minutes or until turkey is no longer pink and onion is tender, breaking up turkey into crumbles. Stir in corn, green chiles and, if desired, pepper sauce. Transfer to a greased 8-in. square baking dish.
2. Meanwhile, in a saucepan, bring water, butter, cream, pepper and remaining salt to a boil. Remove from heat. Stir in potato flakes. Spoon over turkey mixture, spreading to cover. Bake until bubbly and potatoes are light brown, 25-30 minutes.
Freeze option: Thaw unbaked casserole in the refrigerator overnight. Remove from the refrigerator 30 minutes before baking. Bake at 425° as directed until a thermometer inserted in center reads 165°.
1 cup: 312 cal., 12g fat (5g sat. fat), 78mg chol., 583mg sod., 31g carb. (4g sugars, 3g fiber), 22g pro. **Diabetic exchanges:** 3 lean meat, 2 starch, 1 fat.

GOAT CHEESE & SPINACH STUFFED CHICKEN

SHEET-PAN TACO TURKEY MEAT LOAF

I bought a supersized package of ground turkey and wanted something other than turkey burgers for a month! I adapted this meat loaf using what I had on hand and it's become a family favorite with everyone. I serve it for tailgating parties, and it's delicious the next day for sandwiches!
—*Holly Battiste, Barrington, NJ*

PREP: 25 min. • **BAKE:** 70 min. + standing
MAKES: 2 loaves (8 servings each)

- 2 large eggs, lightly beaten
- 1 cup cooked brown rice
- 1 medium onion, grated
- ½ cup shredded Monterey Jack cheese
- ¼ cup dry bread crumbs
- ¼ cup grated Romano cheese
- ¼ cup tomato sauce
- 1 envelope taco seasoning
- 2 garlic cloves, minced
- ½ tsp. pepper
- 3 lbs. ground turkey

TOPPING

- 1 cup tomato sauce
- ½ cup shredded Monterey Jack cheese
- ¼ cup grated Romano cheese

1. Preheat oven to 350°. In a large bowl, combine the first 10 ingredients. Add turkey; mix lightly but thoroughly. Shape into two 7½ x 4½-in. loaves. Place in a greased shallow baking pan.
2. Bake 1 hour. Mix together the topping ingredients; spread over loaves. Bake until a thermometer reads 165°, 10-15 minutes longer. Let stand 10 minutes before slicing.
Freeze option: Bake meat loaves without sauce. Securely wrap and freeze the cooled meat loaves in foil. To use, partially thaw in refrigerator overnight. Unwrap meat loaves and place in a greased shallow baking pan. Prepare topping as directed; spread over meat loaves. Reheat meat loaf in a preheated 350° oven until heated through and a thermometer inserted in center reads 165°. Let stand for 10 minutes before slicing.
1 slice: 211 cal., 11g fat (4g sat. fat), 86mg chol., 456mg sod., 8g carb. (1g sugars, 1g fiber), 22g pro. **Diabetic exchanges:** 3 lean meat, ½ starch, ½ fat.

GOAT CHEESE & SPINACH STUFFED CHICKEN

This spinach-stuffed chicken breast recipe is special to me because it has so much flavor, yet not too many calories. I love Italian food, but most of the time it is too heavy. This is a healthy twist on an Italian dish!
—*Nicole Stevens, Charleston, SC*

PREP: 30 min. • **BAKE:** 20 min.
MAKES: 2 servings

- 1½ cups fresh spinach, chopped
- ⅓ cup julienned soft sun-dried tomatoes (not packed in oil), chopped
- ¼ cup crumbled goat cheese
- 2 garlic cloves, minced
- ½ tsp. pepper, divided
- ¼ tsp. salt, divided
- 2 boneless skinless chicken breasts (6 oz. each)
- 1 Tbsp. olive oil, divided
- ½ lb. fresh asparagus, trimmed
  Aged balsamic vinegar or balsamic glaze, optional

1. Preheat oven to 400°. In small bowl, combine the spinach, sun-dried tomatoes, goat cheese, minced garlic, ¼ tsp. pepper and ⅛ tsp. salt.
2. Cut a pocket horizontally in the thickest part of each chicken breast. Fill with spinach mixture; secure with toothpicks.
3. In an 8-in. cast-iron or ovenproof skillet, heat 1½ tsp. oil over medium heat. Brown chicken on each side. Place in oven; bake 10 minutes.
4. Toss the asparagus with remaining 1½ tsp. oil, ¼ tsp. pepper, and ⅛ tsp. salt; add to the skillet. Bake for 10-15 minutes longer or until a thermometer inserted in chicken reads 165° and asparagus is tender. If desired, drizzle with vinegar. Discard toothpicks before serving.
Note: This recipe was tested with soft sun-dried tomatoes that do not need to be softened in hot water.
1 stuffed chicken breast: 347 cal., 14g fat (4g sat. fat), 111mg chol., 532mg sod., 13g carb. (6g sugars, 5g fiber), 39g pro. **Diabetic exchanges:** 7 lean meat, 1 vegetable, 1 fat.

SHEET-PAN TACO
TURKEY MEAT LOAF

SPINACH TURKEY MEATBALLS

Our children call these Gramby Meatballs because the recipe came from my dear mother-in-law. It's a great way to make spinach palatable to the kids. I usually make a triple batch, bake them all and freeze the extras for a quick meal later.
—*Mimi Blanco, Bronxville, NY*

TAKES: 30 min. • **MAKES:** 4 servings

- 1 pkg. (10 oz.) frozen chopped spinach, thawed and squeezed dry
- 1 large egg, beaten
- 1 cup soft bread crumbs
- 2 Tbsp. grated onion
- 1 tsp. seasoned salt
- 1 lb. ground turkey
  Hot cooked pasta, optional

1. In a bowl, combine spinach, egg, bread crumbs, onion and seasoned salt. Add turkey and mix well. Shape into 2-in. balls.

2. Place meatballs on a greased rack in a shallow baking pan. Bake, uncovered, at 400° for 20 minutes or until the meat is no longer pink. Drain on paper towels. If desired, serve meatballs with pasta.

3 meatballs: 295 cal., 19g fat (6g sat. fat), 130mg chol., 626mg sod., 10g carb. (1g sugars, 2g fiber), 23g pro. **Diabetic exchanges:** 3 medium-fat meat, ½ starch.

BAKED CHICKEN FAJITAS

BAKED CHICKEN FAJITAS

I can't remember when or where I found this baked fajitas recipe, but I've used it nearly every week since. We like it with hot sauce for added spice.
—*Amy Trinkle, Milwaukee, WI*

PREP: 15 min. • **BAKE:** 20 min.
MAKES: 6 servings

- 1 lb. boneless skinless chicken breasts, cut into thin strips
- 1 can (14½ oz.) diced tomatoes and green chiles, drained
- 1 medium onion, cut into thin strips
- 1 medium green pepper, cut into thin strips
- 1 medium sweet red pepper, cut into thin strips
- 2 Tbsp. canola oil
- 2 tsp. chili powder
- 2 tsp. ground cumin
- ¼ tsp. salt
- 12 flour tortillas (6 in.), warmed
  Optional toppings: Sliced avocado, tomato wedges and lime wedges

1. In a 13x9-in. baking dish coated with cooking spray, combine the chicken strips, tomatoes, onion and peppers. Combine the oil, chili powder, cumin and salt. Drizzle over chicken mixture; toss to coat.

2. Bake, uncovered, at 400° until chicken is no longer pink and vegetables are tender, 20-25 minutes. Spoon onto tortillas; fold or roll tortillas to serve. Serve with optional toppings as desired.

2 fajitas: 375 cal., 14g fat (3g sat. fat), 42mg chol., 838mg sod., 40g carb. (3g sugars, 5g fiber), 22g pro.

CREAMY CHICKEN TETRAZZINI CASSEROLE

This creamy tetrazzini has been one of my favorite recipes for over 20 years. I always hear, "Yum. Is there any more?" Even overnight guests ask for leftovers the next day!

—*Amanda Hertz-Crisel, Eagle Point, OR*

PREP: 30 min. • **BAKE:** 30 min.
MAKES: 6 servings

- 12 oz. uncooked spaghetti
- 1 small onion, chopped
- 1 celery rib, chopped
- ¼ cup butter, cubed
- 1 can (14 oz.) chicken broth
- 1½ cups half-and-half cream
- 1 pkg. (8 oz.) cream cheese, cubed
- 2 cups cubed cooked chicken
- 1 can (4 oz.) mushroom stems and pieces, drained
- 2 to 4 Tbsp. sliced pimientos
- ½ tsp. salt
- ¼ tsp. pepper
- ½ cup sliced almonds, toasted
- ¼ cup grated Parmesan cheese
- ¼ cup crushed potato chips

1. Cook spaghetti according to the package directions. Meanwhile, in a large skillet, saute onion and celery in butter until tender. Stir in the broth, cream and cream cheese. Cook and stir just until cheese is melted. Remove from the heat.

2. Stir in the chicken, mushrooms, pimientos, salt and pepper. Drain spaghetti; add to the chicken mixture and toss to coat. Transfer to a greased 13x9-in. baking dish.

3. Bake, uncovered, at 350° for 20 minutes. Sprinkle with almonds, Parmesan cheese and chips. Bake 10-15 minutes longer or until heated through and topping is golden brown.

1½ cups: 665 cal., 37g fat (19g sat. fat), 134mg chol., 871mg sod., 52g carb. (6g sugars, 3g fiber), 29g pro.

CREAMY CHICKEN
TETRAZZINI CASSEROLE

CHIP-CRUSTED CHICKEN

Dijon-mayo and BBQ potato chips might sound strange together, but the flavors combine beautifully in this entree. And really, could it be any easier?

—*Mike Tchou, Pepper Pike, OH*

TAKES: 30 min. • **MAKES:** 6 servings

- ⅔ cup Dijon-mayonnaise blend
- 6 cups barbecue potato chips, finely crushed
- 6 boneless skinless chicken breast halves (5 oz. each)

1. Place mayonnaise blend and potato chips in separate shallow bowls. Dip chicken in mayonnaise blend, then coat with chips.

2. Place on an ungreased baking sheet. Bake at 375° until a thermometer reads 165°, 20-25 minutes.

1 serving: 397 cal., 16g fat (5g sat. fat), 78mg chol., 1015mg sod., 29g carb. (1g sugars, 1g fiber), 30g pro.

CURRY-ROASTED TURKEY & POTATOES

Honey mustard is the preferred condiment around here, so I wanted a healthy recipe to serve it with. Roasted turkey with a dash of curry complements it nicely.
—Carol Witczak, Tinley Park, IL

- -

TAKES: 30 min. • **MAKES:** 4 servings

- 1 lb. Yukon Gold potatoes (about 3 medium), cut into ½-in. cubes
- 2 medium leeks (white portion only), thinly sliced
- 2 Tbsp. canola oil, divided
- ½ tsp. pepper, divided
- ¼ tsp. salt, divided
- 3 Tbsp. Dijon mustard
- 3 Tbsp. honey
- ¾ tsp. curry powder
- 1 pkg. (17.6 oz.) turkey breast cutlets
  Minced fresh cilantro or thinly sliced green onions, optional

1. Preheat oven to 450°. Place potatoes and leeks in a 15x10x1-in. baking pan coated with cooking spray. Drizzle with 1 Tbsp. oil; sprinkle with ¼ tsp. pepper and ⅛ tsp. salt. Stir to coat. Roast 15 minutes, stirring once.
2. Meanwhile, in a small bowl, combine the mustard, honey, curry powder and the remaining oil. Sprinkle turkey with remaining salt and pepper.
3. Drizzle 2 Tbsp. mustard mixture over potatoes; stir to coat. Place turkey over potato mixture; drizzle with remaining mustard mixture. Roast 6-8 minutes longer or until turkey is no longer pink and potatoes are tender. If desired, sprinkle with cilantro.

3 oz. cooked turkey with ¾ cup potato mixture: 393 cal., 9g fat (1g sat. fat), 71mg chol., 582mg sod., 44g carb. (16g sugars, 3g fiber), 33g pro. **Diabetic exchanges:** 4 lean meat, 3 starch, 1½ fat.

TURKEY & VEGETABLE SHEET-PAN SUPPER

My family loves turkey tenderloins so I tried them in a sheet-pan supper. I used ingredients I had on hand including bacon, which gives a nice smoky flavor. It's perfect because it's so quick and easy to prepare.
—Susan Bickta, Kutztown, PA

- -

PREP: 15 min. • **BAKE:** 30 min.
MAKES: 6 servings

- 6 bacon strips
- 2 medium potatoes, cut into ½-in. pieces
- 4 medium carrots, peeled and cut into ½-in. pieces
- 2 medium onions, cut into ½-in. pieces
- 2 tsp. canola oil
- 1 tsp. salt, divided
- ½ tsp. pepper, divided
- 1 pkg. (20 oz.) turkey breast tenderloins
  Minced fresh parsley, optional

1. Preheat oven to 375°. Line a 15x10x1-in. baking pan with aluminum foil. Place bacon on prepared pan; bake 15 minutes.
2. Meanwhile, in a large bowl, toss potatoes, carrots and onions with oil; sprinkle with ½ tsp. salt and ¼ tsp. pepper. Sprinkle remaining salt and pepper on tenderloins.
3. Remove par-cooked bacon from baking pan. Transfer vegetables to pan, spreading evenly. Place the tenderloins on top of the vegetables; cover with bacon slices.
4. Bake until a thermometer reads 165° and vegetables are tender, 30-35 minutes. If desired, top with parsley to serve.

3 oz. cooked turkey with ⅔ cup vegetables: 238 cal., 11g fat (3g sat. fat), 42mg chol., 500mg sod., 15g carb. (3g sugars, 2g fiber), 22g pro. **Diabetic exchanges:** 3 lean meat, 1 vegetable, ½ starch.

CURRY-ROASTED TURKEY & POTATOES

**TURKEY & VEGETABLE
SHEET-PAN SUPPER**

TURKEY & BLACK BEAN
ENCHILADA CASSEROLE

TURKEY & BLACK BEAN ENCHILADA CASSEROLE

When I don't feel like pulling out the slow cooker, my next favorite weeknight meal is a warm casserole! This recipe is easy and tasty, and it's gluten-free.
—*Kristine Fretwell, Mission, BC*

PREP: 25 min. • **BAKE:** 25 min. + standing
MAKES: 8 servings

- 1 lb. lean ground turkey
- 1 medium green pepper, chopped
- 1 medium onion, chopped
- 1½ tsp. garlic powder
- 1½ tsp. ground cumin
- 1 can (15 oz.) tomato sauce
- 1 can (14½ oz.) stewed tomatoes, undrained
- 1½ cups salsa
- 1 can (15 oz.) black beans, rinsed and drained
- 8 corn tortillas (6 in.)
- 2 cups shredded reduced-fat Mexican cheese blend, divided
   Optional: Shredded lettuce, chopped tomatoes, plain Greek yogurt and chopped fresh cilantro

1. Cook the turkey, pepper, onion and spices in a large skillet over medium heat until meat is no longer pink. Stir in tomato sauce, stewed tomatoes and salsa; bring to a boil. Reduce the heat; simmer, uncovered, for 5 minutes, breaking up tomatoes with the back of a spoon. Add beans; heat through.
2. Spread 1 cup meat mixture into a greased 13x9-in. baking dish. Top with 4 tortillas. Spread with half of remaining meat mixture; sprinkle with 1 cup cheese. Layer with remaining tortillas and meat mixture.
3. Cover and bake at 350° for 20 minutes. Sprinkle with the remaining cheese. Bake, uncovered, until bubbly and cheese is melted, 5-10 minutes longer. Let stand 10 minutes. If desired, serve with toppings.
Freeze option: Cover and freeze unbaked casserole. To use, partially thaw in the refrigerator overnight. Remove from the refrigerator 30 minutes before baking. Bake casserole as directed, increasing time as necessary for a thermometer to read 165°.
1 piece: 313 cal., 12g fat (5g sat. fat), 54mg chol., 853mg sod., 31g carb. (6g sugars, 6g fiber), 25g pro. **Diabetic exchanges:** 3 medium-fat meat, 2 starch.

CHICKEN CORDON BLEU
CRESCENT RING

CHICKEN CORDON BLEU CRESCENT RING

A classic cordon bleu has chicken, Swiss cheese and ham. To change it up, roll everything inside crescent dough for a delicious handheld.
—*Stella Culotta, Pasadena, MD*

TAKES: 30 min. • **MAKES:** 6 servings

- 1 tube (8 oz.) refrigerated crescent rolls
- 2 cups shredded Swiss cheese
- 2 cups cubed cooked chicken
- ¾ cup mayonnaise
- ½ cup cubed fully cooked ham
- 2 Tbsp. honey mustard

1. Preheat oven to 375°. Unroll crescent dough and separate into triangles. On an ungreased 12-in. pizza pan, arrange triangles in a ring with points toward the outside and wide ends overlapping. Press overlapping dough to seal.
2. In a large bowl, mix the remaining ingredients. Spoon across wide ends of triangles. Fold pointed ends of triangles over filling, tucking points under to form a ring (filling will be visible).
3. Bake 15-20 minutes or until golden brown and heated through.
1 slice: 603 cal., 45g fat (13g sat. fat), 91mg chol., 772mg sod., 19g carb. (6g sugars, 0 fiber), 29g pro.

CHICKEN & SPAGHETTI SQUASH

While dreaming up a healthier pasta dish, I decided to experiment with spaghetti squash.
—*Christina Morris, Agoura Hills, CA*

PREP: 45 min. • **BAKE:** 20 min.
MAKES: 5 servings

- 1 medium spaghetti squash (4 lbs.)
- 1 can (14½ oz.) diced tomatoes, undrained
- 2 Tbsp. prepared pesto
- ½ tsp. garlic powder
- ½ tsp. Italian seasoning
- ¼ cup dry bread crumbs
- ¼ cup shredded Parmesan cheese
- 1 lb. boneless skinless chicken breasts, cut into ½-in. cubes
- 1 Tbsp. plus 1 tsp. olive oil, divided
- ½ lb. sliced fresh mushrooms
- 1 medium onion, chopped
- 1 garlic clove, minced
- ½ cup chicken broth
- ⅓ cup shredded cheddar cheese

1. Cut squash in half lengthwise; discard seeds. Place the squash cut side down on a microwave-safe plate. Microwave, uncovered, on high for 14-16 minutes or until tender.

2. Meanwhile, in a blender, combine the tomatoes, pesto, garlic powder and Italian seasoning. Cover and process until blended; set aside. In a small bowl, combine bread crumbs and Parmesan cheese; set aside.

3. In a large skillet, cook chicken in 1 Tbsp. oil until no longer pink; remove and keep warm. In the same skillet, saute mushrooms and onion in remaining oil until tender. Add garlic; cook 1 minute longer. Stir in chicken broth, chicken and reserved tomato mixture. Bring to a boil. Reduce heat; simmer, uncovered, for 5 minutes.

4. When squash is cool enough to handle, use a fork to separate the strands. In a large ovenproof skillet, layer half of the squash, chicken mixture and reserved crumb mixture. Repeat layers.

5. Bake, uncovered, at 350° for 15 minutes or until heated through. Sprinkle with cheddar cheese. Broil 3-4 in. from heat until golden brown, 5-6 minutes.

1½ cups: 348 cal., 14g fat (5g sat. fat), 63mg chol., 493mg sod., 32g carb. (6g sugars, 7g fiber), 27g pro.

CHICKEN VERDE QUESADILLAS

CHICKEN VERDE QUESADILLAS

I used the corn, peppers and zucchini in my fridge to create these quick and easy quesadillas. Dollop with sour cream and you're good to go.
—*Julie Merriman, Seattle, WA*

TAKES: 30 min. • **MAKES:** 4 servings

- 2 Tbsp. olive oil, divided
- 1 large sweet onion, halved and thinly sliced
- 1½ cups (about 7½ oz.) frozen corn
- 1 small zucchini, chopped
- 1 poblano pepper, thinly sliced
- 2 cups frozen grilled chicken breast strips, thawed and chopped
- ¾ cup green enchilada sauce
- ¼ cup minced fresh cilantro
- ¼ tsp. salt
- ⅛ tsp. pepper
- 8 flour tortillas (10 in.)
- 4 cups shredded Monterey Jack cheese
  Optional: Pico de gallo and sour cream

1. Preheat oven to 400°. In a large skillet, heat 1 Tbsp. oil over medium-high heat. Add the onion, corn, zucchini and poblano pepper; cook and stir until tender, 8-10 minutes. Add chicken, enchilada sauce, cilantro, salt and pepper; heat through.

2. Brush remaining oil over 1 side of each tortilla. Place half of the tortillas on 2 baking sheets, oiled side down. Sprinkle each with ½ cup cheese and top with 1 cup chicken mixture, remaining cheese and remaining tortillas, oiled side up. Bake until golden brown and cheese is melted, 7-9 minutes. If desired, serve with pico de gallo and sour cream.

1 quesadilla: 1083 cal., 55g fat (27g sat. fat), 132mg chol., 2449mg sod., 94g carb. (13g sugars, 8g fiber), 56g pro.

MIMOSA ROASTED CHICKEN

This aromatic seasoned chicken with a rich and buttery champagne gravy will delight all who taste it.
—Taste of Home *Test Kitchen*

- -

PREP: 15 min. • **BAKE:** 2¼ hours + standing
MAKES: 6 servings

- 2 **medium navel oranges**
- 1 **roasting chicken (6 to 7 lbs.)**
- ¾ **tsp. pepper, divided**
- ¼ **cup butter, softened**
- 4 **garlic cloves, minced**
- 1 **Tbsp. dried basil**
- 1 **tsp. salt**
- ½ **tsp. onion powder**
- ½ **tsp. dried marjoram**
- 2 **cups brut champagne**
- 2 **medium onions, cut into wedges**
- ½ **cup chicken broth**
- ½ **cup orange juice**

GRAVY
- **Chicken broth or water**
- 1 **Tbsp. butter**
- 2 **Tbsp. all-purpose flour**

1. Cut 1 orange into slices; cut remaining orange into wedges. With fingers, carefully loosen the skin from both sides of chicken breast. Place orange slices under the skin. Place orange wedges inside cavity and sprinkle with ¼ tsp. pepper.

2. Tuck wings under chicken. Place breast side up on a rack in a shallow roasting pan. Combine the butter, garlic, basil, salt, onion powder, marjoram and remaining pepper; rub over chicken.

3. Bake, uncovered, at 350° for 30 minutes. Meanwhile, in a large bowl, combine the champagne, onions, broth and orange juice; pour into pan. Bake until a thermometer reads 175°, 1½-2 hours longer, basting occasionally with pan juices. Cover loosely with foil if chicken browns too quickly. Cover and let stand for 15 minutes before slicing.

4. For gravy, pour drippings and loosened browned bits into a measuring cup. Skim fat, reserving 1 Tbsp.. Add enough broth to the drippings to measure 1 cup. In a small saucepan, melt butter and reserved fat. Stir in flour until smooth, gradually add broth mixture. Bring mixture to a boil; cook and stir until thickened, about 2 minutes. Serve with chicken.

6 oz. cooked chicken with 2 Tbsp. gravy: 731 cal., 41g fat (15g sat. fat), 204mg chol., 798mg sod., 17g carb. (9g sugars, 2g fiber), 58g pro.

TEST KITCHEN TIP
Need a special dish for a small holiday gathering? This fragrant orange chicken will be a hit.

MIMOSA ROASTED CHICKEN

**CHICKEN & BROCCOLI
LASAGNA ROLLS**

APPLE CIDER CHICKEN & DUMPLINGS

I came up with this recipe one fall when I had an abundance of apple cider. Adding some to a down-home classic was a delectable decision—everyone loved it!

—Margaret Sumner-Wichmann, Questa, NM

- -

PREP: 10 min. • **BAKE:** 65 min.
MAKES: 4 servings

8	bone-in chicken thighs (3 lbs.), skin removed
2	Tbsp. butter
1	medium red onion, chopped
1	celery rib, chopped
2	Tbsp. minced fresh parsley
	Salt and pepper to taste
3	Tbsp. all-purpose flour
3	cups chicken broth
1	cup apple cider or juice

DUMPLINGS

2	cups all-purpose flour
1	Tbsp. baking powder
½	tsp. salt
1	Tbsp. cold butter
1	large egg, lightly beaten
⅔	cup 2% milk

1. In a Dutch oven, brown chicken in butter; remove and set aside. In same pan, combine the onion, celery, parsley, salt and pepper; cook and stir until vegetables are tender. Sprinkle with flour and mix well. Add broth and cider. Bring to a boil; cook and stir until thickened, about 2 minutes. Add chicken.

2. Cover and bake at 350° for 45-50 minutes. Increase heat to 425°.

3. For dumplings, combine the flour, baking powder and salt in a bowl; cut in butter until crumbly. Combine egg and milk; stir into the dry ingredients just until moistened. Drop batter into 12 mounds onto hot broth.

4. Bake, uncovered, at 425° for 10 minutes. Cover and bake 10 minutes longer or until a toothpick inserted into a dumpling comes out clean.

1 serving: 721 cal., 27g fat (11g sat. fat), 220mg chol., 1548mg sod., 65g carb. (12g sugars, 3g fiber), 50g pro.

❄

CHICKEN & BROCCOLI LASAGNA ROLLS

Take pasta to new heights with these roll-ups. A cheesy mixture of chicken and broccoli fills the lasagna noodles, and the recipe makes enough for two dinners. It's nice to have a pan of these roll-ups in the freezer for unexpected company.

—Darlene Brenden, Salem, OR

- -

PREP: 20 min. • **BAKE:** 45 min.
MAKES: 2 casseroles (3 servings each)

1	small onion, chopped
3	Tbsp. butter
3	Tbsp. all-purpose flour
1	can (14½ oz.) chicken broth
1	cup whole milk
1½	cups shredded Monterey Jack cheese
3	cups diced cooked chicken
6	cups frozen chopped broccoli, thawed and drained
2	large eggs, lightly beaten
¾	cup dry bread crumbs
1	jar (6½ oz.) diced pimientos, drained
¼	cup minced fresh parsley
½	tsp. salt, optional
12	lasagna noodles, cooked and drained

1. In a large saucepan, saute onion in butter until tender. Stir in the flour until blended. Gradually add broth and milk. Bring to a boil; cook and stir for 2 minutes or until thickened. Remove from the heat; stir in cheese. Pour ⅓ cup each into 2 greased 8-in. square baking dishes; set aside.

2. In a large bowl, combine 1 cup cheese sauce, chicken, broccoli, eggs, bread crumbs, pimientos, parsley and salt if desired. Spread about ½ cup over each noodle. Roll up jelly-roll style, beginning with a short side; secure ends with toothpicks.

3. Place 6 roll-ups curly end down in each baking dish. Top with remaining cheese sauce.

4. Cover and freeze 1 casserole for up to 3 months. Cover and bake the second casserole at 350° for 40 minutes or until a thermometer reads 160°. Uncover; bake 5 minutes longer or until bubbly. Discard the toothpicks.

5. To use frozen casserole, thaw in the refrigerator for 8 hours or overnight. Bake as directed.

2 roll-ups: 617 cal., 24g fat (12g sat. fat), 179mg chol., 914mg sod., 58g carb. (6g sugars, 4g fiber), 42g pro.

APPLE CIDER CHICKEN
& DUMPLINGS

OVERNIGHT CHICKEN CASSEROLE

I don't know where this casserole originated, but the recipe was given to me some 40 years ago. It's my family's all-time favorite. Not only is it a great company meal, it's also well-received at potluck dinners.
—Johnie Mae Barber, Oklahoma City, OK

PREP: 20 min. + chilling
BAKE: 1¼ hours + standing
MAKES: 10 servings

- 8   slices day-old white bread
- 4   cups chopped cooked chicken
- 1   jar (4½ oz.) sliced mushrooms, drained
- 1   can (8 oz.) sliced water chestnuts, drained
- 4   large eggs, lightly beaten
- 2   cups whole milk
- ½   cup mayonnaise
- ½   tsp. salt
- 6   to 8 slices process American cheese
- 1   can (10¾ oz.) condensed cream of celery soup, undiluted
- 1   can (10¾ oz.) condensed cream of mushroom soup, undiluted
- 1   jar (2 oz.) chopped pimientos, drained
- 2   Tbsp. butter, melted

1. Remove the crusts from bread and set aside. Arrange the bread slices in a greased 13x9-in. baking dish. Top with chicken; cover with the mushrooms and water chestnuts.
2. In a large bowl, whisk the eggs, milk, mayonnaise and salt. Pour over chicken. Arrange cheese on top. Combine soups and pimientos; pour over cheese. Cover and refrigerate overnight.
3. Remove from the refrigerator 30 minutes before baking. Crumble reserved crusts; toss with melted butter. Sprinkle over top. Bake, uncovered, at 325° for 1¼ hours or until a knife inserted in the center comes out clean. Let stand for 10 minutes before serving.
1 serving: 438 cal., 27g fat (9g sat. fat), 164mg chol., 1093mg sod., 22g carb. (6g sugars, 3g fiber), 26g pro.

GARLIC CHICKEN WITH MAPLE-CHIPOTLE GLAZE

GARLIC CHICKEN WITH MAPLE-CHIPOTLE GLAZE

This herby one-dish garlic chicken dinner is an updated version of an old standby recipe. The smoky flavors pair well with the savory chicken and hint of sweetness from the maple syrup.
—Taste of Home *Test Kitchen*

PREP: 35 min. • **BAKE:** 40 min.
MAKES: 4 servings

- 4   chicken leg quarters
- 1¼ tsp. kosher salt, divided
- ½   tsp. coarsely ground pepper
- 1   cup all-purpose flour
- ½   tsp. dried rosemary, crushed
- ½   tsp. dried thyme
- ½   tsp. rubbed sage
- ½   tsp. dried marjoram
- ¼   tsp. dried parsley flakes
- 1   large egg, lightly beaten
- ½   cup 2% milk
- 1   Tbsp. lemon juice
- ½   cup plus 1 Tbsp. canola oil, divided
- ½   lb. red potatoes, halved
- 1   medium onion, halved and sliced
- 20   garlic cloves, peeled

GLAZE
- ⅓   cup maple syrup
- 2   tsp. finely chopped chipotle peppers in adobo sauce
- 1   tsp. Dijon mustard
- ¾   tsp. kosher salt
- ½   tsp. chili powder

1. With a sharp knife, cut the leg quarters at the joints. Sprinkle chicken with ¾ tsp. salt and pepper.
2. In a large bowl, combine the flour, rosemary, thyme, sage, marjoram and parsley. In a shallow bowl, combine the egg, milk and lemon juice. Add chicken pieces, 1 at a time, to flour mixture. Toss to coat. Dip chicken in egg mixture and coat again with flour mixture.
3. In a 12-in. cast-iron or other ovenproof skillet, heat ½ cup oil. Fry chicken, a few pieces at a time, 5-6 minutes or until golden brown. Remove chicken and keep warm; drain drippings.
4. In the same skillet, cook potatoes in remaining oil 8-10 minutes or until slightly tender. Add onion and remaining salt; cook until onion is tender, 5-6 minutes longer. Stir in garlic; top with chicken.
5. Bake chicken, uncovered, at 375° until a thermometer reads 170°-175° and potatoes are tender, 45-50 minutes.
6. In a small bowl, combine the glaze ingredients. Brush over the chicken just before serving.
1 chicken quarter with about ½ cup potato mixture: 834 cal., 55g fat (8g sat. fat), 142mg chol., 1112mg sod., 49g carb. (20g sugars, 3g fiber), 36g pro.

CHICKEN CHILES RELLENOS CASSEROLE

My husband likes Mexican food and casseroles, so I combined the two. This chicken with poblanos and chiles satisfies our craving for dinner at a Mexican restaurant.
—*Erica Ingram, Lakewood, OH*

PREP: 20 min. • **BAKE:** 35 min. + standing
MAKES: 8 servings

- 2 Tbsp. butter
- 2 poblano peppers, seeded and coarsely chopped
- 1 small onion, finely chopped
- 2 Tbsp. all-purpose flour
- 1 tsp. ground cumin
- 1 tsp. smoked paprika
- ¼ tsp. salt
- ⅔ cup 2% milk
- 1 pkg. (8 oz.) cream cheese, cubed
- 2 cups shredded pepper jack cheese
- 2 cups coarsely shredded rotisserie chicken
- 1 can (4 oz.) chopped green chiles
- 2 pkg. (8½ oz. each) cornbread/muffin mix

1. Preheat oven to 350°. In a large skillet, heat butter over medium-high heat. Add peppers and onion; cook and stir until peppers are tender, 4-6 minutes.
2. Stir in flour and seasonings until blended; gradually stir in milk. Bring to a boil, stirring constantly; cook and stir until thickened, about 1 minute. Stir in cream cheese until blended. Add pepper jack, chicken and green chiles; heat through, stirring to combine. Transfer to a greased 11x7-in. baking dish.
3. Prepare cornbread batter according to package directions. Spread over chicken mixture. Bake, uncovered, until golden brown and a toothpick inserted in topping comes out clean, 35-40 minutes. Let stand for 10 minutes before serving.
1 serving: 610 cal., 34g fat (16g sat. fat), 151mg chol., 987mg sod., 51g carb. (16g sugars, 5g fiber), 27g pro.

KEY LIME CHICKEN THIGHS

I've been cooking since I was a girl, and I like to try new recipes. Key lime juice is a refreshing change of pace from the lemon juice used in many baked chicken dishes.
—*Idella Koen, Metolius, OR*

PREP: 10 min. • **BAKE:** 30 min.
MAKES: 4 servings

- 8 bone-in chicken thighs, skin removed (6 oz. each)
- 3 Tbsp. butter
- 2 to 3 Tbsp. Key lime juice or lime juice
- 12 to 16 drops hot pepper sauce
- 1 tsp. brown sugar
- 1 tsp. chicken bouillon granules
- ½ tsp. salt
- ½ tsp. poultry seasoning
- ½ tsp. dried rosemary, crushed
- ¼ to ½ tsp. pepper
- ¼ tsp. paprika

1. Place chicken in a greased 13x9-in. baking dish. Dot with butter; sprinkle with lime juice and pepper sauce. Combine remaining ingredients; sprinkle evenly over chicken.
2. Bake, uncovered, at 425° 30 minutes or until a thermometer reads 170°-175°.
1 serving: 460 cal., 27g fat (11g sat. fat), 196mg chol., 712mg sod., 2g carb. (2g sugars, 0 fiber), 48g pro.

CHICKEN CHILES RELLENOS CASSEROLE

Pork

STUFFED
PIZZA ROLLS

STUFFED PIZZA ROLLS

After trying a similar dish at a local restaurant, I came up with my own version. It is easy, delicious and fun for potlucks or parties.
—*Sarah Gilbert, Beaverton, OR*

PREP: 20 min. • **BAKE:** 25 min.
MAKES: 1 dozen

- 1   **tube (13.80 oz.) refrigerated pizza crust**
- ¼   **cup prepared ranch salad dressing**
- 6   **oz. pepperoni, finely chopped**
- 1   **cup shredded pepper jack cheese**
- ¼   **cup shredded Romano cheese**
- ¼   **cup thinly sliced green onions**
- ¼   **cup chopped green pepper**
- 4   **cooked bacon strips, chopped**
- 2   **tsp. Italian seasoning**
- 1   **tsp. garlic powder**
      Optional: Marinara sauce or Alfredo sauce, warmed

1. Preheat oven to 350°. Grease 12 muffin cups; set aside.
2. On a lightly floured surface, unroll pizza crust. Spread ranch to within ½-in. of edges. Sprinkle with pepperoni, cheeses, green onions, green pepper, bacon and seasonings. Roll up jelly-roll style; pinch the edge closed. Cut crosswise into 12 slices. Place each slice into prepared muffin cups.
3. Bake until lightly browned, 20-25 minutes. Serve warm with marinara or Alfredo, if desired.

1 roll: 234 cal., 14g fat (6g sat. fat), 28mg chol., 664mg sod., 17g carb. (2g sugars, 1g fiber), 10g pro.

"I made these for the kids and they LOVED them! Very easy...I didn't try them myself as I can't have some of the ingredients, but they got a huge thumbs-up. And they smelled so good!"
—NIGHTSKYSTAR, TASTEOFHOME.COM

TARRAGON-DIJON PORK CHOPS

RIBS, SAUERKRAUT & DUMPLINGS

My grandmother gave me this recipe 40 years ago. It was a favorite at all our family gatherings and church socials. Today my children are grown and off on their own, but whenever they come to visit, they still ask me to prepare this memorable family dinner!
—Betty Kearsch, Ormond Beach, FL

PREP: 20 min. • **BAKE:** 1 hour 50 min.
MAKES: 6 servings

- 3 lbs. pork spareribs or country-style pork ribs, cut into serving-size pieces
- 1 can (27 oz.) sauerkraut, undrained
- ¾ cup water
- 1 tsp. brown sugar
- ½ tsp. caraway seeds
- 2 cups all-purpose flour
- 1 tsp. baking powder
- ½ tsp. salt
- 1 large egg
- 1 cup 2% milk
  Chopped fresh parsley, optional
  Paprika, optional

1. Place ribs in a 3-qt. baking dish. In a bowl, combine sauerkraut, water, brown sugar and caraway seeds; spoon over ribs. Cover and bake at 350° for 1½ hours.
2. In a small bowl, combine flour, baking powder and salt. Beat egg and milk; add to the dry ingredients and stir with a fork just until combined. Drop by tablespoonfuls onto hot sauerkraut mixture. Cover and return to the oven for 20 minutes. Garnish with parsley and paprika if desired.

1 serving: 639 cal., 35g fat (13g sat. fat), 164mg chol., 1249mg sod., 40g carb. (5g sugars, 5g fiber), 39g pro.

TEST KITCHEN TIP
Country-style ribs come from the loin end close to the shoulder. They're generally considered the meatiest type of rib. Spareribs come from the rib portion near the belly, just north of the bacon.

🍎
TARRAGON-DIJON PORK CHOPS

For my smoky chops, I add tarragon for a hint of herbs. If you like a lot of sauce, simply double or triple the ingredients.
—Julie Danler, Bel Aire, KS

TAKES: 30 min. • **MAKES:** 4 servings

- 4 boneless pork loin chops (¾ in. thick and 6 oz. each)
- ½ tsp. garlic powder
- ¼ tsp. pepper
- 2 Tbsp. olive oil, divided
- 1 lb. sliced fresh mushrooms
- 4 green onions, chopped
- ¼ cup Dijon mustard
- 1 to 1½ tsp. chipotle or other hot pepper sauce
- 1 Tbsp. red wine, optional
- 1 Tbsp. minced fresh tarragon

1. Preheat oven to 400°. Sprinkle pork chops with garlic powder and pepper. In a large ovenproof skillet, heat 1 Tbsp. oil over medium heat. Brown chops on both sides; remove from pan.
2. In same skillet, heat remaining oil over medium-high heat. Add mushrooms and green onions; cook and stir 3 minutes. Place chops over mushroom mixture. Bake, uncovered, for 8-10 minutes or until a thermometer inserted in pork reads 145°.
3. Meanwhile, in a small bowl, mix mustard, pepper sauce and, if desired, wine; spread over chops. Bake 2 minutes longer. Sprinkle with tarragon.

1 pork chop with ⅓ cup mushroom mixture: 334 cal., 17g fat (5g sat. fat), 82mg chol., 417mg sod., 8g carb. (3g sugars, 2g fiber), 37g pro. **Diabetic exchanges:** 5 lean meat, 1½ fat, 1 vegetable.

**APPLE BACON
PORK ROLL-UPS**

PORK & CRANBERRY POTPIES

My neighbor gave me this recipe years ago. I love how these pies are different from the usual chicken potpie.
—*Mary Shenk, DeKalb, IL*

PREP: 45 min. • **BAKE:** 15 min.
MAKES: 8 servings

2	cups fresh or frozen cranberries, thawed
4	celery ribs, sliced
1	medium onion, chopped
2½	cups apple cider or juice
3	Tbsp. brown sugar
4	garlic cloves, minced
4	tsp. grated orange zest
1	Tbsp. beef or chicken bouillon granules
1	tsp. dried rosemary, crushed
6	Tbsp. all-purpose flour
¾	cup water
5	cups chopped cooked pork
4	sheets refrigerated pie crust

1. Adjust oven rack to lower third of oven; preheat oven to 450°. In a large saucepan, bring first 9 ingredients to a boil. Reduce heat; simmer, uncovered, until berries pop, about 10 minutes.
2. In a small bowl, mix flour and water until smooth; stir into cranberry mixture. Return to a boil, stirring constantly; cook and stir until thickened, 1-2 minutes. Stir in pork; remove from heat.
3. On a work surface, roll each crust into a 14-in. circle. Using a 5-in. disposable foil pie pan as a guide (upside down), cut out sixteen 6-in. crust circles, rerolling scraps as needed.
4. Press 1 crust circle firmly into bottom and up sides of eight 5-in. disposable foil pans. Divide pork mixture evenly among pans. Place remaining crust circles over tops, pressing bottom and top crusts together firmly; flute edges. Cut slits in crusts.
5. Place potpies on baking sheets. Bake until crust is golden brown and filling is bubbly, 30-35 minutes.
Freeze option: Cover tightly and freeze unbaked potpies. To use, bake frozen pies on baking sheets in a preheated 425° oven until golden brown and a thermometer inserted in center reads 165°, 40-45 minutes.
1 potpie: 727 cal., 34g fat (14g sat. fat), 98mg chol., 746mg sod., 73g carb. (19g sugars, 2g fiber), 30g pro.

APPLE BACON
PORK ROLL-UPS

I am so proud of this delicious creation—it's easy to make, but impressive enough to use for parties.
—*Cyndy Gerken, Naples, FL*

PREP: 25 min. • **BAKE:** 20 min.
MAKES: 8 servings

½	lb. bacon strips, chopped
2	Tbsp. olive oil, divided
2	Tbsp. butter, divided
½	cup chopped red onion
5	medium apples, peeled and finely chopped
½	cup packed brown sugar
2	Tbsp. minced fresh parsley
8	thin-cut boneless pork loin chops (about 3 oz. each)
8	slices Swiss cheese
½	tsp. salt
¼	tsp. pepper

1. Preheat oven to 400°. In a large skillet, cook bacon over medium heat until crisp, stirring occasionally. Remove with a slotted spoon; drain on paper towels. Remove drippings, reserving 1 Tbsp. for cooking pork chops
2. In same skillet, heat 1 Tbsp. each oil and butter over medium heat. Add onion; cook and stir 3-4 minutes or until tender. Add apples and brown sugar; cook and stir 4-5 minutes or until apples are tender. Stir in parsley and bacon; remove from pan. Cool slightly. Remove 1 cup mixture for filling.
3. Pound each pork chop with a meat mallet to ¼-in. thickness. Layer each with 1 slice cheese and 2 Tbsp. filling to within 1 in. of edges. Roll up pork chops from short side; secure with toothpicks. Sprinkle salt and pepper over roll-ups.
4. In same skillet, heat reserved drippings and remaining oil and butter over medium-high heat. Starting with the seam side, brown roll-ups on both sides. Transfer to a 13x9-in. baking pan. Bake 15-20 minutes or until pork is golden brown and tender. Discard toothpicks; serve with the remaining apple mixture.
1 pork roll-up with ⅓ cup apple mixture: 370 cal., 20g fat (8g sat. fat), 70mg chol., 404mg sod., 25g carb. (22g sugars, 2g fiber), 23g pro.

PORK & CRANBERRY
POTPIES

PORK TENDERLOIN WITH PEAR CREAM SAUCE

Pork's mild taste goes well with sweet flavors and many seasonings. Here, I've teamed it with both—luscious pears and a refreshing herb blend.
—*Joyce Moynihan, Lakeville, MN*

PREP: 25 min. • **BAKE:** 20 min.
MAKES: 4 servings

- 1 pork tenderloin (1 lb.)
- 1 Tbsp. herbes de Provence
- ½ tsp. salt
- ¼ tsp. pepper
- 4 Tbsp. butter, divided
- 4 medium pears, peeled and sliced
- 1 Tbsp. sugar
- 4 shallots, chopped
- 1¼ tsp. dried thyme
- ¼ cup pear brandy or pear nectar
- 1 cup heavy whipping cream
- ⅓ cup pear nectar

1. Preheat oven to 425°. Sprinkle pork with the herbes de Provence, salt and pepper. In a large ovenproof skillet, brown pork in 1 Tbsp. butter on all sides. Bake 18-22 minutes or until a thermometer reads 145°. Remove pork from skillet and keep warm. Let meat stand for 5 minutes before slicing.
2. Meanwhile, in a large skillet, saute pears and sugar in 2 Tbsp. butter until golden brown. Remove from pan and keep warm. In the same pan, melt remaining butter. Add shallots; saute until tender. Stir in thyme.
3. Remove from heat. Add brandy; cook over medium heat until liquid is almost evaporated, stirring to loosen browned bits from pan. Add cream and nectar; cook and stir until slightly thickened. Slice pork; serve with pears and cream sauce.
1 serving: 605 cal., 38g fat (22g sat. fat), 175mg chol., 451mg sod., 42g carb. (24g sugars, 6g fiber), 26g pro.

PORK & CHEESY MACARONI SLIDERS

I love sliders! This sweet and savory recipe was created out of leftover ingredients I had in my fridge. They are perfect for a weeknight meal or special-occasion potluck.
—*Rashanda Cobbins, Milwaukee, WI*

PREP: 30 min. • **BAKE:** 10 min
MAKES: 12 servings

- 1 cup uncooked cavatappi pasta
- 1 Tbsp. butter
- 1½ tsp. all-purpose flour
- ¼ tsp. pepper
- ½ cup 2% milk
- ¾ cup shredded sharp cheddar cheese
- 1 pkg. (18 oz.) Hawaiian sweet rolls
- 1 carton (16 oz.) refrigerated fully cooked barbecued shredded pork, warmed
- 2 Tbsp. melted butter
- 1 Tbsp. honey
- ½ tsp. ground mustard
- 1 jalapeno pepper, sliced, optional

1. Preheat oven to 375°. Cook pasta according to package directions.
2. Meanwhile, in a small saucepan, melt butter over medium heat. Stir in flour and pepper until smooth; gradually whisk in the milk. Bring to a boil, stirring constantly; cook and stir until thickened, 3-5 minutes. Stir in cheese until melted. Drain pasta; stir into cheese sauce. Set aside.
3. Place roll bottoms in a greased 13x9-in. baking dish. Top with pork, pasta mixture and roll tops. Combine melted butter, honey and mustard. Brush over roll tops.
4. Bake until tops are golden brown and the filling is hot, 10-12 minutes. If desired, top with jalapeno pepper slices.
1 slider: 305 cal., 10g fat (6g sat. fat), 48mg chol., 466mg sod., 39g carb. (17g sugars, 2g fiber), 14g pro.

PORK & CHEESY MACARONI SLIDERS

**HUNGARIAN
STUFFED CABBAGE**

SAUSAGE NOODLE CASSEROLE

The sausage makes this casserole meaty and hearty, and the blue cheese adds a special flavor. It's simple to prepare, and it only needs to bake for about 30 minutes.
—Julia Livingston, Frostproof, FL

PREP: 20 min. • **BAKE:** 30 min.
MAKES: 2 casseroles (8 servings each)

- 1 pkg. (16 oz.) egg noodles
- 2 lbs. bulk pork sausage
- 2 cans (10¾ oz. each) condensed cream of chicken soup, undiluted
- 2 cups sour cream
- 1 cup crumbled blue cheese
- 2 jars (4½ oz. each) sliced mushrooms, drained
- 1 jar (4 oz.) diced pimientos, drained
- ¼ cup finely chopped green pepper
- 1 cup soft bread crumbs
- 2 Tbsp. butter, melted

1. Cook noodles according to package directions; drain. In a large skillet, cook sausage over medium heat until no longer pink; drain.

2. In a Dutch oven, combine the soup, sour cream and blue cheese; cook and stir over medium heat until cheese is melted. Stir in the noodles, sausage, mushrooms, pimientos and green pepper.

3. Transfer to 2 greased 3-qt. baking dishes. Toss bread crumbs and butter; sprinkle over top. Bake, uncovered, at 350° until edges are bubbly, 30-35 minutes.

1 cup: 401 cal., 26g fat (11g sat. fat), 75mg chol., 828mg sod., 28g carb. (3g sugars, 2g fiber), 14g pro.

"We all liked this one but I did skip the blue cheese as I'm not a fan. We added corn to it as well. Will definitely make this a regular meal in our menu rotation."
—COBYSMOM, TASTEOFHOME.COM

HUNGARIAN STUFFED CABBAGE

European immigrants brought their favorite stuffed cabbage recipes to the New World in the late 19th century. This Hungarian version is one of my top dishes.
—Katherine Stefanovich, Desert Hot Springs, CA

PREP: 20 min. • **BAKE:** 2 hours
MAKES: 4 servings

- 1 medium head cabbage
- 1 can (28 oz.) sauerkraut, divided
- ½ lb. ground beef
- ½ lb. ground pork
- ½ cup long grain rice, cooked
- 1 tsp. salt
- ½ tsp. pepper
- 1 large egg
- 2 bacon strips, diced
- 1 cup chopped onion
- 2 garlic cloves, minced
- 1 Tbsp. Hungarian paprika
- ¼ tsp. cayenne pepper
- 1 can (14½ oz.) diced tomatoes, undrained
- 1 Tbsp. caraway seeds
- 2 cups water
- 2 Tbsp. all-purpose flour
- 1 cup sour cream

1. Remove core from head of cabbage. Place in a large saucepan and cover with water.

Bring to a boil; boil until the outer leaves loosen from head. Lift out cabbage; remove softened leaves. Return to boiling water to soften more leaves. Repeat until all leaves are removed. Remove tough center stalk from each leaf. Set aside 12 large leaves for rolls; set remaining leaves aside.

2. Spoon half of the sauerkraut into a Dutch oven; set aside. In a bowl, combine the beef, ground pork, rice, salt, pepper and egg. In a saucepan, cook bacon until crisp. Drain on paper towels. In drippings, saute onion and garlic until tender. Add bacon and half of onion mixture to meat mixture; mix well.

3. Preheat oven to 325°. Place about 3 Tbsp. filling on each cabbage leaf. Roll up, tucking in sides. Place rolls, seam side down, on sauerkraut in Dutch oven. Coarsely chop reserved cabbage leaves; place over rolls. To remaining onion mixture, add paprika, cayenne, tomatoes, caraway seeds, water and remaining sauerkraut. Cook until heated through. Pour over rolls.

4. Cover and bake for 1 hour 45 minutes. In a small bowl, gradually stir flour into sour cream. Stir in 1 to 2 Tbsp. hot cooking liquid; mix well. Spoon over cabbage rolls. Bake, uncovered, until sauce is thickened, 15-20 minutes.

3 rolls: 451 cal., 23g fat (11g sat. fat), 117mg chol., 1558mg sod., 37g carb. (10g sugars, 9g fiber), 24g pro.

SHEET-PAN BACON & EGGS BREAKFAST

SHEET-PAN BACON & EGGS BREAKFAST

I re-created this recipe from inspiration I saw on social media, and it was a huge hit! Use any cheeses and spices you like. You can try making it with seasoned potatoes, too.
—*Bonnie Hawkins, Elkhorn, WI*

PREP: 20 min. • **BAKE:** 40 min.
MAKES: 8 servings

- 10 bacon strips
- 1   pkg. (30 oz.) frozen shredded hash brown potatoes, thawed
- 1   tsp. garlic powder
- 1   tsp. dried basil
- 1   tsp. dried oregano
- ½   tsp. salt
- ½   tsp. crushed red pepper flakes
- 1½ cups shredded pepper jack cheese
- 1   cup shredded cheddar cheese
- ¼   tsp. pepper
- 8   large eggs
- ¼   cup chopped green onions

1. Preheat oven to 400°. Place bacon in a single layer in a 15x10x1-in. baking sheet. Bake until partially cooked but not crisp, about 10 minutes. Remove to paper towels to drain. When cool enough to handle, chop bacon; set aside.
2. In a large bowl, combine potatoes and seasonings; spread evenly into drippings in pan. Bake until golden brown, 25-30 minutes.
3. Sprinkle with cheeses. With the back of a spoon, make 8 wells in potato mixture. Break an egg in each well; sprinkle with pepper and reserved bacon. Bake until egg whites are completely set and yolks begin to thicken but are not hard, 12-14 minutes. Sprinkle with green onions.

1 serving: 446 cal., 30g fat (13g sat. fat), 246mg chol., 695mg sod., 22g carb. (2g sugars, 1g fiber), 22g pro.

TEST KITCHEN TIP
Forget buttering slice after slice of toast to accompany this crowd-sized brunch dish. Instead, bake up some frozen Texas toast or garlic bread to serve alongside.

QUICK & EASY MEMPHIS-STYLE BBQ RIBS

QUICK & EASY MEMPHIS-STYLE BBQ RIBS

A friend who loves barbecue gave me her recipe for ribs. Use just enough of the spice mixture to rub over them before baking, and sprinkle on the rest later.
—*Jennifer Ross, Arlington, TN*

PREP: 20 min. • **BAKE:** 3½ hours
MAKES: 6 servings

- ¼ cup packed brown sugar
- ¼ cup paprika
- 2 Tbsp. kosher salt
- 2 Tbsp. onion powder
- 2 Tbsp. garlic powder
- 2 Tbsp. coarsely ground pepper
- 3 racks (1½ to 2 lbs. each) pork baby back ribs
   Barbecue sauce, optional

1. Preheat oven to 350°. In a small bowl, mix the first 6 ingredients; rub ¾ cup over ribs. Wrap rib racks in large pieces of heavy-duty foil; seal tightly. Place in a 15x10x1-in. baking pan. Bake 1½ hours. Reduce oven setting to 250°. Bake until tender, 1½ hours longer.
2. Carefully remove ribs from foil; return to baking pan. Sprinkle ribs with remaining spice mixture. Bake 30 minutes longer or until lightly browned, brushing with barbecue sauce, if desired.

1 serving: 497 cal., 32g fat (11g sat. fat), 122mg chol., 2066mg sod., 17g carb. (10g sugars, 3g fiber), 35g pro.

❄

ASIAN PEANUT PORK ROAST

Your family and friends won't believe you when you reveal the secret ingredients for this flavorful pork roast—peanut butter! I've served this roast to guests for years, and can't tell you how many times I've sent copies of the recipe home with guests. For a change of taste, you can substitute toasted walnuts for peanuts and use walnut oil instead of peanut butter.

—*Alice Vidovich, Walnut Creek, CA*

- -

PREP: 20 min. + standing
BAKE: 1¼ hours + standing
MAKES: 6 servings

- 2 lbs. boneless pork loin roast

COATING
- ¼ cup creamy peanut butter
- 3 Tbsp. reduced-sodium soy sauce
- 2 Tbsp. ground coriander
- 1½ tsp. ground cumin
- ½ tsp. chili powder
- 1 large clove garlic, crushed
- 1 Tbsp. lemon juice

PEANUT SAUCE
- 1 cup reduced-sodium soy sauce
- ¼ cup sherry
- 2 Tbsp. pineapple juice
- 1 clove garlic, crushed
- ½ tsp. minced fresh gingerroot
- ½ cup chopped unsalted peanuts

1. Combine coating ingredients in a bowl; rub coating over all exposed surfaces of roast. Let stand for 30 minutes.
2. Preheat oven to 325°. Place the roast in greased baking dish; roast until thermometer reads 140°, about 75 minutes. (Temperature of roast will continue to rise another 5-10° upon standing.)
3. Combine all sauce ingredients except peanuts in saucepan; bring to a boil. Let cool; add peanuts. Set aside. Remove roast from oven; tent with foil. Let stand 15 minutes before slicing. Serve roast with sauce.
Freeze option: Freeze cooled meat with some of the juices in freezer containers. To use, partially thaw in the refrigerator overnight. Heat though in a saucepan, stirring occasionally and adding a little water if necessary.
5 oz. cooked pork with ¼ cup sauce: 390 cal., 21g fat (5g sat. fat), 91mg chol., 1934mg sod., 10g carb. (2g sugars, 3g fiber), 39g pro.

COUNTRY PORK & SAUERKRAUT

COUNTRY PORK & SAUERKRAUT

The secret ingredient in this recipe is the applesauce. When everything's cooked up, you wouldn't know it's in there...yet the taste is just a bit sweeter. My mother and grandmother once ran a beanery for a train crew. That inspired a lot of my cooking. In fact, I adapted this recipe from one of theirs. Luckily for me, my husband likes to eat what I fix as much as I like to cook it! He and I have three children, all now grown, and six grandchildren.

—*Donna Hellendrung, Minneapolis, MN*

- -

PREP: 15 min. • **BAKE:** 1½ hours
MAKES: 4 servings

- 2 lbs. bone-in country-style pork ribs
- 1 medium onion, chopped
- 1 Tbsp. canola oil
- 1 can (14 oz.) sauerkraut, undrained
- 1 cup unsweetened applesauce
- 2 Tbsp. brown sugar
- 2 tsp. caraway seeds
- 1 tsp. garlic powder
- ½ tsp. pepper

1. In a Dutch oven, cook ribs and onion in oil until ribs are browned and onion is tender. Remove from the heat. Combine remaining ingredients and pour over ribs.
2. Cover and bake at 350° until ribs are tender, 1½-2 hours.
1 serving: 477 cal., 24g fat (8g sat. fat), 130mg chol., 757mg sod., 23g carb. (15g sugars, 5g fiber), 41g pro.

SAUSAGE & SPINACH CRESCENT BAKE

A classic Florentine casserole has cheese and spinach. I make a yummy version with mozzarella, mushrooms and sausage. It's gone in the blink of an eye at our house.
—*Noelle Carle, Bristow, OK*

- -

PREP: 20 min. • **BAKE:** 25 min.
MAKES: 8 servings

- 1 **lb. bulk pork sausage**
- 2 **cups sliced fresh mushrooms**
- 1 **medium onion, chopped**
- 2 **garlic cloves, minced**
- 1 **pkg. (10 oz.) frozen chopped spinach, thawed and squeezed dry**
- 1 **cup shredded part-skim mozzarella cheese**
- 4 **oz. cream cheese, softened**
- 1 **cup half-and-half cream**

- 1 **tube (8 oz.) refrigerated crescent rolls**

1. Preheat oven to 350°. In a large skillet, cook sausage, mushrooms, onion and garlic over medium heat until sausage is no longer pink, breaking up sausage into crumbles, 6-8 minutes. Drain.
2. Add spinach, mozzarella cheese, cream cheese and cream to sausage mixture; cook and stir until blended. Transfer to a greased 13x9-in. baking dish.
3. Unroll crescent dough into 1 long rectangle; press perforations to seal. Place over the sausage mixture. Bake, covered, 10 minutes. Bake, uncovered, until golden brown and filling is bubbly, 12-15 minutes longer. Let stand 5-10 minutes before cutting.
1 piece: 401 cal., 29g fat (12g sat. fat), 70mg chol., 758mg sod., 18g carb. (5g sugars, 1g fiber), 15g pro.

❄
LISA'S ALL-DAY SUGAR & SALT PORK ROAST

My family loves this tender, juicy roast, so we eat it a lot. The salty crust is so delicious mixed into the pulled pork.
—*Lisa Allen, Joppa, AL*

- -

PREP: 15 min. + chilling • **COOK:** 6¼ hours
MAKES: 12 servings

- 1 **cup plus 1 Tbsp. sea salt, divided**
- 1 **cup sugar**
- 1 **bone-in pork shoulder butt roast (6 to 8 lbs.)**
- ¼ **cup barbecue seasoning**
- ½ **tsp. pepper**
- ½ **cup packed brown sugar**
- 12 **hamburger buns or kaiser rolls, split**

1. Combine 1 cup sea salt and granulated sugar; rub onto all sides of roast. Place in a shallow dish; refrigerate, covered, overnight.
2. Preheat oven to 300°. Using a kitchen knife, scrape salt and sugar coating from roast; discard any accumulated juices. Transfer pork to a large shallow roasting pan. Rub with barbecue seasoning; sprinkle with pepper. Roast until tender, 6-8 hours.
3. Increase oven temperature to 500°. Combine brown sugar and 1 Tbsp. sea salt; sprinkle over cooked pork. Return pork to oven and roast until a crisp crust forms, 10-15 minutes. Remove; when cool enough to handle, shred meat with 2 forks. Serve warm on fresh buns or rolls.
Freeze option: Freeze cooled meat with some of the juices in freezer containers. To use, partially thaw in refrigerator overnight. Heat in a saucepan, stirring occasionally and adding a little water if necessary.
1 sandwich: 534 cal., 24g fat (9g sat. fat), 135mg chol., 2240mg sod., 33g carb. (14g sugars, 1g fiber), 43g pro.

SAUSAGE & SPINACH CRESCENT BAKE

SUNDAY PORK ROAST

PORK CHOPS WITH APPLES & STUFFING

The heartwarming taste of cinnamon and apples is the perfect accompaniment to tender pork chops. This dish is always a winner with my family. And with only four ingredients, it's a main course I can serve with little preparation.

—Joan Hamilton, Worcester, MA

PREP: 15 min. • **BAKE:** 45 min.
MAKES: 6 servings

- 6 boneless pork loin chops (1 in. thick)
- 1 Tbsp. canola oil
- 1 pkg. (6 oz.) crushed stuffing mix
- 1 can (21 oz.) apple pie filling with cinnamon
   Minced fresh parsley, optional

1. In a large skillet, brown pork chops in oil over medium-high heat. Meanwhile, prepare stuffing according to package directions. Spread pie filling into a greased 13x9-in. baking dish. Place the pork chops on top; spoon stuffing over chops.

2. Cover and bake at 350° for 35 minutes. Uncover; bake until a thermometer reads 145°, about 10 minutes longer. Let stand 5 minutes. If desired, sprinkle with parsley.

1 serving: 527 cal., 21g fat (9g sat. fat), 102mg chol., 550mg sod., 48g carb. (15g sugars, 3g fiber), 36g pro.

"This is a great recipe, but my family found the canned apple pie filling a bit too sweet. I instead slice up 2 or 3 apples in the bottom of the baking dish and sprinkle them with some cinnamon and sugar to taste. I followed the rest of the recipe as written."

—SPDWAIN100, TASTEOFHOME.COM

SUNDAY PORK ROAST

Mom prepared pork roast for our family, friends and customers at the restaurants she and Dad owned. The herb rub and vegetables give it a remarkable flavor. It's one of my favorite pork roast recipes.

—Sandi Pichon, Memphis, TN

PREP: 20 min. • **BAKE:** 1¾ hours + standing
MAKES: 12 servings

- 2 medium onions, chopped
- 2 medium carrots, chopped
- 1 celery rib, chopped
- 4 Tbsp. all-purpose flour, divided
- 1 bay leaf, finely crushed
- ½ tsp. dried thyme
- 1¼ tsp. salt, divided
- 1¼ tsp. pepper, divided
- 1 boneless pork loin roast (3 to 4 lbs.)
- ⅓ cup packed brown sugar

1. Preheat oven to 325°. Place vegetables on bottom of a shallow roasting pan. Mix 2 Tbsp. flour, bay leaf, thyme, and 1 tsp. each salt and pepper; rub over roast. Place roast on top of vegetables, fat side up. Add 2 cups water to the pan.

2. Roast, uncovered, 1½ hours. Sprinkle brown sugar over roast. Roast 15-20 minutes longer or until a thermometer reads 140°. (Temperature of roast will continue to rise another 5-10° upon standing.)

3. Remove roast to a platter. Tent with foil; let stand 15 minutes before slicing.

4. Strain drippings from roasting pan into a measuring cup; skim fat. Add enough water to the drippings to measure 1½ cups.

5. In a small saucepan over medium heat, whisk remaining flour and ⅓ cup water until smooth. Gradually whisk in drippings mixture and remaining salt and pepper. Bring to a boil over medium-high heat, stirring constantly; cook and stir 2 minutes or until thickened. Serve roast with gravy.

Freeze option: Freeze cooled sliced pork and gravy in freezer containers. To use, partially thaw in refrigerator overnight. Heat through in a covered saucepan, gently stirring and adding a little broth or water if necessary.

3 oz. cooked pork with about 2 Tbsp. gravy: 174 cal., 5g fat (2g sat. fat), 57mg chol., 280mg sod., 8g carb. (6g sugars, 0 fiber), 22g pro. **Diabetic exchanges:** 3 lean meat, ½ starch.

PORK CHOPS WITH
APPLES & STUFFING

SPECIAL PORK CHOPS

I work nine hours a day, so I need delicious and simple recipes like this one. My husband thinks I work hard fixing meals, but these chops are deceptively easy. In summer, I can my own salsa and use some to top the chops.
—*LaDane Wilson, Alexander City, AL*

TAKES: 30 min. • **MAKES:** 6 servings

- 6 boneless pork chops (6 oz. each)
- 1 Tbsp. canola oil
- 1 jar (16 oz.) salsa

In a large cast-iron or other ovenproof skillet, brown the pork chops in oil; drain any fat. Pour salsa over chops. Bake, uncovered, at 350° until a thermometer reads 145°, 20-25 minutes. Let stand 5 minutes.

1 pork chop: 273 cal., 12g fat (4g sat. fat), 82mg chol., 350mg sod., 5g carb. (3g sugars, 0 fiber), 33g pro. **Diabetic exchanges:** 5 lean meat, ½ fat.

PEAR, HAM & CHEESE PASTRY POCKETS

I came up with this simple recipe one night for a quick dinner. It's perfect with a cup of soup for a delicious weeknight meal.
—*Terri Crandall, Gardnerville, NV*

TAKES: 30 min. • **MAKES:** 8 servings

- 1 pkg. (17.3 oz.) frozen puff pastry, thawed
- ¼ cup honey Dijon mustard
- 1 large egg, lightly beaten
- 8 slices deli ham
- 4 slices Muenster cheese, halved diagonally
- 1 medium red pear, very thinly sliced
- 1 small red onion, thinly sliced

1. Preheat oven to 400°. Unfold each sheet of puff pastry. Cut each into 4 squares. Spread 1½ tsp. mustard over each square to within ½ in. of edges. Brush beaten egg over edges of pastry.

2. On 1 corner of each square, layer the ham, cheese, pear and onion. Fold opposite corner over filling, forming a triangle; press edges with a fork to seal. Transfer pockets to ungreased baking sheets. Brush tops with remaining egg.

3. Bake 10-14 minutes or until golden brown. Serve warm.

Freeze option: Freeze cooled pockets in a freezer container, separating with waxed paper. To use, reheat pockets on a baking sheet in a preheated 400° oven until crisp and heated through.

1 pocket: 403 cal., 21g fat (6g sat. fat), 43mg chol., 540mg sod., 43g carb. (6g sugars, 6g fiber), 12g pro.

SPECIAL PORK CHOPS

BACON, LETTUCE & TOMATO PIZZA

MUSHROOM LASAGNA

Two types of mushrooms and a hint of wine provide savory flavor to this creamy lasagna. It has just a hint of prosciutto, which you can increase to taste or omit to make this a meatless entree.
—*Gary Bachara, Wilson, NC*

- -

PREP: 45 min. • **BAKE:** 40 min. + standing
MAKES: 12 servings

  9 uncooked lasagna noodles
  1 lb. sliced fresh mushrooms
  2 cups chopped baby portobello mushrooms
  1 large sweet onion, chopped
  3 Tbsp. olive oil
  ½ cup minced fresh parsley
  2 thin slices prosciutto or deli ham, chopped
  2 garlic cloves, minced
  1½ tsp. Italian seasoning
  ⅔ cup white wine or chicken broth
  2 cans (14½ oz. each) diced tomatoes, drained
  1 cup shredded part-skim mozzarella cheese, divided
  1 cup shredded Parmesan cheese, divided
  ½ cup heavy whipping cream
  ¼ cup whole milk

1. Cook noodles according to package directions. Meanwhile, in a Dutch oven, cook and stir the mushrooms and onion in oil until tender. Add the parsley, prosciutto, garlic and Italian seasoning; cook 2 minutes longer. Add wine; cook and stir until liquid is evaporated. Add tomatoes and heat through.
2. Spread 1 cup sauce in a greased 13x9-in. baking dish. Layer with three noodles, 1⅓ cups sauce, and a scant ¼ cup each of mozzarella and Parmesan. Repeat layers twice. In a small bowl, combine the cream, milk and remaining cheeses; spoon over the top.
3. Cover and bake at 350° for 30 minutes. Uncover; bake 10 minutes longer or until cheese is melted. Let stand for 10 minutes before cutting.
1 piece: 230 cal., 11g fat (5g sat. fat), 25mg chol., 279mg sod., 23g carb. (6g sugars, 3g fiber), 10g pro. **Diabetic exchanges:** 2 fat, 1 starch, 1 lean meat, 1 vegetable.

BACON, LETTUCE & TOMATO PIZZA

I bring together two all-time favorites with this recipe: pizza and BLT sandwiches. I brought this fun mashup to a ladies lunch and was met with "oohs" and "ahhs."
—*Bonnie Hawkins, Elkhorn, WI*

- -

TAKES: 30 min. • **MAKES:** 6 servings

  1 tube (13.8 oz.) refrigerated pizza crust
  2 Tbsp. olive oil
  2 Tbsp. grated Parmesan cheese
  1 tsp. garlic salt
  ½ cup mayonnaise
  2 tsp. ranch dip mix
  4 cups shredded romaine
  3 to 4 plum tomatoes, chopped
  ½ lb. bacon strips, cooked and crumbled

1. Preheat oven to 425°. Unroll and press dough onto bottom of a greased 15x10x1-in. baking pan. Brush with oil; top with cheese and garlic salt. Bake until golden brown, 15-18 minutes; cool slightly.
2. Meanwhile, combine mayonnaise and ranch mix. Spread over pizza crust; top with lettuce, tomatoes and bacon.
1 piece: 389 cal., 23g fat (5g sat. fat), 16mg chol., 1236mg sod., 34g carb. (5g sugars, 2g fiber), 11g pro.

TEST KITCHEN TIP
This pizza tastes just like an open-faced BLT. Amp up the flavor even more by adding torn fresh basil along with the romaine.

Fish & Seafood

SAUCY
BARBECUE
SHRIMP

SAUCY BARBECUE SHRIMP

This old-time Cajun dish and is one of our family favorites. Don't remove the shells from the shrimp—the beauty of this dish is peeling the shrimp and dipping it in the sauce. We've doubled and even tripled the recipe to feed a crowd and it's always perfect!
—*Debbie Glasscock, Conway, AR*

- -

PREP: 20 min. • **BAKE:** 20 min.
MAKES: 8 servings

- ½ cup butter, cubed
- 1 medium onion, chopped
- 1 bottle (18 oz.) barbecue sauce
- 1 bottle (12 oz.) pale ale beer or nonalcoholic beer
- 2 lbs. uncooked shell-on shrimp (31-40 per lb.), deveined
  French bread baguette, sliced

1. Preheat oven to 350°. In a large saucepan, melt butter over medium-high heat. Add onion; cook and stir 8-10 minutes or until tender. Stir in barbecue sauce and beer.
2. Place shrimp in a 13x9-in. baking dish. Pour barbecue mixture over top. Bake, uncovered, 20-25 minutes or until shrimp turn pink, stirring halfway through cooking. Serve with baguette slices.
1 cup: 339 cal., 14g fat (8g sat. fat), 168mg chol., 883mg sod., 30g carb. (24g sugars, 1g fiber), 19g pro.

TEST KITCHEN TIP
To stretch this recipe for meat lovers, add some thick slices of andouille or other smoked sausage.

TUNA-FILLED
SHELLS

CHIMICHURRI BAKED FLOUNDER

Chimichurri is a tasty addition to any type of fish. I find that the fresh herbs brighten up this baked flounder dish in particular. To save time, gather your herbs together on your chopping board and chop them all at once.
—*Jennifer Okutman, Westminster, MD*

- -

TAKES: 30 min. • **MAKES:** 4 servings

  4 **flounder or other lean white fish fillets (about 3 oz. each)**
  ¼ **tsp. garlic salt**
  ½ **cup olive oil**
  2 **Tbsp. chopped fresh thyme**
  2 **Tbsp. chopped fresh oregano**
  2 **Tbsp. chopped fresh parsley**
  2 **Tbsp. chopped fresh basil**
  2 **Tbsp. chopped fresh chives**
  4 **tsp. lemon juice**
      Optional: Lemon wedges and additional herbs

1. Preheat oven to 350°. Place fillets in a 15x10x1-in. baking pan. Sprinkle with garlic salt. Bake until fish just begins to flake easily with a fork, 15-20 minutes.
2. Meanwhile, whisk together oil, chopped herbs and lemon juice. Pour over cooked fillets. If desired, serve with lemon wedges and additional herbs.

1 fillet with 3 Tbsp. sauce: 313 cal., 28g fat (4g sat. fat), 40mg chol., 186mg sod., 1g carb. (0 sugars, 0 fiber), 14g pro.

TUNA-FILLED SHELLS

Hot tuna is a hit when you mix it with jumbo pasta shells and a cheesy sauce. Dill complements the fish nicely in this creamy comfort food. It's a great change of pace from the traditional tuna casserole.
—*Connie Staal, Greenbrier, AR*

- -

PREP: 20 min. • **BAKE:** 25 min.
MAKES: 6 servings

 12 **jumbo pasta shells**
  5 **tsp. all-purpose flour**
  2 **cups 2% milk**
  1 **tsp. dill weed**
  ½ **tsp. salt**
  1 **celery rib, diced**
  1 **small onion, diced**
  1 **Tbsp. canola oil**
  2 **slices white bread, crumbled**
  1 **can (12 oz.) light water-packed tuna, drained and flaked**
  ½ **cup reduced-fat ranch salad dressing**
  ½ **cup shredded part-skim mozzarella cheese**

1. Cook pasta shells according to package directions. Meanwhile in a saucepan, combine the flour, milk, dill and salt until smooth. Bring to a boil; cook and stir until thickened, about 2 minutes. Pour 1¼ cups sauce into a 2-qt. baking dish; set aside.
2. In a nonstick skillet, saute celery and onion in oil until tender. Add bread. Stir in the tuna, salad dressing and cheese; mix well. Drain shells; stuff with tuna mixture. Place over sauce. Drizzle with remaining sauce. Cover and bake at 350° until bubbly and heated through, 25-30 minutes.

2 stuffed shells: 291 cal., 9g fat (3g sat. fat), 34mg chol., 733mg sod., 27g carb. (0 sugars, 1g fiber), 24g pro. **Diabetic exchanges:** 2 starch, 2 lean meat, ½ fat.

**SESAME SALMON
WITH WASABI MAYO**

CRAB-TOPPED FISH FILLETS

These fillets are elegant enough for company but truly no trouble to make. Fish is abundant here in South Florida, and we like to get together with friends in the afternoon, so I often need to whip up a quick dinner when we get home. This special dish is one of my husband's favorites.
—*Mary Tuthill, Fort Myers Beach, FL*

- -

TAKES: 30 min. • **MAKES:** 4 servings

 4 sole or cod fillets, or fish fillets of
    your choice (6 oz. each)
 1 can (6 oz.) crabmeat, drained and
    flaked, or 1 cup imitation crabmeat,
    chopped
 ½ cup grated Parmesan cheese
 ½ cup mayonnaise
 1 tsp. lemon juice
 ⅓ cup slivered almonds, toasted
    Paprika, optional

1. Place fillets in a greased 13x9-in. baking dish. Bake, uncovered, at 350° until fish flakes easily with a fork, 18-22 minutes. Meanwhile, in a large bowl, combine the crab, cheese, mayonnaise and lemon juice.
2. Drain cooking juices from baking dish; spoon crab mixture over fillets. Broil 4-5 in. from the heat until topping is lightly browned, about 5 minutes. Sprinkle with almonds and, if desired, paprika.
1 fillet: 429 cal., 31g fat (6g sat. fat), 128mg chol., 1063mg sod., 3g carb. (0 sugars, 1g fiber), 33g pro.

"A favorite with my husband. Made the recipe just as described and served it with rice and salad. Love the almonds with the crab."
—HOMEMADEWITHLOVE, TASTEOFHOME.COM

SESAME SALMON WITH WASABI MAYO

I created this recipe to mimic the flavors of sushi. It's remarkably simple and turns out well every time.
—*Carolyn Ketchum, Wakefield, MA*

- -

PREP: 15 min. • **BAKE:** 20 min.
MAKES: 6 servings

 2 Tbsp. butter, melted
 3 Tbsp. sesame oil, divided
 1 salmon fillet (2 lbs.)
 ¼ tsp. salt
 ¼ tsp. pepper
 ⅓ cup mayonnaise
 1½ tsp. lemon juice
 1 tsp. prepared wasabi
 4 green onions, chopped
 2 Tbsp. sesame seeds, toasted

1. Drizzle butter and 2 Tbsp. oil into a 13x9-in. baking dish; tilt to coat bottom. Place salmon in dish; brush with remaining oil and sprinkle with salt and pepper.
2. Bake, uncovered, at 425° 18-22 minutes or until fish just begins to flake easily with a fork. Meanwhile, combine the mayonnaise, lemon juice and wasabi. Sprinkle salmon with onions and sesame seeds. Serve with sauce.
4 oz. cooked salmon with 1 Tbsp. sauce: 439 cal., 36g fat (8g sat. fat), 90mg chol., 302mg sod., 2g carb. (0 sugars, 1g fiber), 26g pro.

CRAB-TOPPED
FISH FILLETS

LEMONY SALMON PATTIES

Topped with a zippy white sauce, these little patties bake up golden brown in a muffin pan. They're impressive enough for guests, but easy enough that I can prepare them any time we like.
—Lorice Britt, Severn, NC

- -

PREP: 20 min. • **BAKE:** 45 min.
MAKES: 4 servings

1	can (14¾ oz.) pink salmon, drained, skin and bones removed
¾	cup whole milk
1	cup soft bread crumbs
1	large egg, lightly beaten
1	Tbsp. minced fresh parsley
1	tsp. finely chopped onion
½	tsp. Worcestershire sauce
¼	tsp. salt
⅛	tsp. pepper

LEMON SAUCE

2	Tbsp. butter
4	tsp. all-purpose flour
¾	cup whole milk
2	Tbsp. lemon juice
¼	tsp. salt
⅛	to ¼ tsp. cayenne pepper

1. Preheat oven to 350°. In a large bowl, combine first 9 ingredients. Fill 8 greased muffin cups with ¼ cup salmon mixture. Bake 45 minutes or until browned.
2. Meanwhile, melt butter in a saucepan; stir in flour until smooth. Gradually stir in milk; bring to a boil over medium heat. Cook and stir for 2 minutes or until thickened. Remove from heat; stir in the lemon juice, salt and cayenne. Serve with patties.
2 patties with ¼ cup sauce: 328 cal., 18g fat (8g sat. fat), 127mg chol., 1044mg sod., 13g carb. (5g sugars, 0 fiber), 27g pro.

GREEN CURRY SALMON WITH GREEN BEANS

Like many people here in the beautiful Pacific Northwest, my boyfriend, Michael, loves to fish. When we have an abundance of fresh salmon on hand, this is one way we cook it.
—Amy Paul Maynard, Albany, OR

- -

TAKES: 30 min. • **MAKES:** 4 servings

4	salmon fillets (4 oz. each)
1	cup light coconut milk
2	Tbsp. green curry paste
1	cup uncooked instant brown rice
1	cup reduced-sodium chicken broth
⅛	tsp. pepper
¾	lb. fresh green beans, trimmed
1	tsp. sesame oil
1	tsp. sesame seeds, toasted
	Lime wedges

1. Preheat oven to 400°. Place the salmon in an 8-in. square baking dish. Whisk together coconut milk and curry paste; pour over salmon. Bake, uncovered, until the fish just begins to flake easily with a fork, 15-20 minutes.
2. Meanwhile, in a small saucepan, combine the rice, broth and pepper; bring to a boil. Reduce heat; simmer, covered, 5 minutes. Remove from heat; let stand 5 minutes.
3. In a large saucepan, place steamer basket over 1 in. of water. Place the green beans in basket; bring water to a boil. Reduce heat to maintain a simmer; steam, covered, until beans are crisp-tender, 7-10 minutes. Toss with sesame oil and sesame seeds.
4. Serve salmon fillets with rice, green beans and lime wedges. Spoon coconut sauce over the salmon.
Note: This recipe was tested with Thai Kitchen Green Curry Paste.
1 serving: 366 cal., 17g fat (5g sat. fat), 57mg chol., 340mg sod., 29g carb. (5g sugars, 4g fiber), 24g pro. **Diabetic exchanges:** 3 lean meat, 2 starch, 1 fat.

GREEN CURRY SALMON WITH GREEN BEANS

ONE-PAN SWEET CHILI
SHRIMP & VEGGIES

CRAB-STUFFED MANICOTTI

I love pasta, and my husband loves seafood.
I combined the two to create this dish, and
he raved that it's the best meal ever.
—*Sonya Polfliet, Anza, CA*

PREP: 25 min. • **BAKE:** 25 min.
MAKES: 2 servings

- 4   uncooked manicotti shells
- 1   Tbsp. butter
- 4   tsp. all-purpose flour
- 1   cup fat-free milk
- 1   Tbsp. grated Parmesan cheese
- 1   cup lump crabmeat, drained
- ⅓   cup reduced-fat ricotta cheese
- ¼   cup shredded part-skim mozzarella
     cheese
- ¼   tsp. lemon-pepper seasoning
- ¼   tsp. pepper
- ⅛   tsp. garlic powder
      Minced fresh parsley

1. Cook manicotti according to package
directions. In a small saucepan, melt butter.
Stir in flour until smooth; gradually add milk.
Bring to a boil; cook and stir for 2 minutes or
until thickened. Remove from the heat; stir in
Parmesan cheese.
2. In a small bowl, combine the crab, ricotta
cheese, mozzarella cheese, lemon-pepper
seasoning, pepper and garlic powder. Drain
manicotti; stuff with crab mixture. Spread
¼ cup sauce in an 8-in. square baking dish
coated with cooking spray. Top with stuffed
manicotti. Pour remaining sauce over top.
3. Cover and bake at 350° for 25-30 minutes
or until heated through. Just before serving,
sprinkle with parsley.
2 manicotti: 359 cal., 12g fat (7g sat. fat),
98mg chol., 793mg sod., 38g carb. (11g
sugars, 1g fiber), 26g pro. **Diabetic
exchanges:** 2 starch, 2 lean meat, 1 fat,
½ fat-free milk.

ONE-PAN SWEET CHILI
SHRIMP & VEGGIES

This recipe has everything I'm looking for in
a weeknight family dinner: quick, flavorful,
nutritious and all three of my kids will eat it!
My oldest son loves shrimp and I thought it
could work really well as a sheet-pan supper.
For easy cleanup, I like to line my pan with foil
or a silicone mat before greasing the pan.
—*Elisabeth Larsen, Pleasant Grove, UT*

TAKES: 30 min. • **MAKES:** 4 servings

- 1   lb. uncooked shrimp (16-20 per lb.),
     peeled and deveined
- 2   medium zucchini, halved and sliced
- ½   lb. sliced fresh mushrooms
- 1   medium sweet orange pepper,
     julienned
- 3   Tbsp. sweet chili sauce
- 1   Tbsp. canola oil
- 1   Tbsp. lime juice
- 1   Tbsp. reduced-sodium soy sauce
- 3   green onions, chopped
- ¼   cup minced fresh cilantro

1. Preheat oven to 400°. Place the shrimp,
zucchini, mushrooms and orange pepper in a
greased 15x10x1-in. baking pan. Combine chili
sauce, oil, lime juice and soy sauce. Pour over
shrimp mixture and toss to coat.
2. Bake until shrimp turn pink and vegetables
are tender, 12-15 minutes. Sprinkle with green
onions and cilantro.
1 serving: 199 cal., 6g fat (1g sat. fat), 138mg
chol., 483mg sod., 15g carb. (11g sugars, 3g
fiber), 22g pro.

TEST KITCHEN TIP
Lump crabmeat comes from the
crab's body, and these are the
choicest, sweetest, largest bits.
Backfin and flake crab are smaller
pieces from the back and other
parts of the crab, respectively.
They are less expensive than
lump crab.

**TUSCAN
FISH PACKETS**

TUSCAN FISH PACKETS

My husband does a lot of fishing, so I'm always looking for different ways to serve his catches. A professional chef was kind enough to share this recipe with me, and I played around with some different veggie combinations until I found the one my family liked best.

—*Kathy Morrow, Hubbard, OH*

- -

TAKES: 30 min. • **MAKES:** 4 servings

- 1 can (15 oz.) great northern beans, rinsed and drained
- 4 plum tomatoes, chopped
- 1 small zucchini, chopped
- 1 medium onion, chopped
- 1 garlic clove, minced
- ¼ cup white wine
- ¾ tsp. salt, divided
- ¼ tsp. pepper, divided
- 4 tilapia fillets (6 oz. each)
- 1 medium lemon, cut into 8 thin slices

1. Preheat oven to 400°. In a bowl, combine beans, tomatoes, zucchini, onion, garlic, wine, ½ tsp. salt and ⅛ tsp. pepper.
2. Rinse fish and pat dry. Place each fillet on an 18x12-in. piece of heavy-duty foil; season with remaining salt and pepper. Spoon bean mixture over the fish; top with lemon slices. Fold foil around fish and crimp the edges to seal. Transfer packets to a baking sheet.
3. Bake 15-20 minutes or until fish just begins to flake easily with a fork and vegetables are tender. Be careful of escaping steam when opening packet.
1 serving: 270 cal., 2g fat (1g sat. fat), 83mg chol., 658mg sod., 23g carb. (4g sugars, 7g fiber), 38g pro. **Diabetic exchanges:** 5 lean meat, 1 starch, 1 vegetable.

TEST KITCHEN TIP
If you hate to open a bottle of wine just for ¼ cup, look for wine in single-portion plastic bottles. The small bottles are convenient for using in recipes.

SIMPLE HERBED SCALLOPS

SIMPLE HERBED SCALLOPS

Living in Kansas, fresh seafood can be hard to come by. Luckily, frozen scallops aren't. This dish offers coastal flavor to those of us in landlocked areas.
—*Sarah Befort, Hays, KS*

- -

TAKES: 30 min. • **MAKES:** 2 servings

- ½ to ¾ lb. sea scallops
- 3 Tbsp. butter, divided
- ¾ tsp. lemon juice
- 1 tsp. minced fresh parsley or ¼ tsp. dried parsley
- 1½ tsp. minced fresh chives or ½ tsp. dried chives
- ¼ tsp. minced fresh tarragon or ⅛ tsp. dried tarragon
- ⅛ tsp. garlic salt
   Dash pepper
- 2 Tbsp. dry bread crumbs

1. Preheat oven to 350°. Place scallops in a greased 1-qt. baking dish. Mix 2 Tbsp. melted butter, lemon juice, herbs, garlic salt and pepper; drizzle over scallops.
2. Mix bread crumbs with remaining melted butter; sprinkle over top. Bake, uncovered, 20-25 minutes or until the scallops are firm and opaque.
1 serving: 260 cal., 18g fat (11g sat. fat), 73mg chol., 754mg sod., 9g carb. (1g sugars, 1g fiber), 15g pro.

STUFFED TILAPIA

Make a reservation for four at your dining room table. With this elegant, restaurant-quality dish, you can turn any night into a celebration.
—*Linda Stemen, Monroeville, IN*

PREP: 20 min. • **BAKE:** 25 min.
MAKES: 4 servings

- 1 small onion, finely chopped
- 1 celery rib, finely chopped
- ¼ cup plus 6 Tbsp. butter, divided
- 1 cup lump crabmeat, drained
- ⅓ cup dry bread crumbs
- ⅓ cup mayonnaise
- 1 large egg, beaten
- 2 Tbsp. diced pimientos, drained
- ¼ tsp. seafood seasoning
- 4 tilapia fillets (6 oz. each)
- ¼ tsp. salt
- ¼ tsp. paprika

1. In a large skillet, saute onion and celery in ¼ cup butter until tender. Remove from the heat; stir in the crab, bread crumbs, mayonnaise, egg, pimientos and seafood seasoning. Spread ⅓ cup crab mixture over fillets. Roll up each from the pointed end; secure with toothpicks.

2. Place seam side down in a greased 9-in. square baking pan. Melt remaining butter; drizzle over fish. Sprinkle with salt and paprika.

3. Bake, uncovered, at 400° 25-30 minutes or until fish just begins to flake easily with a fork. Discard the toothpicks. Spoon pan juices over fish.

1 serving: 608 cal., 47g fat (21g sat. fat), 248mg chol., 894mg sod., 9g carb. (2g sugars, 1g fiber), 40g pro.

AVOCADO
CRAB BOATS

AVOCADO CRAB BOATS

These boats are wonderful with tortilla chips, beans or rice. You can also cover them, pack them on ice, and take them to a picnic or potluck. Straight from the oven or cold, they're always delicious.
—*Frances Benthin, Scio, OR*

TAKES: 20 min. • **MAKES:** 8 servings

- 5 medium ripe avocados, peeled and halved
- ½ cup mayonnaise
- 2 Tbsp. lemon juice
- 2 cans (6 oz. each) lump crabmeat, drained
- 4 Tbsp. chopped fresh cilantro, divided
- 2 Tbsp. minced chives
- 1 serrano pepper, seeded and minced
- 1 Tbsp. capers, drained
- ¼ tsp. pepper
- 1 cup shredded pepper jack cheese
- ½ tsp. paprika
  Lemon wedges

1. Preheat broiler. Place 2 avocado halves in a large bowl; mash lightly with a fork. Add mayonnaise and lemon juice; mix until well blended. Stir in crab, 3 Tbsp. cilantro, chives, serrano pepper, capers and pepper. Spoon into remaining avocado halves.

2. Transfer to a 15x10x1-in. baking pan. Sprinkle with cheese and paprika. Broil 4-5 in. from heat until cheese is melted, 3-5 minutes. Sprinkle with remaining cilantro; serve with lemon wedges.

Note: Wear disposable gloves when cutting hot peppers; the oils can burn skin. Avoid touching your face.

1 filled avocado half: 325 cal., 28g fat (6g sat. fat), 57mg chol., 427mg sod., 8g carb. (0 sugars, 6g fiber), 13g pro.

RAGIN' CAJUN EGGPLANT & SHRIMP SKILLET

We always have a large summer garden where lots of produce lingers into fall. That's when we harvest our onions, green bell peppers, tomatoes and eggplant, some key ingredients of this dish. This recipe turns Cajun with the Holy Trinity (onion, celery and bell pepper), shrimp and red pepper flakes.

—*Barbara Hahn, Park Hills, MO*

PREP: 30 min. • **BAKE:** 35 min.
MAKES: 4 servings

- 1 medium eggplant, peeled and cut into ½-in. cubes
- 3 Tbsp. olive oil
- 2 celery ribs, diced
- 1 medium onion, diced
- 1 small green pepper, seeded and diced
- 3 plum tomatoes, diced
- 1 tsp. crushed red pepper flakes
- ½ tsp. pepper
- 12 oz. uncooked shell-on shrimp (31-40 per lb.), peeled and deveined
- ½ cup seasoned bread crumbs
- 1½ cups shredded part-skim mozzarella cheese

1. Place eggplant in a large saucepan; add water to cover. Bring to a boil. Reduce heat; simmer, covered, until eggplant is tender, 3-4 minutes. Drain.

2. Preheat oven to 350°. In an ovenproof skillet, heat oil over medium-high heat. Add celery, onion and green pepper; saute until tender, about 5 minutes. Reduce the heat to medium; stir in tomatoes and eggplant. Saute 5 minutes. Stir in seasonings. Add the shrimp and bread crumbs; saute 5 minutes longer, stirring well.

3. Bake 30 minutes. Remove skillet from oven; top with cheese. Bake 5 minutes more.

1 serving: 399 cal., 21g fat (7g sat. fat), 131mg chol., 641mg sod., 26g carb. (9g sugars, 5g fiber), 28g pro.

PARSLEY-CRUSTED COD

Struggling to increase your family's fish servings? You'll appreciate this easy cod with staple ingredients. The flavors are mild and delicious, so even picky eaters won't complain.

—*Judy Grebetz, Racine, WI*

TAKES: 30 min. • **MAKES:** 4 servings

- ¾ cup dry bread crumbs
- 1 Tbsp. minced fresh parsley
- 2 tsp. grated lemon zest
- 1 garlic clove, minced
- ¼ tsp. kosher salt
- ¼ tsp. pepper
- 2 Tbsp. olive oil
- 4 cod fillets (6 oz. each)

1. In a shallow bowl, combine the first 6 ingredients. Brush oil over 1 side of fillets; gently press into crumb mixture.

2. Place crumb side up in a 13x9-in. baking dish coated with cooking spray. Bake at 400° just until fish begins to flake easily with a fork, 15-20 minutes.

1 fillet: 215 cal., 8g fat (1g sat. fat), 65mg chol., 194mg sod., 6g carb. (1g sugars, 0 fiber), 28g pro. **Diabetic exchanges:** 5 lean meat, 1½ fat, ½ starch.

"The flavor is similar to many other breaded fish recipes I've tried, but this one excels with ease of preparation. There's no dipping the fish in liquid, then slopping it into crumbs. There's no mess whatsoever—very quick and easy. And it's baked with minimal fat, so it's healthier than a lot of other recipes. This is a keeper for sure."

—BRKORNHAUS, TASTEOFHOME.COM

RAGIN' CAJUN EGGPLANT & SHRIMP SKILLET

CREAMY SCALLOP CREPES

SALMON LOAF

During the Depression, Mom's tasty salmon loaf was a welcome change from the usual meat loaf everyone made to stretch a meal. I still enjoy a lot of the make-do meals of those days, but this old-fashioned loaf is one of my favorites.
—*Dorothy Bateman, Carver, MA*

PREP: 20 min. • **BAKE:** 40 min. + standing
MAKES: 4 servings

- 1 can (14¾ oz.) salmon, drained, bones and skin removed
- 1 small onion, finely chopped
- ½ cup soft bread crumbs
- ¼ cup butter, melted
- 3 large eggs, separated
- 2 tsp. lemon juice
- 1 tsp. minced fresh parsley
- ½ tsp. salt
- ⅛ tsp. pepper

OLIVE CREAM SAUCE
- 2 Tbsp. butter
- 2 Tbsp. all-purpose flour
- 1½ cups whole milk
- ¼ cup chopped pimiento-stuffed olives

1. In a large bowl, combine the salmon, onion, soft bread crumbs and butter. Stir in the egg yolks, lemon juice, parsley, salt and pepper.
2. In a small bowl, beat the egg whites on high speed until stiff peaks form. Fold into salmon mixture.
3. Transfer mixture to a greased 8x4-in. loaf pan. Place in a larger baking pan. Add 1 in. of hot water to larger pan. Bake at 350° until a knife inserted in the center comes out clean, 40-45 minutes. Let stand for 10 minutes before slicing.
4. Meanwhile, in a small saucepan, melt the butter. Stir in flour until smooth; gradually add milk. Bring to a boil; cook and stir until thickened, 1-2 minutes. Stir in olives. Serve with salmon loaf.

1 serving: 476 cal., 33g fat (15g sat. fat), 264mg chol., 1334mg sod., 13g carb. (6g sugars, 1g fiber), 30g pro.

🍎 CREAMY SCALLOP CREPES

These savory crepes feel so elegant for the holidays. I like to add ¼ teaspoon of fresh dill weed to the crepe batter before refrigerating.
—*Doreen Kelly, Hatboro, PA*

PREP: 45 min. + chilling • **BAKE:** 15 min.
MAKES: 6 servings

- 2 large egg whites
- 1 large egg
- 1½ cups fat-free milk
- 1 cup all-purpose flour
- ½ tsp. salt
- 2 Tbsp. unsalted butter, melted

FILLING
- 1 lb. bay scallops
- ½ cup white wine or reduced-sodium chicken broth
- ⅛ tsp. white pepper
- 1 lb. sliced fresh mushrooms
- 4 green onions, sliced
- 2 Tbsp. butter
- ¼ cup all-purpose flour
- ⅔ cup fat-free evaporated milk
- ½ cup shredded reduced-fat Swiss cheese
  Sliced green onions, optional

1. In a small bowl, beat the egg whites, egg and milk. Combine flour and salt; add to milk mixture and mix well. Chill for 1 hour.
2. Brush an 8-in. nonstick skillet lightly with melted butter; heat. Stir crepe batter; pour 2 Tbsp. into center of pan. Lift and tilt pan to coat bottom evenly. Cook until top appears dry; turn and cook 15-20 seconds longer. Remove to a wire rack. Repeat with remaining batter, brushing skillet with melted butter as needed. When cool, stack crepes with waxed paper or paper towels in between.
3. In a large nonstick skillet, bring scallops, wine and pepper to a boil. Reduce heat; simmer until scallops are firm and opaque, 3-4 minutes. Drain, reserving cooking liquid; set liquid and scallops aside.
4. In the same skillet, saute mushrooms and onions in butter until almost tender. Sprinkle with flour; stir until blended. Gradually stir in evaporated milk and cooking liquid. Bring to a boil; cook and stir until thickened, about 2 minutes. Remove from the heat. Stir in the cheese and scallops.
5. Spread ⅓ cup filling down the center of each crepe; roll up. Place in a 13x9-in. baking dish coated with cooking spray. Cover and bake at 350° 12-15 minutes or until heated through. Sprinkle with onions if desired.

2 crepes: 331 cal., 10g fat (6g sat. fat), 76mg chol., 641mg sod., 33g carb. (9g sugars, 2g fiber), 24g pro. **Diabetic exchanges:** 3 lean meat, 2 starch, 2 fat.

SALMON
LOAF

TANGY PARMESAN TILAPIA

If you want a gluten-free fish coating, this works beautifully! Some reduced-fat mayos may contain gluten, though, so check the label on yours to be sure.
—Deborah Purdue, Westland, MI

- -

TAKES: 15 min. • **MAKES:** 4 servings

- ¼ cup grated Parmesan cheese
- 2 Tbsp. reduced-fat mayonnaise
- 1 Tbsp. butter, softened
- 1 Tbsp. lime juice
- ⅛ tsp. garlic powder
- ⅛ tsp. dried basil
- ⅛ tsp. pepper
  Dash onion powder
- 4 tilapia fillets (5 oz. each)
- ¼ tsp. salt

1. Preheat broiler. Mix the first 8 ingredients until blended.

2. Line a 15x10x1-in. baking pan with foil; coat foil with cooking spray. Place tilapia in pan; sprinkle with salt.

3. Broil 3-4 in. from heat 2-3 minutes per side. Spread cheese mixture over fillets. Broil until topping is golden brown and fish just begins to flake easily with a fork, 1-2 minutes.

1 fillet: 191 cal., 8g fat (4g sat. fat), 84mg chol., 359mg sod., 2g carb. (0 sugars, 0 fiber), 28g pro. **Diabetic exchanges:** 4 lean meat, 1½ fat.

BAKED FISH & RICE

You have to love a delectable fish dinner with veggies and rice that only dirties one dish. Your family will be lining up to dig in!
—Taste of Home *Test Kitchen*

- -

PREP: 10 min. • **BAKE:** 30 min.
MAKES: 4 servings

- 2 cups uncooked instant rice
- 1 pkg. (16 oz.) frozen broccoli-cauliflower blend, thawed
- 4 tilapia or other white fish fillets (6 oz. each)
- 1 can (14½ oz.) chicken broth
- 1 can (14½ oz.) fire-roasted diced tomatoes, undrained
- 1 tsp. garlic powder
- 1 tsp. lemon-pepper seasoning
- ¼ to ½ tsp. cayenne pepper
- ½ cup shredded cheddar cheese

1. Place rice in a greased 13x9-in. baking dish. Layer with the vegetables and fish. Pour the broth and tomatoes over the top; sprinkle with seasonings.

2. Cover and bake at 375° 25-30 minutes or until fish flakes easily with a fork and rice is tender. Sprinkle with cheese; bake until cheese is melted, 5 minutes longer.

1 serving: 442 cal., 7g fat (3g sat. fat), 119mg chol., 1047mg sod., 51g carb. (3g sugars, 3g fiber), 38g pro.

TANGY PARMESAN TILAPIA

FOIL-PACKET SHRIMP & SAUSAGE JAMBALAYA

CRAB MACARONI CASSEROLE

Cold winter evenings are much more tolerable with this comforting casserole. Whole wheat macaroni boosts nutrition, while the melted cheese topping makes it rich and so satisfying. We like it best with a veggie side.
—*Jason Egner, Edgerton, WI*

PREP: 25 min. • **BAKE:** 20 min.
MAKES: 6 servings

- 2 cups uncooked whole wheat elbow macaroni
- 3 Tbsp. chopped onion
- 2 Tbsp. butter
- 3 Tbsp. all-purpose flour
- 1½ cups fat-free milk
- 2 cans (6 oz. each) lump crabmeat, drained
- 1 cup reduced-fat sour cream
- ½ cup shredded Swiss cheese
- ½ tsp. salt
- ½ tsp. ground mustard
- 1 cup shredded fat-free cheddar cheese, divided

1. Cook elbow macaroni according to package directions.
2. Meanwhile, in a large skillet, saute onion in butter until tender. Combine flour and milk until smooth; stir into pan. Bring to a boil; cook and stir for 1-2 minutes or until thickened. Remove from the heat. Drain macaroni. Add the crabmeat, sour cream, Swiss cheese, salt, mustard, macaroni and ¼ cup cheddar cheese to the skillet.
3. Transfer to an 11x7-in. baking dish coated with cooking spray. Sprinkle with remaining cheddar cheese. Bake, uncovered, at 350° for 20-25 minutes or until heated through.
1 cup: 380 cal., 11g fat (6g sat. fat), 86mg chol., 619mg sod., 38g carb. (7g sugars, 4g fiber), 31g pro. **Diabetic exchanges:** 3 lean meat, 2 starch, 1½ fat.

FOIL-PACKET SHRIMP & SAUSAGE JAMBALAYA

This hearty, satisfying dinner has all the flavors of an authentic jambalaya with little effort. The foil packets can be prepared a day ahead and cooked right before serving. These are also good on the grill!
—*Allison Stroud, Oklahoma City, OK*

PREP: 20 min. • **BAKE:** 20 min.
MAKES: 6 servings

- 12 oz. fully cooked andouille sausage links, cut into ½-in. slices
- 12 oz. uncooked shrimp (31-40 per lb.), peeled and deveined
- 1 medium green pepper, chopped
- 1 medium onion, chopped
- 2 celery ribs, chopped
- 3 garlic cloves, minced
- 2 tsp. Creole seasoning
- 1 can (14½ oz.) fire-roasted diced tomatoes, drained
- 1 cup uncooked instant rice
- 1 can (8 oz.) tomato sauce
- ½ cup chicken broth

Preheat oven to 425°. In a large bowl, combine all ingredients. Divide mixture among 6 greased 18x12-in. pieces of heavy-duty foil. Fold foil around mixture and crimp edges to seal, forming packets; place on a baking sheet. Bake until shrimp turn pink and rice is tender, 20-25 minutes.
1 packet: 287 cal., 12g fat (4g sat. fat), 143mg chol., 1068mg sod., 23g carb. (3g sugars, 2g fiber), 23g pro.

TEST KITCHEN TIP
Make sure to use instant rice. If you use long grain or converted rice, the shrimp will be done long before the rice.

FETA
TOMATO-BASIL
FISH

FETA TOMATO-BASIL FISH

I rely on my husband for the main ingredient in this fuss-free dish. He fills our freezer after his summer fishing trip.
—*Alicia Szeszol, Lindenhurst, IL*

TAKES: 20 min. • **MAKES:** 4 servings

- ⅓ cup chopped onion
- 1 garlic clove, minced
- 2 tsp. olive oil
- 1 can (14½ oz.) Italian diced tomatoes, drained
- 1½ tsp. minced fresh basil or ½ tsp. dried basil
- 1 lb. walleye, bass or other white fish fillets
- 4 oz. crumbled feta cheese

1. In a saucepan, saute onion and garlic in oil until tender. Add tomatoes and basil. Bring to a boil. Reduce heat; simmer, uncovered, for 5 minutes.

2. Meanwhile, broil fish 4-6 in. from the heat for 5-6 minutes. Top each fillet with tomato mixture and cheese. Broil 5-7 minutes longer or until fish just begins to flake easily with a fork.

1 serving: 241 cal., 8g fat (4g sat. fat), 113mg chol., 660mg sod., 12g carb. (7g sugars, 2g fiber), 28g pro. **Diabetic exchanges:** 4 lean meat, 1 vegetable, 1 fat.

"I've made this twice for lunch now and really enjoy it. Quick, easy, tasty and healthy!"
—DANICALIFORNIA, TASTEOFHOME.COM

ROAST LEMON BUTTER SHRIMP

ROAST LEMON BUTTER SHRIMP

This baked shrimp is a quick and easy weeknight meal that has lots of great flavor!
—*Anne Ormond, Dover, NH*

TAKES: 30 min. • **MAKES:** 4 servings

- 6 Tbsp. unsalted butter, cubed
- ¼ cup Worcestershire sauce
- 2 garlic cloves, minced
- 3 Tbsp. lemon juice
- 1 fresh rosemary sprig
- ½ tsp. salt
- ¼ tsp. pepper
- 1 lb. uncooked shrimp (26-30 per lb.), peeled and deveined, tails removed
- 1 pkg. (8½ oz.) ready-to-serve jasmine rice
- 3 Tbsp. heavy whipping cream
  Hot pepper sauce, optional

1. Preheat oven to 400°. Place the first 7 ingredients in a 13x9-in. baking dish. Place dish in oven 3-5 minutes or until butter is melted. Add shrimp. Bake, uncovered, until shrimp turn pink, 12-15 minutes, stirring halfway. Meanwhile, cook rice according to package directions.

2. Discard rosemary; stir in cream. Serve shrimp mixture with rice and, if desired, hot pepper sauce.

1 serving: 431 cal., 24g fat (14g sat. fat), 196mg chol., 607mg sod., 32g carb. (2g sugars, 1g fiber), 22g pro.

Bonus: Cast-Iron Desserts

BERRY WHIRLIGIG

BERRY WHIRLIGIG

Blackberries are an Oregon treasure. We love to go out and pick our own. Whatever we don't eat fresh, we freeze to enjoy whenever we start dreaming of this irresistible treat.
—*Pearl Stanford, Medford, OR*

PREP: 25 min. • **BAKE:** 25 min.
MAKES: 9 servings

- ½ cup sugar
- 2 Tbsp. cornstarch
- ½ tsp. salt
- ¼ tsp. ground cinnamon
- 1 cup water
- 3 cups fresh or frozen blackberries or a mixture of berries

ROLLS

- 1 cup all-purpose flour
- 2 tsp. baking powder
- ½ tsp. salt
- 2 Tbsp. shortening
- 1 large egg, room temperature, lightly beaten
- 2 Tbsp. 2% milk
- ¼ cup butter, softened
- ½ cup sugar
- 1 tsp. grated lemon zest
- ¼ tsp. ground cinnamon

1. In a large saucepan, combine the sugar, cornstarch, salt and cinnamon. Stir in water until smooth. Cook until mixture boils and thickens. Stir in berries; cook over low heat for 5 minutes.

2. Pour into a greased 9- or 10-in. cast-iron skillet or 8-in. square baking pan; set aside. In a large bowl, combine the flour, baking powder and salt. Cut in shortening until coarse crumbs form.

3. In a small bowl, mix egg and milk. Add to flour mixture; stir until mixture forms a soft ball. Knead several minutes. Roll into a 12x8-in. rectangle. Spread with butter. Combine sugar, zest and cinnamon; sprinkle over dough.

4. Starting at a long end, roll up; seal edges. Cut into 9 slices. Place slices over berry mixture. Bake at 400° until golden brown, 22-25 minutes.

1 serving: 248 cal., 9g fat (4g sat. fat), 38mg chol., 412mg sod., 41g carb. (26g sugars, 3g fiber), 3g pro.

CARIBBEAN WONTONS

MILK CAKE

This is a simple recipe—and especially easy in a well-seasoned cast-iron skillet. The result is a deliciously light, airy cake.
—*Suzanne Coleman, Rabun Gap, GA*

- -

PREP: 20 min. • **BAKE:** 30 min.
MAKES: 8 servings

- ½ cup whole milk
- ¾ cup all-purpose flour
- 1 tsp. baking powder
- ¼ tsp. salt
- 3 large eggs, room temperature
- 1 tsp. vanilla extract
- 1 cup sugar

TOPPING
- ⅓ cup packed brown sugar
- ½ cup chopped pecans
- 2 Tbsp. butter, softened
- 2 Tbsp. whole milk
- 1 cup sweetened shredded coconut

1. Scald milk by bringing it almost to a boil; set aside to cool. Combine flour, baking powder and salt; set aside. In a bowl, beat eggs until thick and lemon-colored; stir in vanilla. Gradually add sugar, blending well. On low speed, alternately mix in milk and dry ingredients. Pour batter into a greased 10-in. cast-iron skillet.

2. Bake at 350° for 25-30 minutes or until the cake springs back when lightly touched. Remove cake and preheat broiler. Combine all topping ingredients and sprinkle over cake. Broil 5 in. from the heat until topping bubbles and turns golden brown. Serve warm.

1 slice: 349 cal., 15g fat (7g sat. fat), 90mg chol., 220mg sod., 51g carb. (39g sugars, 2g fiber), 5g pro.

"Mother always made this cake for us kids. If baking in a skillet, you can cut a round circle of parchment paper for the bottom to make sure the cake easily comes out."
—WONKYGIRL, TASTEOFHOME.COM

CARIBBEAN WONTONS

I first served these fresh and fruity treats as an appetizer at a summer luau. My family and friends now enjoy them as a fun dessert for occasions throughout the year.
—*Melissa Pelkey Hass, Waleska, GA*

- -

PREP: 30 min. • **COOK:** 5 min./batch
MAKES: 2 dozen (1¼ cups sauce)

- 4 oz. cream cheese, softened
- ¼ cup sweetened shredded coconut
- ¼ cup mashed ripe banana
- 2 Tbsp. chopped walnuts
- 2 Tbsp. canned crushed pineapple
- 1 cup marshmallow creme
- 24 wonton wrappers
  Oil for deep-fat frying

SAUCE
- 1 lb. fresh strawberries, hulled
- ¼ cup sugar
- 1 tsp. cornstarch
  Confectioners' sugar and ground cinnamon

1. In a small bowl, beat cream cheese until smooth. Stir in the coconut, banana, walnuts and pineapple. Fold in marshmallow creme.

2. Position a wonton wrapper with 1 point toward you. Keep the remaining wrappers covered with a damp paper towel until ready to use. Place 2 tsp. of filling in the center of wrapper. Moisten the edges with water; fold opposite corners together over filling and press to seal. Repeat with the remaining wrappers and filling.

3. In a cast-iron or electric skillet, heat oil to 375°. Fry wontons, a few at a time, until golden brown, 15-20 seconds on each side. Drain on paper towels.

4. Place strawberries in a food processor; cover and process until pureed. In a small saucepan, combine sugar and cornstarch. Stir in pureed berries. Bring to a boil; cook and stir until thickened, 2 minutes. If desired, strain mixture, reserving sauce; discard the seeds. Sprinkle wontons with confectioners' sugar and cinnamon. Serve with sauce.

1 wonton with 1½ tsp. sauce: 95 cal., 4g fat (2g sat. fat), 6mg chol., 66mg sod., 13g carb. (7g sugars, 1g fiber), 1g pro.

DATE PUDDING
COBBLER

CANDIED SWEET POTATO PIES

My grandmother made the best candied sweet potatoes. She was also famous for her incredible fried apricot pies. This recipe combines the best of both.
—*Angela Eshelman, Phoenix, AZ*

- -

PREP: 1 hour 35 min.
MAKES: 12 pies

- 6 cups all-purpose flour
- 2 tsp. salt
- 2 cups shortening
- ⅔ cup water
- 2 large eggs, room temperature
- 2 Tbsp. white vinegar
- 1 large sweet potato, peeled and cut into 1-in. cubes
- ¾ cup sugar
- ¼ cup butter, cubed
- 1½ tsp. lemon juice
- ½ tsp. salt
- ¼ tsp. vanilla extract
   Oil for deep-fat frying
   Confectioners' sugar

1. In a large bowl, combine flour and salt; cut in shortening until mixture resembles coarse crumbs. Combine water, eggs and vinegar; gradually add to dry ingredients, tossing with a fork until a ball forms. Cover and chill until easy to handle, 1-1½ hours.
2. Meanwhile, place sweet potato in a small saucepan; cover with water. Bring to a boil. Reduce heat; cover and cook just until tender, 10-15 minutes. Drain.
3. In a large skillet, combine the sugar, butter and potatoes; cook and stir until the syrup is golden brown, 15-20 minutes. Remove from the heat and mash. Stir in the lemon juice, salt and vanilla. Cool to room temperature.
4. Roll out dough to ¼-in. thickness. Cut out 12 circles with a floured 5½-in. round cookie cutter. Spoon 2 Tbsp. filling onto half of each circle. Moisten edges with water; fold crust over filling and press edges with a fork to seal.
5. In a deep cast-iron or electric skillet, heat 1 in. oil to 375°. Fry pies in batches until golden brown, about 5 minutes, turning once. Drain pies on paper towels. Dust with confectioners' sugar.
1 pie: 771 cal., 51g fat (12g sat. fat), 41mg chol., 538mg sod., 67g carb. (16g sugars, 3g fiber), 8g pro.

DATE PUDDING COBBLER

There were eight children in my family when I was a girl, and we all enjoyed this homestyle cobbler. I now serve it for everyday and special occasions alike.
—*Carolyn Miller, Guys Mills, PA*

- -

PREP: 15 min. • **BAKE:** 25 min.
MAKES: 8 servings

- 1 cup all-purpose flour
- 1½ cups packed brown sugar, divided
- 2 tsp. baking powder
- 1 Tbsp. cold butter
- ½ cup 2% milk
- ¾ cup chopped dates
- ¾ cup chopped walnuts
- 1 cup water
   Optional: Whipped cream and ground cinnamon

1. In a large bowl, combine the flour, ½ cup brown sugar and baking powder. Cut in the butter until crumbly. Gradually add the milk, dates and walnuts.
2. In a large saucepan, combine the water and the remaining brown sugar; bring to a boil. Remove from the heat; add the date mixture and mix well.
3. Transfer to a greased 10-in. cast-iron skillet or 8-in. square baking pan. Bake at 350° for 25-30 minutes or until top is golden brown and fruit is tender. Serve warm, with whipped cream and cinnamon if desired.
1 serving: 347 cal., 9g fat (2g sat. fat), 5mg chol., 150mg sod., 65g carb. (50g sugars, 2g fiber), 4g pro.

CANDIED SWEET
POTATO PIES

DEEP-FRIED CANDY BARS ON A STICK

Why wait in line at the state fair for deep-fried candy bars when you can satisfy your curious taste buds in your very own home? Be sure to make a lot—these novelties go fast!
—Taste of Home *Test Kitchen*

- -

PREP: 20 min. • **COOK:** 5 min./batch
MAKES: 2 dozen

1½ cups all-purpose flour
4½ tsp. baking powder
 1 Tbsp. sugar
 1 Tbsp. brown sugar
⅛ tsp. salt
⅛ tsp. ground cinnamon
 1 large egg
½ cup water
½ cup 2% milk
¼ tsp. vanilla extract
 Oil for deep-fat frying
24 fun-size Snickers and/or Milky Way candy bars, frozen
 Wooden skewers
 Confectioners' sugar, optional

1. Whisk together the first 6 ingredients. In another bowl, whisk together egg, water, milk and vanilla; add to dry ingredients, stirring just until moistened.
2. In a deep cast-iron or electric skillet, heat oil to 375°. Dip candy bars, a few at a time, into batter; fry until golden brown, about 30 seconds per side. Drain on paper towels.
3. Insert skewers into bars. If desired, dust with confectioners' sugar.
1 fried candy bar: 136 cal., 7g fat (2g sat. fat), 11mg chol., 130mg sod., 16g carb. (9g sugars, 1g fiber), 2g pro.

GRILLED CRANBERRY PEAR CRUMBLE

My husband loves dessert. Fruit crisps are easy and quick to prepare, so I make them often. I created this fall-flavored grilled version with fresh pears and items I had on hand. We declared it a keeper!
—*Ronna Farley, Rockville, MD*

- -

TAKES: 30 min. • **MAKES:** 6 servings

 3 medium ripe pears, sliced
½ cup dried cranberries
¼ cup sugar
 2 Tbsp. all-purpose flour
¼ tsp. ground cinnamon
 1 Tbsp. butter
TOPPING
 2 Tbsp. butter, melted
¼ tsp. ground cinnamon
 1 cup granola without raisins

1. Toss pears and cranberries with sugar, flour and cinnamon. Place 1 Tbsp. butter in a 9-in. cast-iron skillet. Place on grill rack over medium heat until butter is melted. Stir in the fruit; grill, covered, until pears are tender, 15-20 minutes, stirring occasionally.
2. For topping, mix melted butter and cinnamon; toss with granola. Sprinkle over pears. Grill, covered, 5 minutes. Serve warm.
1 serving: 258 cal., 9g fat (4g sat. fat), 15mg chol., 54mg sod., 47g carb. (29g sugars, 7g fiber), 4g pro.

DEEP-FRIED CANDY BARS ON A STICK

CAST-IRON
PEACH CROSTATA

SKILLET CARAMEL APRICOT GRUNT

Here's an old-fashioned pantry dessert made with items you likely have on hand. Mix up a second batch of the dry ingredients for the dumplings to save a few minutes the next time you prepare it.
—*Shannon Norris, Cudahy, WI*

PREP: 20 min. + standing • **BAKE:** 20 min.
MAKES: 8 servings

- 2 cans (15¼ oz. each) apricot halves, undrained
- 2 tsp. quick-cooking tapioca
- ⅓ cup packed brown sugar
- 1 Tbsp. butter
- 1 Tbsp. lemon juice

DUMPLINGS

- 1½ cups all-purpose flour
- ½ cup sugar
- 2 tsp. baking powder
- 2 Tbsp. cold butter
- ½ cup whole milk

TOPPING

- ¼ cup packed brown sugar
- 1 Tbsp. water
  Half-and-half cream, optional

1. In a large saucepan, combine apricots and tapioca; let stand for 15 minutes. Add the brown sugar, butter and lemon juice. Cook and stir until the mixture comes to a full boil. Reduce heat to low; keep warm.
2. For dumplings, in a large bowl, combine the flour, sugar and baking powder; cut in butter until crumbly. Add milk; mix just until combined. Pour warm fruit mixture into an ungreased 9- or 10-in. cast-iron skillet. Drop the batter in 6 mounds onto fruit mixture.
3. Bake, uncovered, at 425° until a toothpick inserted into a dumpling comes out clean, about 15 minutes. Stir together brown sugar and water; microwave until sugar is dissolved, stirring frequently, about 30 seconds. Spoon over dumplings; bake 5 minutes longer. Serve with cream if desired.
1 serving: 336 cal., 5g fat (3g sat. fat), 13mg chol., 170mg sod., 71g carb. (51g sugars, 2g fiber), 4g pro.

CAST-IRON PEACH CROSTATA

While the crostata, an open-faced fruit tart, has Italian origins, my peach-filled version is American all the way.
—*Lauren Knoelke, Des Moines, IA*

PREP: 45 min. + chilling • **BAKE:** 45 min.
MAKES: 10 servings

- 1½ cups all-purpose flour
- 2 Tbsp. plus ¾ cup packed brown sugar, divided
- 1¼ tsp. salt, divided
- ½ cup cold unsalted butter, cubed
- 2 Tbsp. shortening
- 3 to 5 Tbsp. ice water
- 8 cups sliced peaches (about 7-8 medium)
- 1 Tbsp. lemon juice
- 3 Tbsp. cornstarch
- ½ tsp. ground cinnamon
- ¼ tsp. ground nutmeg
- 1 large egg, beaten
- 2 Tbsp. sliced almonds
- 1 Tbsp. coarse sugar
- ⅓ cup water
- 1 cup fresh raspberries, optional

1. Mix flour, 2 Tbsp. brown sugar and 1 tsp. salt; cut in the butter and shortening until crumbly. Gradually add ice water, tossing mixture with a fork until the dough holds together when pressed. Shape into a disk. Cover and refrigerate 1 hour or overnight.
2. Combine peaches and lemon juice. Add remaining brown sugar, cornstarch, spices and remaining salt; toss gently. Let stand 30 minutes.
3. Preheat oven to 400°. On a lightly floured surface, roll dough into a 13-in. circle; transfer to a 10-in. cast-iron skillet, letting excess hang over edge. Using a slotted spoon, transfer peaches into crust, reserving liquid. Fold crust edge over filling, pleating as you go, leaving center uncovered. Brush folded crust with beaten egg; sprinkle with almonds and coarse sugar. Bake until crust is dark golden and filling bubbly, 45-55 minutes.
4. In a small saucepan, combine reserved liquid and water; bring to a boil. Simmer until thickened, 1-2 minutes; serve warm with pie. If desired, top with fresh raspberries.
1 slice: 322 cal., 13g fat (7g sat. fat), 43mg chol., 381mg sod., 49g carb. (30g sugars, 3g fiber), 4g pro.

SKILLET CHOCOLATE
CHUNK WALNUT BLONDIES

CHOCOLATE CHIP DUTCH BABY

I modified a traditional Dutch baby recipe a friend gave me to come up with this version. My family loves it, and it's so easy to make!
—*Mary Thompson, LaCrosse, WI*

- -

TAKES: 30 min. • **MAKES:** 4 servings

- ¼ cup miniature semisweet chocolate chips
- ¼ cup packed brown sugar

DUTCH BABY
- ½ cup all-purpose flour
- 2 large eggs, room temperature
- ½ cup half-and-half cream
- ⅛ tsp. ground nutmeg
  Dash ground cinnamon
- 3 Tbsp. butter
  Maple syrup and additional butter, optional

1. In a small bowl, combine chocolate chips and brown sugar; set aside. In a small bowl, beat the flour, eggs, cream, nutmeg and cinnamon until smooth.
2. Place butter in a 9-in. pie plate or an 8-in. cast-iron skillet. Heat in a 425° oven until

melted, about 4 minutes. Pour batter into hot pie plate or skillet. Sprinkle with the chocolate chip mixture. Bake until top edges are golden brown, 13-15 minutes. Serve immediately with syrup and butter if desired.

1 piece: 313 cal., 17g fat (10g sat. fat), 144mg chol., 140mg sod., 33g carb. (21g sugars, 1g fiber), 6g pro.

SKILLET CHOCOLATE CHUNK WALNUT BLONDIES

Bring these beauties to a potluck and you'll find only crumbs on your platter when it's time to head home. Everyone will ask who made the scrumptious blondies, so be sure to bring copies of the recipe!
—*Peggy Woodward, Shullsburg, WI*

- -

PREP: 15 min. • **BAKE:** 30 min.
MAKES: 3 blondies (8 servings each)

- 1 cup butter, melted
- 2 cups packed brown sugar
- 2 tsp. vanilla extract
- 2 large eggs, room temperature
- 2 cups all-purpose flour
- ½ cup ground walnuts
- 1 tsp. baking powder
- ½ tsp. salt
- ⅛ tsp. baking soda
- 1 cup chopped walnuts, toasted
- 1 cup semisweet chocolate chunks

1. Preheat oven to 350°. Grease three 6½-in. cast-iron skillets.
2. In a large bowl, mix butter, brown sugar and vanilla until blended. Add eggs, 1 at a time, whisking to blend after each addition. In another bowl, mix flour, ground walnuts, baking powder, salt and baking soda; stir into butter mixture. Fold in chopped walnuts and chocolate chunks.
3. Spread into skillets. Bake until a toothpick inserted in center comes out with moist crumbs and top is golden, 30-35 minutes. Cool slightly; serve warm.

Note: Recipe may also be prepared in a parchment-lined greased 13x9-in. baking pan. Bake 30-35 minutes or until a toothpick inserted in center comes out with moist crumbs and top is golden brown.

1 serving: 262 cal., 15g fat (7g sat. fat), 36mg chol., 149mg sod., 32g carb. (22g sugars, 1g fiber), 3g pro.

PEACH PIE

CARAMEL-APPLE SKILLET BUCKLE

My grandma used to make a version of this for me when I was a girl. She used fresh apples from the tree in her yard. I've adapted her recipe because I love the combination of apple, pecans and caramel.
—*Emily Hobbs, Springfield, MO*

PREP: 35 min. • **BAKE:** 1 hour + standing
MAKES: 12 servings

- ½ cup butter, softened
- ¾ cup sugar
- 2 large eggs, room temperature
- 1 tsp. vanilla extract
- 2 cups all-purpose flour
- 2½ tsp. baking powder
- 1¾ tsp. ground cinnamon
- ½ tsp. ground ginger
- ¼ tsp. salt
- 1½ cups buttermilk

TOPPING
- ⅔ cup packed brown sugar
- ½ cup all-purpose flour
- ¼ cup cold butter
- ¾ cup finely chopped pecans
- ½ cup old-fashioned oats
- 6 cups thinly sliced peeled Gala or other sweet apples (about 6 medium)
- 18 caramels, unwrapped
- 1 Tbsp. buttermilk
  Vanilla ice cream, optional

1. Preheat oven to 350°. In a large bowl, cream butter and sugar until light and fluffy, 5-7 minutes. Add eggs, 1 at a time, beating well after each addition. Beat in vanilla. In another bowl, whisk flour, baking powder, cinnamon, ginger and salt; add to creamed mixture alternately with buttermilk, beating well after each addition. Pour into a greased 12-in. cast-iron or other ovenproof skillet.
2. For topping, in a small bowl, mix brown sugar and flour; cut in butter until crumbly. Stir in pecans and oats; sprinkle over batter. Top with apples. Bake until the apples are golden brown, 60-70 minutes. Cool in pan on a wire rack.
3. In a microwave, melt the caramels with buttermilk; stir until smooth. Drizzle over cake. Let stand until set. If desired, serve with ice cream.
1 slice: 462 cal., 19g fat (9g sat. fat), 64mg chol., 354mg sod., 68g carb. (42g sugars, 3g fiber), 7g pro.

PEACH PIE

I acquired this recipe for delicious peach pie filling some 40 years ago, when my husband and I first moved to southern Iowa and had peach trees growing in our backyard. It's been a family favorite since then and always brings back memories of both summer and those happy early years.
—*June Mueller, Sioux City, IA*

PREP: 35 min. + standing
BAKE: 50 min. + cooling
MAKES: 8 servings

- ½ cup sugar
- ¼ cup packed brown sugar
- 4½ cups sliced peeled peaches
  Pastry for double-crust pie (9 in.)
- 3 Tbsp. cornstarch
- ¼ tsp. ground nutmeg
- ¼ tsp. ground cinnamon
- ⅛ tsp. salt
- 2 tsp. lemon juice
- 1 Tbsp. butter
  Vanilla ice cream

1. In a large bowl, combine sugars; add the peaches and toss gently. Cover and let stand for 1 hour. Line a 9-in. pie plate or cast-iron skillet with bottom pastry; trim even with edge. Set crust aside. Drain the peaches, reserving juice.
2. In a small saucepan, combine the cornstarch, nutmeg, cinnamon and salt; gradually stir in reserved juice. Bring to a boil; cook and stir until thickened, about 2 minutes. Remove from the heat; stir in lemon juice and butter. Gently fold in the peaches. Pour filling into crust.
3. Roll out remaining pastry; make a lattice crust. Trim, seal and flute edges. Cover edges loosely with foil. Bake at 400° until the crust is golden brown and the filling is bubbly, 50-60 minutes. Remove foil. Cool on a wire rack. If desired, serve with vanilla ice cream.
1 piece: 380 cal., 16g fat (7g sat. fat), 14mg chol., 254mg sod., 59g carb. (29g sugars, 2g fiber), 3g pro.

CARAMEL-APPLE
SKILLET BUCKLE

POT OF
S'MORES

POT OF S'MORES

This easy Dutch-oven version of the popular campout treat is utterly melty, gooey and good. The hardest part is waiting for it to cool a bit so you can dig in. Yum!
—*June Dress, Meridian, ID*

TAKES: 25 min. • **MAKES:** 12 servings

- 1 pkg. (14½ oz.) graham crackers, crushed
- ½ cup butter, melted
- 1 can (14 oz.) sweetened condensed milk
- 2 cups semisweet chocolate chips
- 1 cup butterscotch chips
- 2 cups miniature marshmallows

1. Prepare grill or campfire for low heat, using 16-18 charcoal briquettes or large wood chips.

2. Line a cast-iron Dutch oven with a piece of heavy-duty aluminum foil. Combine cracker crumbs and butter; press into bottom of pan. Pour condensed milk over the crust and sprinkle with chocolate and butterscotch chips. Top with marshmallows.

3. Cover Dutch oven. When the briquettes or wood chips are covered with white ash, place the Dutch oven directly on top of 6 of them. Using long-handled tongs, place remaining briquettes on pan cover.

4. Cook until marshmallows begin to melt, about 15 minutes. To check for doneness, use the tongs to carefully lift the cover.

1 serving: 584 cal., 28g fat (17g sat. fat), 31mg chol., 326mg sod., 83g carb. (47g sugars, 3g fiber), 8g pro.

TEST KITCHEN TIP

A Dutch oven will stay warm long after you remove it from the grill or campfire. Take advantage of those properties by using the pot as a serving vessel. It works the other way, too; fill Dutch oven with ice water for about 10 minutes. Then drain it and use it to keep cold dishes like potato salad and other picnic foods even colder.

SKILLET STOUT BROWNIES

SKILLET STOUT BROWNIES

These stout brownies are so rich and fudgy. I love that you only need one bowl and a skillet to make this quick dessert, making it perfect for busy weeknights when you don't want a sink full of dishes.
—*Mandy Naglich, New York, NY*

PREP: 30 min. • **BAKE:** 25 min. + cooling
MAKES: 12 servings

- 8 oz. semisweet chocolate, chopped
- 1 cup butter, cubed
- 1 cup milk stout beer
- 1 large egg, room temperature
- 2 large egg yolks, room temperature
- ¾ cup sugar
- ¼ cup packed brown sugar
- ¾ cup all-purpose flour
- ⅓ cup baking cocoa
- ½ tsp. salt
  Vanilla ice cream, optional

1. Preheat oven to 350°. Place semisweet chocolate in a large bowl. In a 10-in. cast-iron or other ovenproof skillet, combine butter and stout. Bring to a boil; reduce heat. Simmer 10 minutes, stirring constantly. Pour over chocolate; stir with a whisk until smooth. Cool slightly. In another large bowl, beat egg, egg yolks and sugars until blended. Stir in chocolate mixture. In another bowl, mix the flour, baking cocoa and salt; gradually add to chocolate mixture, mixing well.

2. Spread into skillet. Bake until set, 25-30 minutes. Cool completely in skillet on a wire rack. If desired, serve with vanilla ice cream.

1 piece: 363 cal., 24g fat (14g sat. fat), 87mg chol., 229mg sod., 29g carb. (21g sugars, 1g fiber), 4g pro.

BERRY JAM FUNNEL CAKES

When I was in high school, I made these funnel cakes every Sunday after church for my family. They are crisp and tender, just like the kind we always ate at the state fair.
—*Susan Tingley, Portland, OR*

- -

PREP: 15 min. • **COOK:** 5 min./batch
MAKES: 8 servings

- 2 cups 2% milk
- 3 large eggs
- ¼ cup sugar
- 2 cups all-purpose flour
- 2 tsp. baking powder
   Oil for deep-fat frying
   Confectioners' sugar
   Lingonberry jam or red currant jelly

1. In a large bowl, combine the milk, eggs and sugar. Combine flour and baking powder; beat into egg mixture until smooth.
2. In a cast-iron or electric skillet, heat 2 in. oil to 375°. Cover the bottom of a funnel spout with your finger; ladle ½ cup batter into the funnel. Holding the funnel several inches above the skillet, release your finger and move the funnel in a spiral motion until all the batter is released. Scrape funnel with a rubber spatula if needed.
3. Fry until golden brown, 1 minute on each side. Drain on paper towels. Repeat with remaining batter. Dust with confectioners' sugar. Serve warm with jam.
1 funnel cake: 300 cal., 15g fat (2g sat. fat), 84mg chol., 157mg sod., 33g carb. (10g sugars, 1g fiber), 8g pro.

ORANGE & PEAR UPSIDE-DOWN CAKE

I love cooking with my cast-iron skillet, whether it's to make a main dish or a dessert. This upside-down cake is a fall version of a typical summer standby.
—*Linda Persall, Cullman, AL*

- -

PREP: 25 min. • **BAKE:** 45 min. + cooling
MAKES: 10 servings

- ½ cup butter, cubed
- ½ cup packed brown sugar
- 2 medium ripe pears, peeled and quartered
- 2 Tbsp. grated orange zest, divided
- ⅔ cup sugar
- ⅓ cup coconut oil
- 1 large egg, room temperature
- 1⅓ cups all-purpose flour
- 1½ tsp. baking powder
- ½ tsp. salt
- ¾ cup half-and-half cream

1. Preheat oven to 350°. Place butter in a 10-in. cast-iron or other ovenproof skillet; place pan in oven until butter is melted, 3-5 minutes. Carefully tilt pan to coat bottom and sides with butter. Sprinkle with brown sugar and 1 Tbsp. orange zest. Arrange pears in a single layer over sugar.
2. In a large bowl, beat sugar, coconut oil, egg and remaining 1 Tbsp. orange zest until well blended. In another bowl, whisk flour, baking powder and salt; gradually beat into sugar mixture alternately with cream.
3. Spoon over pears. Bake until a toothpick inserted in center of cake comes out clean, 45-50 minutes. Cool 10 minutes before inverting onto a serving plate. Serve warm.
1 slice: 352 cal., 19g fat (14g sat. fat), 52mg chol., 283mg sod., 43g carb. (28g sugars, 2g fiber), 3g pro.

ORANGE & PEAR UPSIDE-DOWN CAKE

STRAWBERRY
BUTTERMILK SKILLET
SHORTCAKE

PEACH & BERRY COBBLER

This is one of my favorite summer recipes because it features in-season peaches and berries, but is just as delicious with frozen fruit, too. The quick biscuit topping brings it all together.
—Lauren Knoelke, Des Moines, IA

- -

PREP: 20 min. • **BAKE:** 40 min.
MAKES: 8 servings

- ½ cup sugar
- 3 Tbsp. cornstarch
- ½ tsp. ground cinnamon
- ¼ tsp. ground cardamom
- 10 medium peaches, peeled and sliced (about 6 cups)
- 2 cups mixed blackberries, raspberries and blueberries
- 1 Tbsp. lemon juice

TOPPING
- 1 cup all-purpose flour
- ¼ cup sugar
- 2 tsp. grated orange zest
- ¾ tsp. baking powder
- ¼ tsp. salt
- ¼ tsp. baking soda
- 3 Tbsp. cold butter
- ¾ cup buttermilk
  Vanilla ice cream, optional

1. Preheat oven to 375°. In a large bowl, mix sugar, cornstarch, cinnamon and cardamom. Add peaches, berries and lemon juice; toss to combine. Transfer to a 10-in. cast-iron or other ovenproof skillet.
2. In a small bowl, whisk the first 6 topping ingredients; cut in butter until the mixture resembles coarse crumbs. Add buttermilk; stir just until moistened. Drop mixture by tablespoonfuls over peach mixture.
3. Bake, uncovered, until topping is golden brown, 40-45 minutes. Serve warm. If desired, top with vanilla ice cream.
1 serving: 279 cal., 5g fat (3g sat. fat), 12mg chol., 238mg sod., 57g carb. (38g sugars, 5g fiber), 4g pro.

STRAWBERRY BUTTERMILK SKILLET SHORTCAKE

This from-scratch buttermilk shortcake is a summer tradition in my family, and one that my grandma carries on to this day. Baking it in a skillet gives it an old-fashioned appeal.
—Claudia Lamascolo, Melbourne, FL

- -

PREP: 25 min. • **BAKE:** 50 min.
MAKES: 10 servings

- 10 Tbsp. shortening
- ¼ cup butter, softened
- 1 cup sugar
- 2 large eggs, room temperature
- 2½ cups all-purpose flour
- 3 tsp. baking powder
- ½ tsp. salt
- ⅔ cup buttermilk

STREUSEL TOPPING
- ⅔ cup all-purpose flour
- ½ cup sugar
- 1 tsp. ground cinnamon
- ¼ tsp. ground allspice
- ½ cup butter, softened
- 2 cups sliced fresh strawberries
  Whipped cream

1. Preheat oven to 350°. In a large bowl, cream shortening, butter and sugar until light and fluffy, 5-7 minutes. Add eggs, 1 at a time, beating well after each addition. In another bowl, whisk flour, baking powder and salt; add to creamed mixture alternately with buttermilk, beating well after each addition. Transfer to a 12-in. cast-iron or other ovenproof skillet.
2. For streusel topping, in a small bowl, mix flour, sugar, cinnamon and allspice; cut in butter until crumbly. Sprinkle over batter. Top with strawberries. Bake until center is puffed and edges are golden brown, 50-60 minutes. Serve warm with whipped cream.
1 slice: 526 cal., 27g fat (12g sat. fat), 74mg chol., 418mg sod., 64g carb. (33g sugars, 2g fiber), 6g pro.

SHOOFLY CHOCOLATE PIE

SHOOFLY CHOCOLATE PIE

If you like traditional shoofly pie, you'll love this chocolate version. I sometimes serve it with a scoop of vanilla ice cream, but it's just as good on its own.
—*Gwen Brounce Widdowson, Fleetwood, PA*

PREP: 20 min. • **BAKE:** 45 min. + cooling
MAKES: 8 servings

     Pastry for single-crust pie (9 in.)
½ **cup semisweet chocolate chips**
1½ **cups all-purpose flour**
½ **cup packed brown sugar**
3 **Tbsp. butter-flavored shortening**
1 **tsp. baking soda**
1½ **cups water**
1 **large egg, lightly beaten**
1 **cup molasses**

1. Line a 9-in. cast-iron skillet or deep-dish pie plate with crust. Trim to ½ in. beyond edge of plate; flute edges. Sprinkle chocolate chips into crust; set aside.

2. In a large bowl, combine flour and brown sugar; cut in shortening until crumbly. Set aside 1 cup for topping. Add the baking soda, water, egg and molasses to the remaining crumb mixture and mix well. Pour over chips. Sprinkle with reserved crumb mixture.

3. Bake at 350° until a knife inserted in the center comes out clean, 45-55 minutes. Let stand on a wire rack for 15 minutes before cutting. Serve warm.

1 piece: 526 cal., 20g fat (10g sat. fat), 53mg chol., 341mg sod., 83g carb. (49g sugars, 2g fiber), 6g pro.

GRANDMA PRUIT'S VINEGAR PIE

TEST KITCHEN TIP

If you use your cast-iron skillet on a regular basis, you might notice food starting to stick, even if you clean it daily. That means it's time to reseason the pan. Here's how. Line the lower oven rack with foil and preheat oven to 350°. Scrub the pan with hot, soapy water and a stiff brush to remove any rust. Towel-dry and apply a thin coat of cooking oil to the entire pan, outside and handle included. Place on top oven rack, upside down; bake 1 hour. Turn off the oven and leave the pan inside to cool. Now you're ready to cook.

GRANDMA PRUIT'S VINEGAR PIE

My grandma's beloved recipe for this vintage pie has been in our family for generations. We serve it at all our get-togethers.
—*Suzette Pruit, Houston, TX*

PREP: 40 min. • **BAKE:** 1 hour + cooling
MAKES: 8 servings

2 **cups sugar**
3 **Tbsp. all-purpose flour**
¼ **to ½ tsp. ground nutmeg**
    Pastry for double-crust pie
½ **cup butter, cubed**
⅔ **cup white vinegar**
1 **qt. hot water**

1. Preheat oven to 450°. Whisk together sugar, flour and nutmeg; set aside. On a lightly floured surface, roll one-third of pie dough to a ⅛-in.-thick circle; cut into 2x1-in. strips. Layer a deep 12-in. enamel-coated cast-iron skillet or ovenproof casserole with half the strips; sprinkle with half the sugar mixture. Dot with half the butter. Repeat sugar and butter layers.

2. Roll remaining two-thirds of pie dough to a ⅛-in.-thick circle. Place over filling, pressing against sides of skillet or casserole. Cut a slit in top. Add vinegar to hot water; slowly pour vinegar mixture through slit. Liquid may bubble up through crust (this is normal). Line an oven rack with foil to catch spills.

3. Bake until crust is golden brown, about 1 hour. Cover edge loosely with foil during the last 15-20 minutes if needed to prevent overbrowning. Remove foil. Cool pie on a wire rack.

1 slice: 545 cal., 25g fat (13g sat. fat), 41mg chol., 316mg sod., 78g carb. (50g sugars, 0 fiber), 2g pro.

🍎 GINGER MANGO GRUNT

These tender dumplings swimming in a chunky fruit sauce are comfort food at its finest. Refreshing mango and zesty ginger combine for a burst of flavor.
—*Roxanne Chan, Albany, CA*

PREP: 25 min. • **COOK:** 20 min.
MAKES: 8 servings

½	cup all-purpose flour
3	Tbsp. yellow cornmeal
4½	tsp. sugar
1	tsp. baking powder
¼	tsp. ground ginger
⅛	tsp. salt
2	Tbsp. cold butter
3	Tbsp. egg substitute
¾	cup mango nectar, divided
1	jar (20 oz.) refrigerated mango slices, drained
½	cup reduced-sugar orange marmalade
1	Tbsp. lemon juice
½	cup golden raisins
¼	cup chopped crystallized ginger
¼	cup sliced almonds
	Low-fat frozen yogurt, optional

1. In a small bowl, combine the first 6 ingredients. Cut in butter until mixture resembles coarse crumbs. Combine egg substitute and ¼ cup nectar; stir into the flour mixture just until moistened.

2. Coarsely chop mango slices; combine with orange marmalade, lemon juice and the remaining nectar.

3. Transfer mixture to an 8-in. cast-iron or other ovenproof skillet; stir in raisins. Bring to a boil. Drop flour mixture in 8 mounds onto the simmering mango mixture. Reduce heat; cover and simmer for 12-15 minutes or until a toothpick inserted in a dumpling comes out clean (do not lift the cover while simmering). Sprinkle with crystallized ginger and sliced almonds; if desired, serve with frozen yogurt.

1 serving: 232 cal., 5g fat (2g sat. fat), 8mg chol., 136mg sod., 47g carb. (31g sugars, 2g fiber), 3g pro.

CARAMEL-PECAN CHEESECAKE PIE

I'm proud to serve this rich, nutty pecan pie. It's a snap to prepare, and cream cheese and caramel make it even more luscious. It's perfect for fall or any time of year.
—*Becky Ruff, McGregor, IA*

PREP: 15 min. • **BAKE:** 35 min. + chilling
MAKES: 8 servings

1	sheet refrigerated pie crust
1	pkg. (8 oz.) cream cheese, softened
½	cup sugar
4	large eggs, room temperature
1	tsp. vanilla extract
1¼	cups chopped pecans
1	jar (12¼ oz.) fat-free caramel ice cream topping
	Additional fat-free caramel ice cream topping, optional

1. Preheat oven to 375°. Line a 9-in. cast-iron skillet or deep-dish pie plate with pastry. Trim and flute edges. In a small bowl, beat cream cheese, sugar, 1 egg and vanilla until smooth. Spread into pastry shell; sprinkle with pecans.

2. In a small bowl, whisk remaining eggs; gradually whisk in caramel topping until blended. Pour slowly over pecans.

3. Bake 35-40 minutes or until pie is lightly browned (loosely cover edges with foil after 20 minutes if pie browns too quickly). Cool on a wire rack 1 hour. Refrigerate 4 hours or overnight before slicing. If desired, garnish with additional caramel ice cream topping.

Note: This recipe was tested with Smucker's ice cream topping.

1 piece: 502 cal., 33g fat (11g sat. fat), 142mg chol., 277mg sod., 45g carb. (26g sugars, 2g fiber), 8g pro.

CRAN-APPLE COBBLER

My family isn't big on traditional pies, but we love this hot and bubbly cranberry-packed cobbler. It's the crowning glory of many of our late fall and winter meals and our top pick for holiday celebrations, too. The sweet aroma of cinnamon and fruit is irresistible.
—Jo Ann Sheehan, Ruther Glen, VA

- -

PREP: 35 min. • **BAKE:** 30 min.
MAKES: 8 servings

2½ cups sliced peeled apples
2½ cups sliced peeled firm pears
1   to 1¼ cups sugar
1   cup fresh or frozen cranberries, thawed
½   cup water
3   Tbsp. quick-cooking tapioca
3   Tbsp. Red Hots
½   tsp. ground cinnamon
2   Tbsp. butter

TOPPING
¾   cup all-purpose flour
2   Tbsp. sugar
1   tsp. baking powder
¼   tsp. salt
¼   cup cold butter, cubed
3   Tbsp. 2% milk
    Vanilla ice cream

1. In a large cast-iron or other ovenproof skillet, combine first 8 ingredients; let stand 5 minutes. Cook and stir over medium heat until mixture comes to a full rolling boil, about 18 minutes. Dot the fruit mixture with butter.

2. In a small bowl, combine the flour, sugar, baking powder and salt. Cut in butter until mixture resembles coarse crumbs. Stir in milk until a soft dough forms.

3. Drop topping by heaping tablespoons onto hot fruit. Bake at 375° until golden brown, 30-35 minutes. Serve warm with ice cream.

1 serving: 384 cal., 13g fat (8g sat. fat), 38mg chol., 222mg sod., 67g carb. (48g sugars, 3g fiber), 3g pro.

**PEACH &
BERRY COBBLER**

BERRY-APPLE-
RHUBARB PIE

DEEP-FRIED COOKIES

My kids love this indulgent treat. I give the
batter a kick by adding a pinch of cinnamon
and a teaspoon of vanilla extract.
—*Margarita Torres, Bayamon, AE*

- -

TAKES: 25 min. • **MAKES:** 1½ dozen

  18 Oreo cookies
      Oil for deep-fat frying
   1 cup biscuit/baking mix
   1 large egg
   ½ cup 2% milk
      Confectioners' sugar

1. On each of eighteen 4-in. wooden skewers,
thread 1 cookie, inserting pointed end of
skewer into filling. Freeze until firm, about
1 hour.
2. In a deep cast-iron skillet or deep fryer,
heat oil to 375°. Place biscuit mix in a shallow
bowl. In another bowl, combine egg and milk;
whisk into biscuit mix just until moistened.
3. Holding skewer, dip cookie into biscuit
mixture to coat both sides; shake off excess.
4. Fry cookies, a few at a time, until golden
brown, 1-2 minutes on each side. Drain on
paper towels. Dust with confectioners' sugar
before serving.

1 cookie: 100 cal., 5g fat (1g sat. fat), 11mg
chol., 123mg sod., 13g carb. (5g sugars, 1g
fiber), 1g pro.

TEST KITCHEN TIP
When frying, use oils that have
a high smoking point. Smoking
point is the temperature it takes
for the oil to start to break down
and smoke. Once it starts to
smoke, it's not good for frying
anymore. We recommend peanut
oil, canola oil, sunflower oil,
safflower oil, corn oil or vegetable
oil. Avoid butter, shortening
and olive oil, as they have a low
smoking point. And make sure
you have enough oil to fully
submerge food, with plenty of
room to cook.

BERRY-APPLE-RHUBARB PIE

I make this family favorite every year for an
annual gathering at my sister's house, where
the recipe has been dubbed Uncle Mike's Pie.
I use only fresh berries, apples and rhubarb
that I grow myself.
—*Michael Powers, New Baltimore, VA*

- -

PREP: 30 min. + chilling
BAKE: 65 min. + cooling • **MAKES:** 8 servings

  2⅔ cups all-purpose flour
   1 tsp. salt
   1 cup butter-flavored shortening
   6 to 8 Tbsp. cold water
  FILLING
   2 cups thinly sliced peeled tart apples
   1 Tbsp. lemon juice
   1 tsp. vanilla extract
   1 cup halved fresh strawberries
   1 cup fresh blueberries
   1 cup fresh raspberries
   1 cup fresh blackberries
   1 cup sliced fresh or frozen rhubarb
   ⅓ cup all-purpose flour
   1 tsp. ground allspice
   1 tsp. ground cinnamon
  1½ cups plus 1 tsp. sugar, divided
   2 Tbsp. butter
   1 Tbsp. 2% milk

1. In a large bowl, combine flour and salt; cut
in shortening until crumbly. Gradually add
water, tossing with a fork until dough forms
a ball. Divide dough in half so that 1 portion
is slightly larger than the other; wrap each in
plastic. Refrigerate 30 minutes or until easy
to handle.
2. Preheat oven to 400°. On a lightly floured
surface, roll out larger portion of dough to fit
a cast-iron skillet or 9-in. deep-dish pie plate.
Transfer pastry to skillet.
3. In a large bowl, toss apples with lemon
juice and vanilla; add berries and rhubarb.
Combine the flour, allspice, cinnamon and
1½ cups sugar; add to apple mixture and
toss gently to coat. Spoon into crust; dot
with butter.
4. Roll out remaining pastry; make a lattice
crust. Trim, seal and flute edges. Brush milk
over lattice top. Sprinkle the remaining sugar
over top.
5. Bake 15 minutes. Reduce heat to 350°;
bake 50-60 minutes longer or until crust is
golden brown and filling is bubbly. Cover
edges with foil during the last 15 minutes to
prevent overbrowning if necessary. Cool on
a wire rack.

1 piece: 615 cal., 28g fat (8g sat. fat), 8mg
chol., 318mg sod., 86g carb. (46g sugars, 5g
fiber), 6g pro.

DEEP-FRIED
COOKIES

FUNNEL
CAKES

FUNNEL CAKES

Funnel cakes have been a favorite of ours since we came across them living in the Ozarks. This recipe is easier to make than doughnuts, and it's just as good.
—*Mary Faith Yoder, Unity, WI*

PREP: 15 min. • **COOK:** 5 min./batch
MAKES: 8 cakes

- 2 large eggs, room temperature
- 1 cup 2% milk
- 1 cup water
- ½ tsp. vanilla extract
- 3 cups all-purpose flour
- ¼ cup sugar
- 3 tsp. baking powder
- ¼ tsp. salt
  Oil for deep-fat frying
  Confectioners' sugar

1. In a large bowl, beat eggs. Add milk, water and vanilla until well blended. In another bowl, whisk flour, sugar, baking powder and salt; beat into egg mixture until smooth. In a deep cast-iron or electric skillet, heat the oil to 375°.
2. Cover the bottom of a funnel spout with your finger; ladle ½ cup batter into the funnel. Holding the funnel several inches above the oil, release your finger and move the funnel in a spiral motion until all the batter is released, scraping with a rubber spatula if needed.
3. Fry until golden brown, 2 minutes on each side. Drain on paper towels. Dust with confectioners' sugar; serve warm.

1 serving: 316 cal., 12g fat (2g sat. fat), 50mg chol., 256mg sod., 44g carb. (8g sugars, 1g fiber), 7g pro.

TEST KITCHEN TIP
Make classic funnel cakes extra indulgent by adding whipped cream and fresh berries. Or go al-out with a big scoop of ice cream, a drizzle of chocolate syrup, colored sprinkles and a maraschino cherry for a funnel cake sundae. The creative possibilities are endless!

RHUBARB
UPSIDE-DOWN CAKE

RHUBARB UPSIDE-DOWN CAKE

I bake this cake every spring, and my family loves it. It gets eaten up quickly at parties and potlucks, even by folks who don't normally go for rhubarb. Use your own fresh rhubarb, hit up a farmers market or find a neighbor who will trade stalks for the recipe!
—*Helen Breman, Mattydale, NY*

PREP: 20 min. • **BAKE:** 35 min.
MAKES: 10 servings

- 3 cups sliced fresh or frozen rhubarb
- 1 cup sugar
- 2 Tbsp. all-purpose flour
- ¼ tsp. ground nutmeg
- ¼ cup butter, melted

BATTER
- ¼ cup butter, melted
- ¾ cup sugar
- 1 large egg, room temperature
- 1½ cups all-purpose flour
- 2 tsp. baking powder
- ½ tsp. ground nutmeg
- ¼ tsp. salt
- ⅔ cup 2% milk
  Sweetened whipped cream, optional

1. Place rhubarb in a greased 10-in. cast-iron or other heavy ovenproof skillet. Combine sugar, flour and nutmeg; sprinkle over rhubarb. Drizzle with butter; set aside. For batter, in a large bowl, beat the butter and sugar until blended. Beat in the egg. Combine the flour, baking powder, nutmeg and salt. Gradually add to egg mixture alternately with milk, beating well after each addition.
2. Spread over rhubarb mixture. Bake at 350° until a toothpick inserted in the center comes out clean, about 35 minutes. Loosen edges immediately and invert cake onto a serving dish. Serve warm. If desired, serve with whipped cream.

1 piece: 316 cal., 10g fat (6g sat. fat), 48mg chol., 248mg sod., 53g carb. (36g sugars, 1g fiber), 4g pro.

KHRUSTYKY

MAINE BLUEBERRY PIE WITH CRUMB TOPPING

I make this delicious, fruity pie with small Maine berries, but any variety can be used. Instead of the thyme and lemon peel, I prefer to use fresh lemon thyme. The shortbread topping adds crunch and sweetness.

—Jessie Grearson, Falmouth, ME

PREP: 15 min. • **BAKE:** 45 min. + cooling
MAKES: 8 servings

- 1 sheet refrigerated pie crust
- 6 cups fresh or frozen wild blueberries
- ¾ cup sugar
- 3 Tbsp. all-purpose flour
- ⅛ tsp. ground cinnamon
- 1 tsp. minced fresh thyme, optional
- ½ tsp. grated lemon zest, optional
- 1 Tbsp. butter, cubed

TOPPING
- 12 shortbread cookies
- 3 Tbsp. quick-cooking oats
- 3 Tbsp. brown sugar
- 3 Tbsp. butter, cubed
- 2 Tbsp. all-purpose flour
- ¼ tsp. ground cinnamon
     Dash salt
     Whipped cream, optional

1. Preheat oven to 400°. Unroll pie crust into a 9-in. cast-iron skillet or deep-dish pie plate; flute edges.

2. In a large bowl, combine the blueberries, sugar, flour, cinnamon and, if desired, thyme and lemon zest; toss gently. Spoon into crust; dot with butter.

3. In a food processor, cover and process the cookies until coarsely chopped. Add the oats, brown sugar, butter, flour, salt and cinnamon; process until crumbly. Sprinkle over berry mixture.

4. Bake until crust is golden brown and filling is bubbly, 45-55 minutes. Cover edges with foil during the last 15 minutes if necessary to prevent overbrowning. Cool on a wire rack. If desired, serve with whipped cream.

1 piece: 462 cal., 19g fat (8g sat. fat), 25mg chol., 264mg sod., 72g carb. (36g sugars, 3g fiber), 4g pro.

KHRUSTYKY

Khrustyky, a crispy, delicate pastry dusted with confectioners' sugar, has an eggy flavor similar to cream puffs. I honor my Ukrainian heritage by serving it on Christmas Eve as part of the traditional feast of 12 dishes. Each dish symbolizes one of the apostles.

—Carol Funk, Richard, SK

PREP: 25 min. • **COOK:** 20 min.
MAKES: 1½ dozen pastries

- 2 large eggs, room temperature
- 3 large egg yolks, room temperature
- 1 Tbsp. heavy whipping cream
- 1 Tbsp. vanilla extract
- 2 Tbsp. sugar
- 1½ cups all-purpose flour
- ½ tsp. salt
     Oil for deep-fat frying
     Confectioners' sugar

1. In a large bowl, beat the eggs, egg yolks, cream and vanilla. Beat in sugar. Combine flour and salt; stir into the egg mixture just until smooth (dough will be soft). Divide into 4 portions.

2. On a well-floured surface, roll out 1 dough portion to ⅛-in. thickness. Cut into 1½-in. strips; cut strips diagonally into 3 pieces. Cut a 1½-in. slit lengthwise into the center of each piece; pull 1 end of strip through slit to make a loop. Cover shaped pieces while rolling out and cutting the remaining dough.

3. In a deep cast-iron or electric skillet, heat 2-3 in. of oil to 375°. Fry pastries, in batches, until golden brown, turning once. Drain on paper towels. Dust with confectioners' sugar.

1 pastry: 83 cal., 4g fat (1g sat. fat), 52mg chol., 75mg sod., 10g carb. (2g sugars, 0 fiber), 2g pro.

MAINE BLUEBERRY PIE
WITH CRUMB TOPPING

Recipe Index

A

All-American Meat Loaf, 166
Apple Bacon Pork Roll-Ups, 202
Apple Betty with Almond Cream, 89
Apple Cider Chicken & Dumplings, 196
Apricot Salsa Chicken, 115
Arrabbiata Sauce with Zucchini
   Noodles, 105
Artichoke Tuna Toss, 151
Asian Peanut Pork Roast, 208
Asparagus Beef Cashew Stir-Fry, 93
Avocado Crab Boats, 222

B

Back Porch Meatballs, 81
Bacon-Feta Stuffed Chicken, 130
Bacon, Lettuce & Tomato Pizza, 213
Bacon-Ranch Spinach Dip, 87
Bacon-Wrapped Scallops with
   Pineapple Quinoa, 147
Baked Chicken Fajitas, 188
Baked Fish & Rice, 226
Balsamic Chicken & Pears, 130
Barbecued Beef Chili, 70
Batter-Fried Fish, 154
BBQ Chicken & Smoked Sausage, 49
BBQ Turkey Meatballs, 82
Beef & Biscuit Bake, 162
Beef & Veggie Soup, 70
Beef Gyros, 97
Beef Ragu with Ravioli, 108
Beefy Tortellini Skillet, 109
Beer-Braised Beef, 13
Beergarita Chicken Tacos, 24
Berry-Apple-Rhubarb Pie, 248
Berry Jam Funnel Cakes, 242
Berry Whirligig, 230
Braciole, 93
Breaded Chicken with Avocado, 127
Breaded Steaks, 96
Broiled Steak Fajitas, 167
Broiled Steaks with Parmesan-Sage
   Potatoes, 174
Buffalo Chicken Biscuits, 180
Buffalo Chicken Sliders, 56
Butternut Squash, Cauliflower
   & Beef Shepherd's Pie, 164

C

Cajun Sirloin with Mushroom
   Leek Sauce, 99
Candied Sweet Potato Pies, 232
Cantonese Pork , 38
Caramel-Apple Skillet Buckle, 238
Caramel-Pecan Cheesecake Pie, 246
Caribbean Wontons, 231
Carnitas Huevos Rancheros, 51
Carnitas Tacos, 40
Carrot & Lentil Chili , 69
Cast-Iron Peach Crostata, 235
Cast-Iron Skillet Steak, 102
Cauliflower Pork Soup, 133
Cheese-Stuffed Sweet Onions, 60
Cheeseburger Crescent Ring, 177
Chicken & Broccoli Lasagna Rolls, 196
Chicken & Garlic with Fresh Herbs, 112
Chicken & Spaghetti Squash, 194
Chicken & Sweet Potato Potpie, 183
Chicken Chiles Rellenos Alfredo, 114
Chicken Chiles Rellenos Casserole, 199
Chicken Cordon Bleu Crescent Ring, 193
Chicken Cordon Bleu Sliders, 89
Chicken Dinner Poppers, 182
Chicken Paprikash, 117
Chicken Parmesan Burgers, 111
Chicken Potpie, 179
Chicken Spareribs, 118
Chicken Veggie Alfredo, 34
Chicken Verde Quesadillas, 194
Chicken with Stuffing, 27
Chickpea Sausage Skillet, 145
Chimichurri Baked Flounder, 215
Chinese Cashew Chicken Pizza, 185
Chip-Crusted Chicken, 189
Chocolate Chip Dutch Baby, 237
Coconut Mango Thai Beef Curry, 101
Comforting Tuna Patties, 151
Cornmeal Oven-Fried Chicken, 180
Country Pork & Sauerkraut, 208
Crab Egg Foo Yong, 153
Crab Macaroni Casserole, 227
Crab-Stuffed Manicotti, 219
Crab-Topped Fish Fillets, 216
Cran-Apple Cobbler, 247
Cranberry Apple Cider, 87
Cranberry Chili Meatballs, 75
Creamy Chicken Tetrazzini Casserole, 189

Creamy Scallop Crepes, 224
Curried Chicken Cacciatore, 27
Curried Sweet Potato Pineapple
   Chicken , 37
Curry-Roasted Turkey & Potatoes, 190

D

Date Pudding Cobbler, 232
Deep-Dish Beef & Bean Taco Pizza, 177
Deep-Fried Candy Bars on a Stick, 234
Deep-Fried Cookies, 248
Deluxe Pizza Casserole, 175
Down-Home Chicken, 131

E

East Coast Shrimp & Lentil Bowls, 146
Easy Beef Pies, 170
Easy Lemon-Rosemary Chicken, 35

F

Fajita-Style Shrimp & Grits, 150
Feta Shrimp Skillet, 154
Feta Tomato-Basil Fish, 229
Flank Steak Roll-Up, 17
Foil-Packet Shrimp & Sausage
   Jambalaya, 227
Funnel Cakes, 251

G

Game-Night Nacho Pizza, 169
Garlic Beef Stroganoff, 17
Garlic Chicken with Maple-Chipotle
   Glaze, 198
Garlic-Ginger Turkey Tenderloins, 179
General Tso's Chicken Soup, 73
German Bratwurst with Sauerkraut
   & Apples, 54
German Schnitzel & Potatoes
   with Gorgonzola Cream, 45
Ginger Mango Grunt, 246
Goat Cheese & Spinach Stuffed
   Chicken, 186
Golden Seafood Chowder, 159
Gooey Peanut Butter & Chocolate
   Cake, 79
Grandma Pruit's Vinegar Pie, 245
Greek-Style Chicken with Green Beans, 37
Green Beans with Smoked Turkey
   Bacon, 65

Green Chile Adobado Poutine, 46
Green Curry Salmon with Green
   Beans, 218
Grilled Cheese Burgers with Sauteed
   Onions, 102
Grilled Cranberry Pear Crumble, 234
Ground Pork Taco Salad, 143

H

Ham Steaks with Gruyere, Bacon
   & Mushrooms, 139
Hearty Ground Beef Stew, 21
Hearty Manhattan Clam Chowder, 60
Herbed Slow-Cooker Turkey Breast, 31
Homemade Cincinnati Chili, 11
Honey Mustard Apple Chicken
   Sausage, 119
Honey Walleye, 148
Hungarian Stuffed Cabbage, 205

I

Indian Curried Beef with Rice, 13
Italian Sausages with Provolone, 66
Italian Stuffed Beef Rolls, 172

J

Jamaica-Me-Crazy Chicken Tropicale, 35
Jamaican Chicken with Couscous, 122
Key Lime Chicken Thighs, 199
Khrustyky, 252
Kimchi Cauliflower Fried Rice, 145

K

Korean Beef & Rice, 100
Korean Sausage Bowl, 140

L

Lauren's Bouillabaisse, 153
Lemon Cream Chicken, 120
Lemony Greek Beef & Vegetables, 107
Lemony Salmon Patties, 218
Light Ham Tetrazzini, 48
Lisa's All-Day Sugar & Salt Pork Roast , 209

M

Maine Blueberry Pie with Crumb
   Topping, 252
Make-Ahead Cabbage Rolls, 171
Maple Sausage Skillet, 138
Marinara-Mozzarella Dip, 79
Meat & Potato Patties, 104
Meat Lover's Pizza Rice Skillet, 134
Mediterranean Turkey Skillet, 114
Mexican Pie, 175
Mexican Pork & Hominy Soup, 67
Mexican Turkey Hash Brown Bake, 182

Milk Cake, 231
Mimosa Roasted Chicken, 195
Modern Tuna Casserole, 148
Mojito Pulled Pork, 65
Mom's Chicken & Buttermilk
   Dumplings, 118
Mom's Hazelnut & Chocolate Bread
   Pudding, 78
Moroccan Lamb Lettuce Wraps, 52
Moroccan Pot Roast, 23
Mughali Chicken, 122
Mushroom Beef & Noodles, 20
Mushroom Lasagna, 213
Mushroom Pork Ragout, 51

N

Naked Fish Tacos, 156
New Zealand Rosemary Lamb Shanks, 39

O

Old-Fashioned Beef Brisket, 170
Old-Fashioned Steamed Molasses
   Bread, 76
Olive & Fig Chicken, 119
One-Dish Turkey Dinner , 120
One-Pan Sweet Chili Shrimp
   & Veggies, 219
One-Pot Dinner, 101
Open-Faced Bratwurst Sandwiches
   with Beer Gravy, 135
Open-Faced Breakfast Banh Mi, 136
Orange & Pear Upside-Down Cake, 242
Osso Buco, 163
Overnight Bacon & Swiss Breakfast, 44
Overnight Chicken Casserole, 198

P

Parsley-Crusted Cod, 223
Pasta with Chorizo & Spinach, 142
Peach & Berry Cobbler, 243
Peach Pie, 238
Peachy Summer Cheesecake, 82
Pear, Ham & Cheese Pastry Pockets, 212
Pepper Beef Goulash, 16
Philly Cheesesteak Gnocchi, 94
Philly Cheesesteak Rolls, 174
Pineapple-Glazed Chicken Thighs, 125
Pineapple RumChata Shortcakes, 76
Pizza Rigatoni, 41
Pork & Cranberry Potpies, 202
Pork & Cheesy Macaroni Sliders, 204
Pork Chop Dinner, 40
Pork Chops with Apples & Stuffing, 210
Pork Piperade, 142
Pork Roast with Peach Sauce, 45
Pork Stew with Cornbread
   Dumplings, 137

Pork Tenderloin with Pear Cream
   Sauce, 204
Pot of S'mores, 241
Prime Rib with Horseradish Cream, 169
Prosciutto Chicken Cacciatore, 31
Pumpkin Latte Custard, 74
Pumpkin Spice Oatmeal, 46

Q

Quick & Easy Memphis-Style BBQ
   Ribs, 207
Quick Beef & Noodles, 96
Quick Chicken Piccata, 110

R

Ragin' Cajun Eggplant & Shrimp
   Skillet, 223
Raspberry Coconut French Toast
   Slow-Cooker Style, 52
Reuben Bread Pudding, 164
Rhubarb Beef, 97
Rhubarb Upside-Down Cake, 251
Ribs, Sauerkraut & Dumplings, 201
Roast Beef Caribbean Style, 167
Roast Lemon Butter Shrimp, 229
Root Beer Pulled Pork Nachos, 75

S

Salmon Croquette Bagel Sandwich, 155
Salmon Loaf, 224
Salmon with Tomato-Goat Cheese
   Couscous, 147
Santa Fe Chili, 62
Saucy Barbecue Shrimp, 214
Saucy Thai Chicken Pizzas, 30
Sausage & Spinach Crescent Bake, 209
Sausage & Squash Penne , 139
Sausage & Asparagus Pasta with
   Cajun Cream Sauce, 143
Sausage Cobb Salad Lettuce Wraps, 133
Sausage Noodle Casserole, 205
Sausage Pasta with Vegetables, 131
Sausage, Kale & Squash Bread
   Pudding, 62
Savory Beef Fajitas, 12
Seared Salmon with Balsamic
   Sauce, 150
Sesame Salmon with Wasabi Mayo, 216
Sheet-Pan Bacon & Eggs Breakfast, 207
Sheet-Pan Taco Turkey Meat Loaf, 186
Sheet-Pan Tandoori Chicken, 178
Shoofly Chocolate Pie, 245
Shredded Green Chile Beef, 15
Simple Herbed Scallops, 221
Simple Mediterranean Chicken, 126
Simply Incredible Grits, 59
Skillet Caramel Apricot Grunt, 235

Skillet Chocolate Chunk Walnut Blondies, 237
Skillet Nachos, 108
Skillet Plum Chicken Tenders, 127
Skillet Stout Brownies, 241
Sloppy Joe Biscuit Cups, 166
Sloppy Joe Stew, 109
Slow-Cooked Chai Tea, 81
Slow-Cooked Corned Beef, 16
Slow-Cooked Goose, 26
Slow-Cooked Pizzaiola Meat Loaf, 29
Slow-Cooked Ropa Vieja, 18
Slow-Cooked Shredded Pork, 70
Slow-Cooked Stuffed Apples, 86
Slow-Cooked Thai Drunken Noodles, 43
Slow-Cooked Vegetable Curry, 41
Slow-Cooked Vegetables with Cheese Sauce, 69
Slow-Cooker Asian Short Ribs, 15
Slow-Cooker Bacon Mac & Cheese, 67
Slow-Cooker Baked Potatoes, 57
Slow-Cooker Beef & Broccoli, 23
Slow-Cooker Beef Tostadas, 10
Slow-Cooker Beef with Red Sauce, 10
Slow-Cooker Berry Compote, 84
Slow-Cooker Breakfast Burritos, 43
Slow-Cooker Buffalo Chicken Salad, 32
Slow-Cooker Chicken Tikka Masala , 34
Slow-Cooker Citrus Carrots, 59
Slow-Cooker Cordon Bleu Soup, 63
Slow-Cooker Crab & Green Onion Dip, 84
Slow-Cooker Goetta, 54
Slow-Cooker Honey Nut Granola, 86
Slow-Cooker Malaysian Chicken, 26
Slow-Cooker Meat Loaf, 21
Slow-Cooker Mongolian Beef, 18
Slow-Cooker Pear Butter, 83
Slow-Cooker Potato & Ham Soup, 73

Slow-Cooker Red Beans & Sausage, 44
Slow-Cooker Sausage Lasagna, 48
Slow-Cooker Southwestern Chicken, 25
Slow-Cooker Spumoni Cake, 83
Slow-Cooker Sriracha Corn, 66
Smothered Round Steak, 12
So-Easy Sticky Chicken Wings, 78
Soda Pop Chops with Smashed Potatoes, 140
Southern Fried Chicken with Gravy, 115
Southern Seafood Gumbo, 155
Southwest Shredded Pork Salad, 39
Southwest-Style Shepherd's Pie, 185
Spaghetti Squash & Sausage Easy Meal, 137
Special Pork Chops, 212
Spicy Corned Beef Tacos, 99
Spicy Kale & Herb Porchetta, 49
Spicy Sausage Meatball Sauce, 53
Spicy Shrimp Fettuccine Alfredo, 159
Spinach Turkey Meatballs, 188
Steakhouse Pizza, 163
Steaks with Crab Sauce, 100
Strawberry Buttermilk Skillet Shortcake, 243
Stuffed Pizza Rolls, 200
Stuffed Tilapia, 222
Sunday Pork Roast, 210
Sunshine Chicken, 117
Sweet & Tangy Chicken, 30
Sweet & Savory Slow-Cooked Beef, 57
Sweet Hoosier Dog Sauce, 107
Sweet Onion & Sausage Spaghetti, 125

T
Taco Baked Potatoes, 172
Tacos in a Bowl, 92
Tangy Parmesan Tilapia, 226

Tarragon-Dijon Pork Chops, 201
Tempting Teriyaki Chicken Stew, 32
Texas Stew, 20
Thai Scallop Saute, 158
Three-Meat Spaghetti Sauce, 138
Tilapia with Citrus Sauce, 158
Tomato & Pepper Sirloin, 104
Tomato-Poached Halibut, 156
Tortellini with Sausage & Mascarpone, 132
Triple-Citrus Steaks with Jicama & Mango, 94
Tuna-Filled Shells, 215
Turkey & Black Bean Enchilada Casserole, 193
Turkey & Vegetable Sheet-Pan Supper, 190
Turkey Crepes, 123
Turkey Lo Mein, 128
Turkey Pea Skillet, 111
Turkey Salisbury Steaks, 128
Turkey Sausage Cabbage Rolls, 25
Turkey Scallopini, 126
Turkey Tostadas, 112
Tuscan Fish Packets, 221

V
Veggie Pork Saute, 136

W
Wine-Poached Pears, 87

Z
Za'atar Chicken, 29